POSTMORTAL SPIRIT WORLD

POSTMORTAL SPIRIT WORLD

Our Next Temporary Home

Compendium of Questions & Answers

MARK W. SHEFFIELD

SHILOH PRESS

Postmortal Spirit World

Jacket illustration by Ron Peterson www.ronpetersonart.com

Text illustrations by Rachel Anne Jones

Printed in the United States of America by Sheridan Books Inc.

ISBN: 978-0-9829147-4-8

$27.00

First Printing: July 2011

10 9 8 7 6 5 4 3 2 1

Published by Shiloh Press Inc.
San Jose, California

For information, correspondence and catalog go to www.shilohpress.com
Library of Congress Cataloging-in-Publication Data is available upon request.

CONTENTS

INTRODUCTION

Since Eden, millions have pondered Job's age-old question: "If a man die, shall he live again?" *(Job 14:14).* Man's age-old hope is for immortality. Yet the world and science can't come up with the answer. We need angels and revelation from God to tell us. Hugh Nibley wrote:

> There is only one justification for religion, one sole question, so let us not talk about the endless, abstract problems . . . The real question, of course, is, Is this all there is? Tell us what everybody wants to know, the only question that bothers us. If you can answer that definitely, then our troubles are over; there is nothing left to worry about . . . Religion exists to answer that question *(CWHN 12:339).*

Clement of Rome (d.101 AD) pondered the real question and other related questions. Clement, who was called by Peter to the office of Bishop in Rome, was among the first of the apostolic fathers (early Christian authors—some had contact with Jesus' Apostles). He was born in a wealthy family and was well-educated in his youth, with the means to attend the finest universities when he reached college age. He was studious and inquisitive by nature. He was asking the real question by the time he was twelve but he could not find the answer even after years of searching at the institutions. Finally, he met the Apostle Barnabas who was preaching in Rome. The message of Barnabas made perfect sense to Clement, but not to the hostile crowd so Clement took him to his home for protection. They discussed his questions, and Barnabas persuaded him to go to Palestine to meet Peter at the approaching Church of Christ conference. Clement was converted and joined the Church.

Clement's story is a favorite of Hugh Nibley. Nibley refers to inquiries such as Clement's as the "terrible questions." They're terrible, because the world can't answer them. Here's part of the story as told by Nibley:

> In the . . . earliest Christian writing we have after the New Testament, we learn the legitimate questions that interested the early Christians, questions which the church would ordinarily say, "You're not supposed to ask that." Clement said he had been to the university, and the professors couldn't answer his questions; the only person who could answer them was Peter. Clement's questions were "Is there a preexistence? Is there life after death? If we live after, will we remember this life? Why don't we remember the premortal existence? When was the world created? What existed before that? If the world was created, will it pass away? And then what? Will we feel things we cannot feel now?" Clement says he could not shake from his mind the *immortalitatis cupido*, the desire to go on living. It was such questions, he said, that led him to seek the true light. Notice these are primarily scientific questions, but they are actually the basic religious questions, too. The scientists say this doesn't have anything to do with religion; we say that it does. Clement complained that the Doctors could not give him any answers, only a lot of clever talk, but nothing else . . . Finally he went to Palestine, where he met Peter at a conference of the church. When he put these questions to Peter straight, he got his answers. "Is the soul mortal or immortal? Was the world created? Why? Can it be dissolved? Will another world take its place? Will there be something better after it? Or will there be anything at all after this world?" Then Peter explained to him how it is, adding that it is important to find answers to these things *(CWHN 12:523-524).*

Perhaps no religious topic generates more questions than the hereafter. So what better way to study the hereafter than with questions . . . and answers? The purpose of this book is to answer the real questions: questions about the future, questions that bother us, questions that people like Clement would ask. Because there is so much we don't know about the postmortal spirit world, the answers might simply raise more questions. Having questions and pondering is a good thing. The Lord repeatedly counsels us to ask questions to understand His words *(2 Nephi 32:4)* and to obtain wisdom and answers (*Matthew 7:7; 1 Nephi 15:11)*. We are "commanded in all things to ask of God" *(D&C 46:7).* When we ask questions, we signify that we are ready to learn, and the doors to knowledge are opened to us through the Holy Ghost. It was, after all, questions that triggered most of the revelations we have today that came through the Prophet Joseph Smith.

To understand the postmortal spirit world, we will briefly reflect on life before birth in the premortal existence, our divine genealogy, why we are here on earth, and questions about death. We will review spirit world terminology, which can be confusing because it has not been used uniformly in the past. We will learn about the nature of spirits, the Spirit element or light, the veil, places and conditions in the spirit world, angels and ministering beings, and the resurrection which is our ticket out of the spirit world.

Before we embark on our journey, a warning from a modern day Apostle is in order. Dallin H. Oaks gave a talk at BYU in 1992 entitled "Our Strengths Can Become Our Downfall." Here is a passage from his remarks:

> Another strength Satan can exploit to seek our downfall is a strong desire to understand everything about every principle of the gospel. How could that possibly work to our detriment? Experience teaches that if this desire is not disciplined, it can cause some to pursue their searchings past the fringes of orthodoxy, seeking answers to mysteries rather than a firmer understanding and a better practice of the basic principles of the gospel. Some seek answers to questions God has not chosen to answer. Others receive answers—or think they receive answers—in ways that are contrary to the order of the Church. For such searchers, Satan stands ready to mislead through sophistry or spurious revelation. Persons who hunger after a full understanding of all things must discipline their questions and their methods or they can get close to apostasy without even knowing it. It may be just as dangerous to exceed orthodoxy as it is to fall short of it. The safety and happiness we are promised lies in keeping the commandments, not in discounting them or multiplying them *(BYU Speeches, June 7, 1992).*

Questions can be a powerful and motivating tool for learning. But there are many curiosities and questions about the spirit world that God has not yet answered. Some of these uncertainties are acknowledged in the text. Imagine how many of these questions will be answered soon enough when we get there! Because the spirit world is so unfamiliar to mortals, without language to precisely describe it, the quotes and opinions in this book should be taken at face value. We know we don't have all the details and answers about the hereafter, so we do the best we can under our present circumstances. Regarding the spirit world, Hugh Nibley explained:

> Today people are talking in terms of dimensions that are real but absolutely inconceivable . . . we cannot describe it, we cannot imagine it, but it is absolutely real. You will try to understand everything all at once. *Doctrine and Covenants 93:30* says that everything must be understood in the sphere in which it exists . . . If you [say] "Take away the boundaries; I want to know about everything now," you will never get anything *(CWHN 9:298, 304).*

The numerous sources quoted herein should not be given equal standing. Latter-day Saints (LDS) place the most credence in the scriptures *(Bible, Book of Mormon, Doctrine & Covenants, and Pearl of Great Price)* and the words of modern prophets and Apostles. Insights from LDS and non-LDS scholars, authors and others are included to amplify our spirit world understanding. The author's words and opinions are the least authoritative and have been included to correlate, summarize, evaluate research from multiple sources and improve readability of the book. Because truth is truth no matter the origin, Latter-day Saints seek knowledge from all merited sources. However, readers should be cognizant of the range of credibility among so many quoted opinions. Appendix D provides brief biographical data to assist in the assessment. Readers should also seek the guidance of the Holy Spirit to discern any unintended but possible errors.

The author's objective is to do some good by facilitating learning only within the bounds of orthodoxy described by Elder Oaks. Such learning is not the end goal. The ultimate hope is that increased knowledge and perspective will provide motivation for readers to better prepare for our next temporary home.

ILLUSTRATIONS

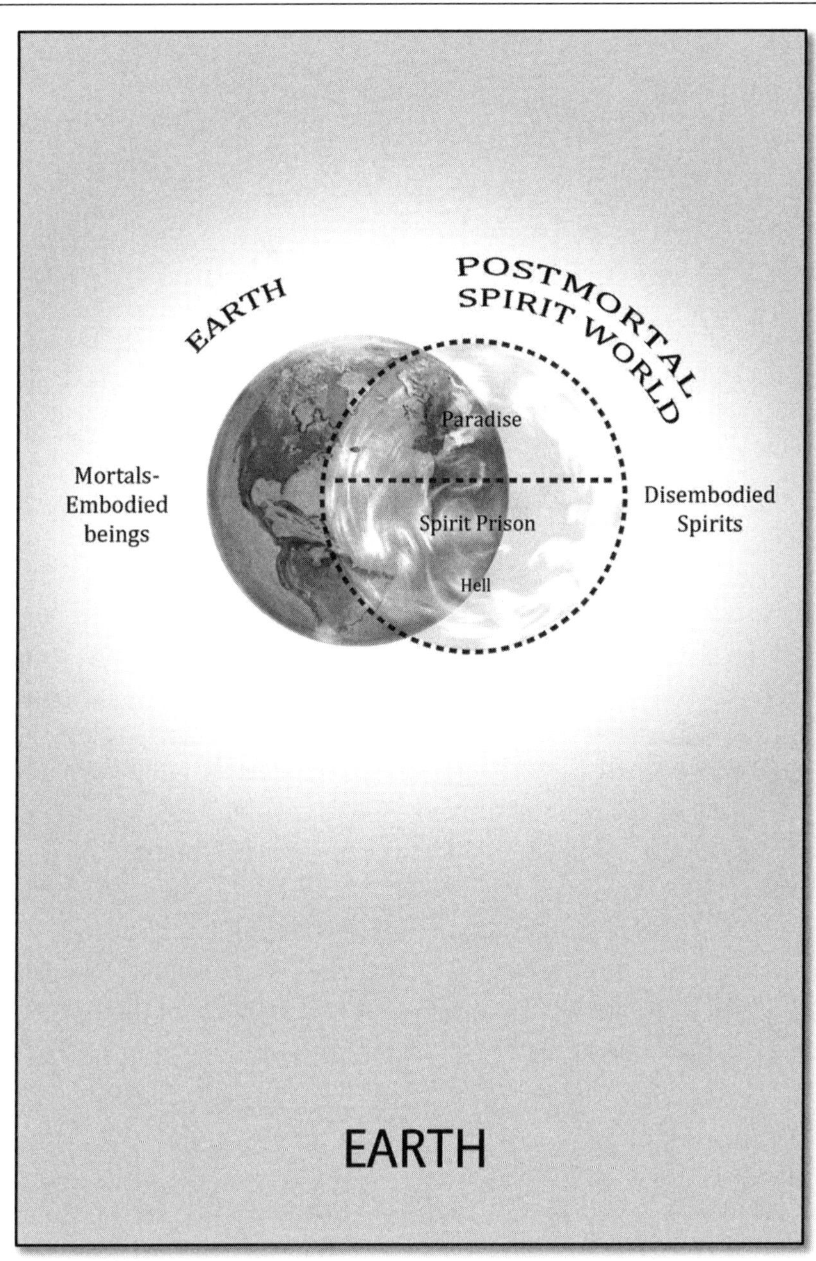

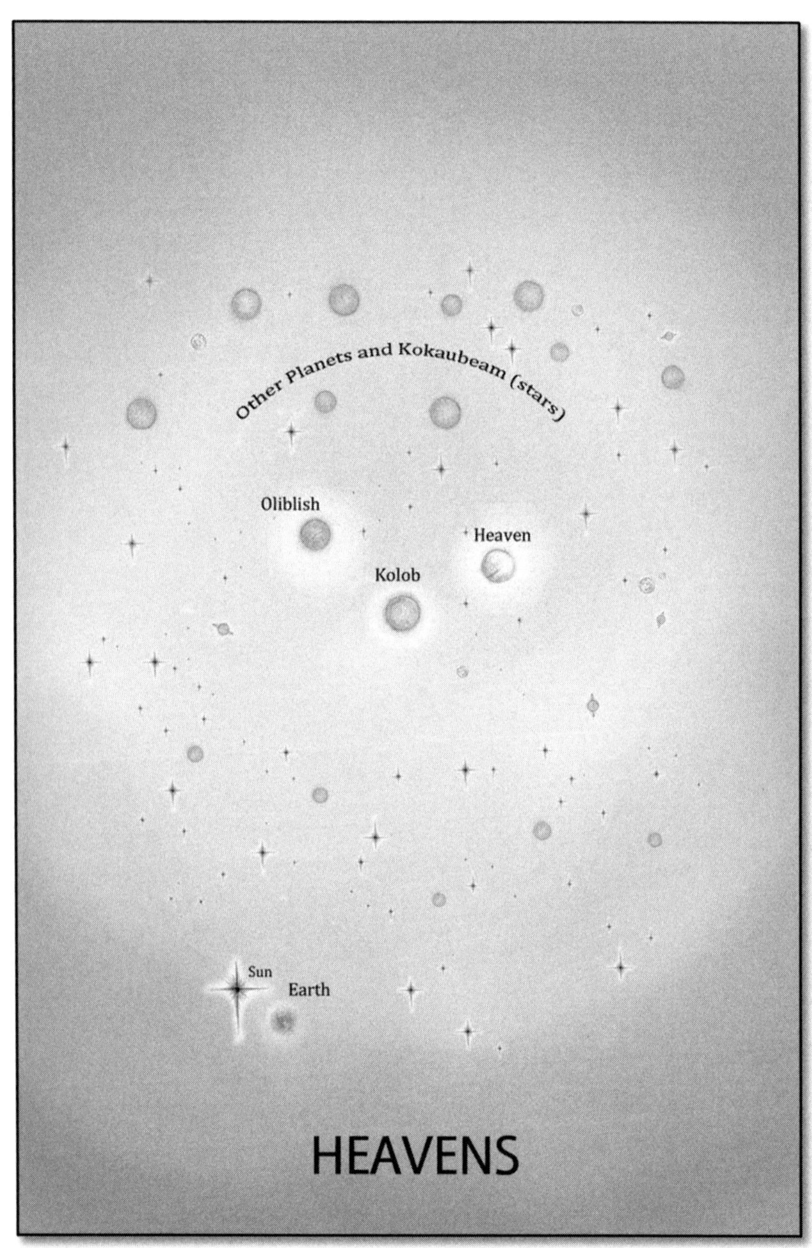
Other Planets and Kokaubeam (stars)
Oliblish
Heaven
Kolob
Sun
Earth
HEAVENS

Premortal Existence
In Premortal Spirit World in the Heavens

Premortal Spirit Birth

Partial Judgment

Veil

Mortal Existence
On Earth

Mortal Birth

Mortal Death

Partial Judgment

Veil

Postmortal Existence
In Postmortal Spirit World on Earth

Spirit Enters the Spirit World

Partial Judgment

Veil

Resurrected Beings Existence
In the Heavens or on Earth during Millenium

Resurrection

Final Judgment

Veil

Outer Darkness

Glorified Existence
In the Kingdoms of Glory: Celestial, Terrestrial, Telestial

THE PLAN OF SALVATION

KEYS
TO BOOK STRUCTURE AND ABBREVIATIONS

Book Structure

To readily identify sources and facilitate referencing:

- Questions are numbered, not the pages
- Scripture references (including within quotes) are *italicized* with *chapter: verse*
- Multiple volume references include *volume: page*
- Quotes are in "quotation marks" or, if lengthy, in indented blocks
- Appendix D lists brief biographies of quoted individuals
- Appendix E lists all the questions

Abbreviations

To simplify frequent references in the text, the following abbreviations are used. More complete publication details are found in Sources at the back.

Latter-day Saint Scriptures

Bible Sources Quoted:

Old Testament: Genesis, Exodus, 1 Kings, Job, Psalms, Ecclesiastes, Isaiah, Ezekial, Daniel

New Testament: Matthew, Mark, Luke, John, Acts, Romans, 1 Corinthians, 2 Corinthians, Galations, Ephesians, Phillippians, Hebrews, James, 1 Peter, 2 Peter, 1 John, Revelation

Book of Mormon Sources Quoted: 1 Nephi, 2 Nephi, Jacob, Mosiah, Alma, 3 Nephi, Ether, Moroni

ABBREVIATIONS

D&C: Doctrine and Covenants of The Church of Jesus Christ of Latter-day Saints

Pearl of Great Price Sources Quoted: Abraham, Moses, Joseph Smith-History (JS-History), Articles of Faith

Other Sources

AD: American Dictionary, Noah Webster, 1828 Edition

AGQ: Joseph Fielding Smith, *Answers to Gospel Questions*

AHD: American Heritage Dictionary, 2006 Edition

Answers: Joseph Fielding McConkie, Answers: Straightforward Answers toTough Gospel Questions.

BD: Bible Dictionary, The Church of Jesus Christ of Latter-day Saints

BofMC: Monte Nyman, *Book of Mormon Commentary*

CA: 2011 Church Almanac

CR: Conference Reports from The Church of Jesus Christ of Latter-day Saints

CWHN: The Collected Works of Hugh Nibley

DCBofM: Robert Millet and Joseph Fielding McConkie, *Doctrinal Commentary on the Book of Mormon*

DNTC: Bruce R. McConkie, *Doctrinal New Testament Commentary*

DBY: Brigham Young, Discourses of Brigham Young

DS: Joseph Fielding Smith, *Doctrines of Salvation*

EB: Encyclopaedia Britannica

EM: Encyclopedia of Mormonism

Ensign: Ensign of The Church of Jesus Christ of Latter-day Saints

Evidence: Jeffrey Long, MD, *Evidence of the Afterlife*

GD: Joseph F. Smith, *Gospel Doctrine*

ABBREVIATIONS

Glimpses: Brent L. Top and Wendy C. Top, *Glimpses Beyond Death's Door*

HC: Joseph Smith, *History of The Church of Jesus Christ of Latter-day Saints*

HQH: Heber Q. Hale, *Vision Given to Heber Q. Hale*

Hymns: Hymns of The Church of Jesus Christ of Latter-day Saints.

IE: Improvement Era of The Church of Jesus Christ of Latter-day Saints

JD: Journal of Discourses

JNDS: Journal of Near-Death Studies

JST: Joseph Smith Translation of the Bible

KST: Parley P. Pratt, *Key to the Science of Theology*

MD: Bruce R. McConkie, *Mormon Doctrine*

MM: Bruce R. McConkie, *Millennial Messiah*

Messages: Messages of the First Presidency

NW: Bruce R. McConkie, *A New Witness for the Articles of Faith*

OLDH: Our Latter-day Hymns

SW: Selected Writings of Daniel H. Ludlow

TD: Spencer W. Kimball, *Tragedy or Destiny*

TG: Topical Guide, with Selected Concordance and Index, The Church of Jesus Christ of Latter-day Saints

TPJS: Joseph Smith, *Teachings of the Prophet Joseph Smith*

WJS: Joseph Smith, *Words of Joseph Smith*

CHAPTER ONE

SPIRIT WORLD IN GENERAL

I saw the hosts of the dead, both small and great.
—Joseph F. Smith, D&C 138:11

1. What is the postmortal spirit world?

It is the abode of the dead. Upon death, our spirits leave the physical body and enter the postmortal spirit world (hereinafter called spirit world). It is a temporary and intermediate state. We live there until the resurrection, when our spirits reunite with the body. Bruce R. McConkie said: "After all men are resurrected, the spirit world will be without inhabitants" (*MD, 762*). (*See Chapter 2 for location of the spirit world; and Chapter 3 for spirit world terminology.*)

2. Why should we learn about the spirit world?

Because we all go there when we die.[i] How we live now greatly impacts our individual spirit world conditions then. Working knowledge of the spirit world helps motivate us to prepare for the hereafter. To be so mired in earthly affairs that we ignore the looming spiritual sphere is a regrettable oversight.

The poet John Greenleaf Whittier wrote:

Alas for him who never sees
The stars shine through his cypress-trees!
Who, hopeless, lays his dead away,
Nor looks to see the breaking day
Across the mournful marbles play.
(*Snow-Bound: A Winter Idyl*)

The prophet Joseph Smith taught the importance of learning about the spirit world:

> All men know they must die. And it is important that we should understand . . . the designs and purposes of God in our coming into the world, our sufferings here, and our departure hence. What is the object of our coming into existence, then dying and falling away, to be no more? It is but reasonable to suppose that God would reveal something in reference to the matter, and it is a subject we ought to study more than any other. We ought to study it day and night, for the world is ignorant in reference to their true condition and relation. If we have any claim on our Heavenly Father for anything, it is for knowledge on this important subject (*TPJS, 324*).

3. Why learn about the spirit world from Latter-day Saints (LDS)?

Because Latter-day Saints have compiled the revelations from God and angels to ancient and modern prophets that answer many questions about the spirit world. This knowledge comes with responsibility, not status. As the "least and the servant of all" (*D&C 50:26*), there is no place for intellectual smugness especially considering the Lord's admonition to us:

> For there are many yet on the earth among all sects, parties, and denominations, . . . who are only kept from the truth because they know not where to find it—Therefore, that we should waste and wear out our lives in bringing to light all the hidden things of darkness, wherein we know them; and they are truly manifest from heaven—These should then be attended to with great earnestness (*D&C 123:12-14*).

Of course, there is much that Latter-day Saints don't know about the spirit world. The Lord intended it that way so we would exercise faith. However, there is much we do know, and should make known, about the "state of the soul between death and the resurrection" (*Alma 40:11*).

4. Is knowledge of the spirit world consistent among all Latter-day Saints?

No. There is some commonality on basic principles, but there is also puzzlement and lack of clarity for many. Certainly spirit world knowledge varies among the Saints. Some, by personal experience, inspiration, or study, undoubtedly have insights beyond the coverage of this book.

As with all gospel concepts we learn on an individual basis as we make our own efforts to study and allow the Lord to tutor us personally. The pattern is to learn and then hearken or apply the principles, to earn the right to learn more. The Lord described how this works:

> I will give unto the children of men line upon line, precept upon precept, here a little and there a little; and blessed are those who hearken unto my precepts, and lend an ear unto my counsel, for they shall learn wisdom; for unto him that receiveth I will give more (*2 Nephi 28:30*).

The Lord promised that in this, the dispensation of the fulness of times, "God shall give unto you knowledge by his Holy Spirit . . . that has not been revealed since the world was until now" (*D&C 121:26*).

5. What constitutes official doctrine regarding the spirit world?

Whatever is true. "Truth is knowledge of things as they are, and as they were, and as they are to come" (*D&C 93:24*). How do we determine truth? The foundation of truth is revelation from God in the scriptures and from living Apostles and prophets. What about truth beyond the general foundation of what is clearly taught in the scriptures and words of Apostles and prophets today? There is much truth left to the individual to seek, study, learn, and discern, using the measuring rod of the scriptures. The First Presidency only rarely makes official doctrinal interpretations or pronouncements. Hugh Nibley affirmed "one of the greatest strengths of the Church: We don't have a professional clergy—a paid ministry that gives official interpretations of the scriptures . . .

We're to read the scriptures for ourselves, as guided by the Spirit." (*CWHN 12:336-337*).

Joseph Smith declared: "One of the grand fundamental principals of 'Mormonism' is to receive truth, let it come from whence it may" (*TPJS, 313*).

As Latter-day Saints, we don't have to wait on a hierarchy to declare what's official. We can learn as much as we want. How liberating! Joseph Fielding McConkie wrote:

> The issue is not whether something is official . . . At issue is truth—finding and complying with the principles that bring salvation . . . Is it in harmony with all other laws and ordinances of the gospel? Does it sanctify the soul? Does it lead us closer to God? Surely any principle that responds affirmatively to such questions can be numbered among the doctrines of the Latter-day Saints (*Answers, 220*).

6. How do we identify misinformation taught about the spirit world?

Jesus Christ gave us the key: "And that which doth not edify is not of God" (*D&C 50:23*). Information received by the "Spirit of truth" is "of God" (*see D&C 50:18-19*). "That which is of God is light" (*D&C 50:24*). Joseph Fielding Smith explained:

> But if a man is humble and true and faithful . . . and trying to draw nearer to God day by day, he'll have the guidance of that Spirit and he'll know the truth. And that Spirit that is given to us—that is the guidance of the Holy Ghost . . . gives us the power to discern between truth and error. A great many of our people are led astray because they don't have the power to discern between truth and error. Well, the Spirit of the Lord will direct us so that we will know when something that isn't true is presented to us, we'll feel it (*The Fundamentals of the Gospel, Address to Seminary and Institute Personnel, BYU, August 25, 1954*).

The Holy Spirit witnesses the truth of things written (*see D&C 18:2*) and confirms whether activities associated with spirits from the spirit world are of God, "then ye may know that it is not of God" (*see D&C 50:27-35*).

7. How can we recognize the feeling of the guidance of the Spirit?

Speaking of the "spirit of revelation," the Lord admonished Oliver Cowdery, "Therefore, this is thy gift; *apply unto it*" (*D&C 8:4, italics for emphasis*), "therefore thou shalt *exercise thy gift*" (*D&C 6:11*). Applying and exercising the Gift of the Holy Ghost suggests thoughtful focus, effort, and practice. Jesus said inspiration would "be signalized unto you by the peace and power of my Spirit" (*D&C 111:8*). Joseph Smith said "it will whisper peace and joy to their souls" (*Manuscript History of Brigham Young, February 23, 1847, 529*). (*See also #43.*)

Recognizing inspiration from the Holy Ghost is a lifelong process one can practice daily. For example, when we read or hear a story about an angel or a ministering spirit or a near-death experience, one might have a tendency to either believe or disbelieve the story offhandedly depending on our own nature or past experiences. We should never forget that we have been promised, if worthy, to always have His Spirit with us. President Lorenzo Snow said it is a "grand privilege of every Latter-day Saint . . . to have the manifestations of the Spirit every day of our lives" (*CR, April 1899*). So, we should be careful not to judge too quickly, deny "the power of God" and "quench the Holy Spirit" (*Jacob 6:8*). We trust the Lord will help us discern the truth.

We can then consider whether the story has a meaningful purpose. Is it uplifting and comforting which are fruits of the Spirit? Does the story ring true, emanating spiritual light? Or is it sinister, with a ghostly, sensational quality? It may be real, but consider the source, whether it be from Satan or God. For example, a spirit or ghost could factually manifest itself in some way to a mortal being, making elements of the story true, but Satan may have a hand in it (*see #38, #44*). Maybe it is without any discernible meaning or purpose. We are to cast away "idle thoughts" (*D&C 88:69*) and "imaginations" (*2 Corinthians 10:5*). Joseph Smith taught that the test of a godly manifestation is whether there is "any intelligence [Spirit] communicated? Are the curtains of heaven withdrawn, or the purposes of God developed?" (*TPJS, 204*). Watch for inaccurate terminology and exaggerations.

We are to be open-minded and prayerful to recognize the truth through the Spirit. Anciently, Jesus rebuked the close-minded and unbelieving Sadducees and Pharisees. In modern times too, many reject unfamiliar teachings. For example, when Joseph Smith taught strange doctrine, such as the premortal existence, many of the early Saints apostatized. Hugh Nibley wrote:

> Brigham Young said that more Saints apostatized because of the doctrine of premortal existence than any other doctrine—more than polygamy, more than tithing, more than jealousies, or anything else. Over it, people left the Church in droves, yet today, everybody accepts the doctrine as the most natural thing in the world (*CWHN 12:370*).

Just because some unfamiliar concept is remarkable or new, doesn't mean it isn't true. However, some truths do take time to ponder and gel. We learn incrementally, milk before meat. "Precept upon precept" (*Isaiah 28:10*). Sometimes it is best not to dwell on new, unsettling information for a period of time. "Put it on a shelf for now," is often sound advice.

8. What are the principle scriptures and revelations from God on the spirit world and the hereafter?

There are several primary sources:

(a) *Vision of the Glories (Joseph Smith): D&C 76 and Joseph's poetic version*
(b) *Revelations on Spirit, light and glory (Joseph Smith): D&C 84, 93*
(c) *Olive Leaf plucked from the Tree of Paradise (Joseph Smith): D&C 88*
(d) *Vision of the Celestial Kingdom (Joseph Smith): D&C 137*
(e) *Vision of the Redemption of the Dead (Joseph F. Smith): D&C 138*
(f) *Vision of the Tree of Life interpretation: 1 Nephi 15*
(g) *Jacob's great sermon on the atonement and salvation: 2 Nephi 9*
(h) *King Benjamin's address made known by an angel: Mosiah 3*
(i) *Amulek's sermon on salvation: Alma 34*
(j) *Alma's spirit world revelation from an angel: Alma 40*
(k) *Jesus' parable of Lazarus and the rich man in the spirit world: Luke 16:19-31*

(l) *Apocalypse: Revelation of John*
(m) *Abraham's face to face talk with the Lord about spirits and creation: Abraham 3*
(n) *Moses' transfiguration and vision: Moses 1*
(o) *King Follett Sermon (Joseph Smith's last conference address): TPJS, 343-361*

9. Will more be revealed about the spirit world?

Yes. "We believe all that God has revealed, all that He does now reveal, and we believe that He will yet reveal many great and important things pertaining to the Kingdom of God" (*Ninth Article of Faith*). In fact, the past 190 years illustrates the pattern of expanding knowledge. Starting in 1820, the Lord revealed through Joseph Smith much of what we know about the spirit world, as part of the "restitution of all things" (*Acts 3:21*). In the late 1800s, such prophets as Brigham Young, Wilford Woodruff, and Jedediah M. Grant added more information. Joseph F. Smith obtained new, clarifying revelation in his vision of the redemption of the dead in 1918, wherein he "saw the hosts of the dead, both small and great" (*D&C 138:11*).

More recent Apostles and prophets, such as Joseph Fielding Smith, Bruce R. McConkie, and Neal A. Maxwell have blessed us with further understanding. The library of credible, sacred encounters with the spirit world and its inhabitants is substantial and growing with the passage of time and with increasing numbers of faithful Latter-day Saints and others privileged to receive these manifestations. Joel prophesied that before the second coming, the Lord will "pour out my spirit" with dreams and visions among sons, daughters, old men, young men, servants, and handmaids (*Joel 2:28-29*). We frequently sing: "The Lord is extending the Saints' understanding" (William W. Phelps, *The Spirit of God, Hymns, 2*).

10. How familiar was the Prophet Joseph Smith with the spirit world?

William Taylor, Joseph Smith's companion for some time in 1842 said: "He seemed to be just as familiar with the spirit world, and as well acquainted with the other side, as he was with this world" (*Young Woman's Journal 17:548, December 1906*).

George Q. Cannon said about Joseph: "He was visited constantly by angels" (*JD 23:362*). Joseph Smith himself stated that he "received many visits from the angels of God" (*HC 4:537*). In fact, as Neal A. Maxwell points out: "more books or pages of scripture have come to us through Joseph Smith than from any other prophet—more even than from Moses, Luke, Paul, and Mormon combined!" (*A Wonderful Flood of Light, 18*).

11. Do mortal beings grasp the scope of the spirit world?

Many of us do not. It is easy to overlook the magnitude of the billions that have died and gone there. Most are unaware of the fervor of activity in the spirit world that impacts the salvation and advancement of mankind. Neal A. Maxwell put it in perspective:

> Often Church members [and others] suffer from a lack of perspective, perhaps understandably, as to the vastness and intensity of the Lord's work in the spirit world. The scope is enormous! Demographers estimate that some sixty to seventy billion people have lived on this planet thus far. Without diminishing in any way the importance of the absolutely vital and tandem work on this side of the veil, we do need a better grasp of "things as they really will be" (*Jacob 4:13*). Otherwise, we can so easily come to regard family history as a quaint hobby and its resulting temple work as something we will get around to later. Not only does the word *vastness* characterize the work there but so does *intensity.* Of course, we still lack many details and would like to know more. Even so, we ought to pay closer attention to what has been given about the spirit world so that we can truly "cite [our] minds forward" in appropriate ways (*Alma 13:1*) (*The Promise of Discipleship, 105*).

> Is one reason we are not told more about the details of God's work in the spirit world perhaps the intimidating larger scale of things there? The scope of the work there is so large that it might embarrass those of us here. Probably twelve times the earth's present population live there. For sure, twelve [now fifteen] times as many presidents of the Church in this dispensation alone are in residence and at work there! Perhaps God thus protects us in our present provinciality from feeling diminished by considerations of scale (*That Ye May Believe, 93*).

> Much of our continuing to work out our own salvation in the spirit world consists of our further correcting our personal deficiencies. If, for instance, we fully accept Christ as our Savior this includes accepting the fact that he asks us to become more like Him (*see 3 Nephi 27:27*). Clearly, in this rigorous process, not all gets done on this side of the veil of death (*That Ye May Believe, 93*).

12. Do Christians today, in general, believe in the spirit world?

No. Although most Christians believe in immortality, beliefs about the afterlife vary widely among denominations and individuals. The concept of a temporary and intermediate abode for all the disembodied dead, good and bad (i.e., postmortal spirit world) is not universally accepted today in Christian thought (*e.g., see EB, Christianity-Concepts of Life after Death*).

This has not always been the case. In the *Bible*, there are numerous references to the spirit world that are translated as *hell* (*TG, 207*). Christian scholars note: "In Jesus' day, Hell (*Sheol* in Hebrew and *Hades* in Greek) was understood not as a place of eternal damnation, but as the resting place of all dead souls" (Heidi J. Hornik and Mikeal C. Parsons, *The Harrowing of Hell, Bible Review, June 2003, 20*). Today, hell has such a negative connotation (*e.g., Dante's Inferno*) no wonder many Christians have a problem with the spirit world. Few Christians want to go to hell!

In spite of the word hell, some modern Christian scholars allude to the spirit world. Matthew George Easton, a Scottish Presbyterian minister known for his masterful *Bible* dictionary, defined hell (translated from the Hebrew Sheol or Greek Hades) as "the place of disembodied spirits" or "the congregation of the dead" (*Proverbs 21:16*). "It is the abode of the wicked" and "of the good." "The righteous and the wicked are separated. The blessed dead are in that part of hades called paradise" (*Easton's Bible Dictionary*). The prolific lexicographer William Smith defined hell as "the word generally and unfortunately used by our translators to render the Hebrew Sheol. It really means the place of the dead, the unseen world, without deciding whether it be the place of misery or of happiness" (*Smith's Bible Dictionary*). (*See also #24.*)

Some Christians believe the ancient teaching that Christ went to the spirit world to bring salvation to the ignorant. The highly regarded and oft-quoted *Apostles' Creed* declares where Jesus went after His death: "He descended into hell" (*The Apostles' Creed, 22*). There He "preached unto the spirits in prison" (*1 Peter 3:19*). The well-known Christian scholar and author William Barclay wrote:

> *He descended into hell.* It would surely be true to say that this is the most neglected sentence in the *Apostles' Creed* . . . What happens to the millions upon millions of men who never hear of Jesus Christ? This doctrine means symbolically that either in this life or in the life beyond death all men are offered the gospel of truth and the love of God (*The Apostles' Creed, 22-23*).

Prominent reformers disputed the ancient tradition of Christ's descent. John Calvin said it was "nothing but a fable" (*Institutes of the Christian Religion 2:442*). Martin Luther declared it "figments of some stupid and bungling sophist" (*Luther's Works II, 175*). By 1700 the convention of Christ descending into the spirit world between His crucifixion and His resurrection "had virtually disappeared" from Christian awareness (Heidi J. Hornik and Mikeal C. Parsons, *The Harrowing of Hell, Bible Review, June 2003, 50*).

In writing about the early Christian tradition of a spirit world, Hugh Nibley quoted from numerous early Christian sources describing the

Savior's and Apostles' teachings about the gospel being taught in spirit world and the ordinance of baptism for the dead, which is performed by the living, in proxy for the dead who are in the spirit world.[ii] Latter-day Saints believe in the spirit world and the opportunity there for all to hear the gospel. The *Encyclopedia of Mormonism* states:

> [T]he dead as well as the living may receive the gospel of Jesus Christ. Every man, woman, and child who has ever lived or whoever will live on this earth will have full opportunity, if not in this life then in the next, to embrace or reject the gospel in its purity and fulness (*EM, 1257*).

13. Do Christians today, in general, believe in a premortal existence?

Not anymore. Today, Christian theology mostly rejects the notion, although that has not always been the case. The Christian theologian, Robert Hamerton-Kelly explained: "While Orthodox Christian doctrine insists that humanity did not pre-exist, there are those who postulate that the biblical tradition says otherwise" (*Pre-Existence, Wisdom, and the Son of Man, 273*).

Indeed, it was widely accepted in the early Church. Several biblical prophets taught about this existence (*see Jeremiah 1:5; Romans 8:29; Ephesians 1:4; Moses 3:5; Abraham 3:22-23*). The doctrine was commonly taught and accepted until the Council of AD 543. Hugh Nibley quotes numerous early Christian sources, such as Josephus, Origen, Pastor of Hermas, Odes of Solomon, and Patrologia, evidencing the early Christian doctrine of a premortal existence. Clement said, "Well, if I live after, I must have lived before" (*CWHN 12:367-369*).

Joseph Smith, through modern revelation, restored and taught the truth that mankind lived as spirits with God before birth (*see Abraham 3:22-23*). The premortal spirit world is in yonder heavens and includes spirits waiting to be born.

CHAPTER TWO

SPIRIT WORLD GEOGRAPHY

Dear Mother Earth, who day by day
Unfoldest blessings on our way,
Alleluia! Alleluia!
—St. Francis of Assisi, All Creatures of Our God and King, Hymns, 62

14. Where is the postmortal spirit world?

"It is right here" (*JD 3:369*); "The spirit world . . . is on this earth" (*JD 3:372*), taught Brigham Young. Parley P. Pratt said the same:

> [I]t is here on this very planet where we were born . . . the earth and all other planets of a like sphere, have their inward or spiritual spheres, as well as their outward, or temporal. The one is peopled by temporal tabernacles, and the other by spirits. A veil is drawn between the one sphere and the other, whereby all the objects in the spiritual sphere are rendered invisible to those in the temporal (*KST, 129-130*).

15. Explain, so where on earth is the spirit world?

Joseph Smith said spirits "are not far from us" (*HC 6:52*). Brigham Young said spirits do not "go beyond the boundaries of this organized earth" (*JD 3:369*). He explained:

> It is incorporated within this celestial [earth] system. Can you see it with your natural eyes? No. (*JD 3:368*). [Spirits] dwell everywhere . . . on this continent; it is full of them. If you could see . . . you would see millions on millions of the spirits of those who have been slain on this continent. Would you see the spirits of those who were as good in the flesh as they

> know how to be? Yes. Would you see the spirits of the wicked? Yes. Could you see the spirits of devils? Yes . . . They do not pass out of the organization of this earth on which we live (*JD 3:368*).

Jesus Christ and the early Apostles understood the spirit world was here, using terminology suggesting the spirit world is within or somehow part of the earth. Matthew quoted Jesus: "For as Jonas was three days and three nights in the whale's belly; so shall the Son of man be three days and three nights in the heart of the earth" (*Matthew 12:40*). Paul taught that before Christ ascended to His Father in heaven, "he also descended first into the lower parts of the earth" (*Ephesians 4:9*). John said Satan "was cast out into the earth, and his angels were cast out with him" (*Revelation 12:9*). They "encompasseth [us] round about (*D&C 76:29*; *see #165*).

Mother earth is alive. She has a spirit and a gender. Jesus said the "earth rolls upon her wings" (*D&C 88:45*). Spirits fill the physical body they are given. Just as our spirit bodies are within our physical bodies, the spirit world is within the physical world (*see #14 and #75*). Some find it helpful to imagine the spirit world as a fourth dimension, not discernible by us in our three dimensional existence.

16. Do the righteous and wicked go to the same spirit world?

Yes. Joseph Smith was clear on this: "The righteous and the wicked all go to the same world of spirits until the resurrection" (*HC 5:425*). Brigham Young queried: "Do the good and evil spirits go together? Yes they do. Do they inhabit one kingdom? Yes, they do" (*JD 3:369*) (*see also #174*).

17. Do spirits from other worlds go to our spirit world?

No. Harold B. Lee taught: "the spirit world is right here round about us, and the only spirits who can live here are those who are assigned to fill their missions here on earth. This is the spirit world. And if our eyes could be opened we could see those who have departed from us—a father, mother, brother, a sister, a child" (*Teachings of Harold B. Lee, 58*). (*See also DBY, 376-377; KST, 117.*)

Brigham Young said the spirit world is "on this earth that was organized for the people that have lived and that do and will live upon it" (*JD 3:372*).

18. Can mortals go to the spirit world?

No. Mortals (earthlings with flesh and blood) cannot go there. However, resurrected beings can go there. Joseph Smith said: "Flesh and blood cannot go there [the spirit world]; but flesh and bones, quickened by the Spirit of God, can" (*HC 6:52*). On occasion, spirits have momentarily left their mortal bodies of flesh and blood, visited the spirit world, and then returned to mortality (*see Appendix A*).

19. Are the spirit world and the world of resurrected beings the same place?

No. Disembodied spirits go to the spirit world, a different place than the world of resurrected beings (*see also #78*). However, resurrected beings can minister in the spirit world. Brigham Young explained where righteous spirits go upon death:

> [W]hen they pass through the veil they are in happiness, they are in glory, they go among the disembodied spirits; but they do not go where there are resurrected bodies, for they cannot live there. Do they commune with the Father and Son? The Father communes with them as He pleases, through the means of angels, or otherwise the Son and Holy Ghost (*JD 6:293*). When a person passes beyond the veil, he can only officiate in the spirit world; but when he is resurrected he officiates as a resurrected being . . . (*JD 9:88-89*).

Parley P. Pratt declared:

> The [postmortal] spirit world is not the heaven where Jesus Christ, his Father, and other beings dwell, who have, by resurrection or translation,

ascended to eternal mansions, and been crowned and seated on thrones of power; but it is an intermediate state, a probation, a place of preparation, improvement, instruction, or education, where spirits are chastened and improved, and where, if found worthy, they may be taught a knowledge of the Gospel" (*KST, 129*). (*See also #77.*)

20. Are the premortal spirit world and the postmortal spirit world the same place?

No. The premortal spirit world is beyond our solar system in the heavens where God dwells (*see #56*; *Isaiah 55:9*). The postmortal spirit world is here on earth. In *The Family: A Proclamation to the World* the First Presidency and Council of the Twelve Apostles declared: "In the premortal realm, spirit sons and daughters knew and worshiped God as their Eternal Father and accepted His plan by which His children could obtain a physical body and gain earthly experience."

The Encyclopedia of Mormonism explains:

Since spirits exist before mortality, as well as afterward, there is both a premortal and a postmortal spirit world. The premortal spirit existence, for mankind at least, was "in heaven," in the kingdom where God lives. Explaining this phase of the Creation, the Lord said, "I, the Lord God, created all things, of which I have spoken, spiritually, before they were naturally upon the face of the earth . . . for in heaven created I them (*Moses 3:5*)" (*EM, 1408*).

CHAPTER THREE

SPIRIT WORLD TERMINOLOGY

Oh say, what is truth?'Tis the brightest prize
To which mortals or Gods can aspire.
Go search in the depths where it glittering lies,
Or ascend in pursuit to the loftiest skies:
'Tis an aim for the noblest desire.
—John Jaques, Oh Say, What Is Truth? Hymns, 272

21. What terms are used for the entire postmortal world of spirits?

There are many words employed such as *spirit world, spirit prison, paradise, hell, Hades* (Greek), *Sheol* (Hebrew), *underworld, netherworld, abode of the dead,* and *place of departed spirits* (*see AHD, #12, #22, #131*). Some of these terms, such as *spirit prison, paradise,* and *hell* also have other meanings which are defined in this chapter. Joseph Smith often used the term *world of spirits* (*see TPJS, 310; HC 5:424-426*). Brigham Young and later prophets used the term *spirit world* (*DBY, 376-380; D&C 138:16*) and *postearthly spirit world* (Russell M. Nelson, *Ensign, May 1987*). Today we often use the term *postmortal spirit world* to differentiate from the *premortal spirit world* (*see EM, 1404; Gospel Principles, 241*). *Heaven* has several diverse meanings (*see Chapter 7*) and is normally differentiated from the *postmortal spirit world.*

An unborn spirit in the *premortal spirit world* is *unembodied.* When the spirit enters mortality it is *embodied.* Upon death, the spirit is *disembodied* in the *postmortal spirit world.* In the resurrection, the spirit is *reembodied* never again to be separated (*see EM, 1404*).

Words in the scriptures have different meanings and are understood on various levels. Accordingly, terms describing the hereafter both in and outside the scriptures mean a number of things. Also, bear in mind our language isn't perfect. Given these circumstances, we need not zealously fret over semantics. There is really nothing we can do to change the way words have been used to describe the hereafter. Rather than demanding or inventing exclusive definitions, we will focus on principles and gospel doctrine. Robert Millet wrote: "I have begun to notice in myself that when my study of the scriptures becomes wholly an intellectual endeavor, when it becomes more definitional than devotional, I have taken a detour" (*Within Reach, 23-24*). To understand the spirit world, we will briefly review the terminology that has historically been used, recognizing that the context and intent of the writer is paramount. We also recognize that the Lord has not yet chosen to completely map out the details of the spirit world for us.

22. In the scriptures is the spirit world called the spirit prison?

Yes. In this broad view, the scriptures don't differentiate between the *spirit world* and *spirit prison.*[iii] Joseph Fielding McConkie explained: "The spirit world and spirit prison are one and the same place. 'Spirit prison' as used in the scriptures refers to the entire spirit world. 'Spirit prison' embraces both paradise and the place of torment to which wicked spirits are consigned" (*Answers, 98-101*).

Bruce R. McConkie noted that in Joseph F. Smith's vision of the redemption of the dead, *D&C 138*, "It is clearly set forth that the whole spirit world, and not only that portion designated as hell, is considered to be a spirit prison" (*Ensign, August 1976*).

23. How is the entire spirit world a prison?

The *spirit world* is a *spirit prison* in one sense because spirits do not have physical bodies there. Spirits look upon the "long absence of their spirits from their bodies as a bondage" (*D&C 138:50*). Disembodied spirits regard their state as a bondage because "when separated, man cannot receive a fulness of joy" (*D&C 93:34*).

Joseph Smith taught about the importance of a body:

> We came to this earth that we might have a body and present it pure before God in the celestial kingdom. The great principle of happiness consists in having a body. The devil has no body, and herein is his punishment. He is pleased when he can obtain the tabernacle of man, and when cast out by the Savior he asked to go into the herd of swine, showing that he would prefer a swine's body to having none [*Luke 8:33*]. All beings who have bodies have power over those who have not (*TPJS, 181*).

24. In what sense is the entire spirit world sometimes called hell?

Hell is not necessarily a bad place in this context. Historically it was a word for the entire underworld, the world of the dead. Joseph Smith explained: "Hades, the Greek, or Sheol, the Hebrew, these two significations mean a world of spirits. Hades, Sheol, paradise, spirits in prison, are all one: it is a world of spirits. The righteous and the wicked all go to the same world of spirits until the resurrection" (*TPJS, 310*) (*see also #12 and #21*).

25. What are the major divisions in the spirit world?

There are two major divisions: *paradise* and *spirit prison* (*see Gospel Fundamentals, 196*). These are narrower definitions for these terms than the broad definitions used for the entire spirit world (*#21, #24*). "When a person dies who has accepted the gospel and been a faithful follower of Jesus, that person's spirit goes to paradise" (*Gospel Fundamentals, 196; see also Chapter 12*). Three kinds of people go to spirit prison: "those who were wicked in this life, those who lived good lives but did not accept the gospel, and those who never had the opportunity to hear the gospel (*Gospel Fundamentals, 196; see also Chapter 13*). *Hell* in common speech (*see #26*) is the place of torment for the wicked within *spirit prison* (*see Chapter 14*).

Joseph F. Smith said that upon death the spirit is "assigned to its place, either to associate with the good and the noble ones who have lived in the paradise of God, or be confined in the 'prison-house' to await the resurrection of the body from the grave" (*GD, 566*).

The *Bible Dictionary* elaborates: "it has been often held, both in Jewish and the Christian churches, that Hades (meaning broadly the place of departed spirits) consists of two parts, *paradise* and *Gehenna* [*hell* in common speech], one the abode of the righteous and the other of the disobedient" (*BD, 699*). The righteous in paradise are in a state of happiness and the wicked in hell are in a state of torment (*see Alma 12:13; 40:12-14; 42:1; 1 Nephi 15:30-36; 2 Nephi 9:27*).

The Savior referred to *paradise* as *Abraham's Bosom* (*see Luke 16:22-23*). "It connotes the harmony that exists among the righteous in paradise, as they await the resurrection" (*BD, 602*). Abraham no longer resides in paradise because he is now a resurrected and exalted god (*see D&C 132:37; 133:55*).

In *paradise* and *spirit prison*, there are various states or conditions (*see Chapters 12, 13 and 14*).

26. What is hell in common speech?

Hell in familiar terminology means the undesirable abode of the disobedient within the *spirit prison* part of the *spirit world*. The *Bible Dictionary* defines *hell* as commonly used today:

> In common speech, it generally denotes the place of torment for the wicked . . . In latter-day revelation hell is spoken of . . . as the temporary abode in the spirit world of those who were disobedient in this mortal life. It is between death and the resurrection, and persons who receive the telestial glory will abide there until the last resurrection at which time they will go to the telestial glory (*BD, 700*; *see D&C 76: 84-85*).

Sometimes *hell* refers to what we commonly call *spirit prison*, which is the entire *spirit world* excluding *paradise*. *Hell* can also mean the permanent habitation of Satan and his followers including the sons of *perdition* (*see EM 585*). Previously we noted that *hell* can mean the entire *spirit world* (*see #12, #21, #24*). Obviously, with so many definitions of *hell*, we must look at the context to decipher the writer's intent.

27. What is outer darkness?

In the scriptures, *outer darkness* usually means the common definition of *hell*, or *Gehenna*. Robert L. Millet and Joseph Fielding McConkie wrote: "With but few exceptions, outer darkness refers to hell, the place of suffering and sadness and confrontation in the spirit world" (*The Life Beyond, 169*). (*See also Alma 40:13-14; 41:7; D&C 38:5; 138:22, 30, 57; Isaiah 49:9.*)

In common speech, Latter-day Saints often use the term *outer darkness* as the post-resurrection, never-ending, second state of hell, called *perdition*. "*Outer darkness* is where Satan and those who have followed him will live" *(Gospel Fundamentals, 202*). These "sons of perdition are not merely wicked; they are incorrigibly evil" (*EM, 1391*).

CHAPTER FOUR

EVIDENCE OF LIFE AFTER DEATH

Prove all things; hold fast that which is good.
—1 Thessalonians 5:21

28. Can it be proven that there is life after death and a spirit world?

Maybe, depending on the kind of proof required. If the required proof is irrefutable evidence upon which all scientists can agree, then no. However, there are many proofs available to the honest and open-minded seeker of truth:

(a) ***Jesus went to the spirit world after He died***, "being put to death in the flesh, but quickened by the Spirit: By which also he went and preached unto the spirits in prison [spirit world]" (*1 Peter 3:18-19; see also D&C 138*).

(b) ***Jesus was resurrected*** on the third day after His death, demonstrating that life continues. After His resurrection Jesus appeared to Mary Magdalene (*Mark 16:9*) then to several other women, the Apostles, Cleopas and Luke on the road to Emmaus (*MM, 509*) and to over 500 brethren at once on a mountain (*1 Corinthians 15:6*). Jesus showed his resurrected body to a multitude of about twenty-five hundred in the Americas; and he let them, one by one, feel with their hands the "prints of the nails in his hands and in his feet . . . and [they] did know of a surety and did bear record, that it was he" (*see 3 Nephi 11:8-17*). Howard W. Hunter, an accomplished attorney and modern prophet, noted: "The testimony of those who saw [Jesus] as a living person after his death has never been contradicted . . . We can come to only one conclusion: the resurrection is a historical fact amply proved by authenticated documentary evidence and the testimony of competent witnesses" (*The Teachings of Howard W. Hunter, 17-18*).

(c) ***Many deceased Saints rose from their graves*** after Jesus' resurrection on both continents. Witnesses bear record of the resurrection of these people in the *New Testament* (*Matthew 27:52*) and *Book of Mormon* (*3 Nephi 23:9-11*). The *Book of Mormon* prophets testify at length of the hereafter and the resurrection for all mankind.

(d) ***Modern witnesses have seen resurrected beings***. There are three witnesses of the Book of Mormon who saw the resurrected Angel Moroni and the gold plates and another eight witnesses who handled the gold plates (*Book of Mormon, Introduction*). In the Doctrine & Covenants and Pearl of Great Price there are testimonies of Joseph Smith and others who saw Jesus Christ (*D&C 76; 110; JS-History*) and resurrected angels such as John the Baptist (*D&C 13*); Peter and James (*D&C 27:12*); Elijah (*D&C 110:13*); and Moses (*D&C 110:11*).

(e) ***Millions of people say they know there is life after death***.[iv] Some testify from a witness of the Spirit, powerful enough to create certainty. Many have experienced a vision, vivid dream, near-death experience (NDE), communication with the deceased, or other spiritual epiphany. In these experiences, many have seen and talked to deceased loved-ones, resulting in life-changing behavior and a firm belief in the hereafter (*see also #35 and #36*). Moroni taught that God is "merciful" to all his children "from the creation of Adam" (*Moroni 10:3*). We are admonished to "deny not the gifts of God" and the "different ways that these gifts are administered" by the Spirit of Christ "unto every man severally [separately] according as he will" (*Moroni 10:8,17*). One of the gifts is "the beholding of angels and ministering spirits" (*Moroni 10:14*).

The above proofs are convincing for many but not all. For some, "though we, or an angel from heaven" (*Galations 1:8*) told them, they would not believe. This kind of religious knowledge is learned by the Spirit, by those who want to believe. Paul explained: "But the natural man receiveth not the things of the Spirit of God: for they are foolishness unto him: neither can he know *them*, because they are spiritually discerned" (*1 Corinthians 2:14*). The Lord gives us evidence and conviction if we look for it with a believing heart. One has to believe it to see it (*see 1 Nephi 15:11; D&C 11:14; 35:8; Ether 4:11*; *12:6*). For those who don't believe, the prophet Alma advised: "even if ye can no more than desire to believe, let this desire work in you" (*Alma 32:27*).

Do these evidences provide scientific proof that can be verified and duplicated at a moments notice using scientific methods? No. Is our knowledge perfect? No. So we still need faith? Yes, so what else is new? Walking by faith is the Lord's way for us. Apparently, with the veil separating mortality from eternity in place, God intends to limit our knowledge and try our faith. Can we obtain our own testimony, our own spiritual proof, without having a near-death or other extraordinary spiritual experience? Absolutely, such is the unsurpassed validation: "converting the soul: the testimony of the Lord is sure" (*Psalm 19:7*).

29. What is an NDE (near-death experience)?

There is no official, agreed-upon definition. The pioneer of modern NDE research, Dr. Raymond Moody defined NDEs as "profound spiritual events that happen, uninvited, to some individuals at the point of death."*(cited in Evidence, 24*). Dr. Jeffrey Long defined NDEs as "events that take place as a person is dying, or indeed, is already clinically dead." Near-death experiencers in his research were "generally unconscious and often apparently clinically dead, with absence of heartbeat and breathing" (*Evidence, 5*). Skeptics say NDEs are dreams, hallucinations, or brain-induced imaginations; while NDE scientists and researchers exclude those experiences from the definition. LDS scholars explain the NDE, in general, in terms of the spirit entering a spiritual state or spirit realm, an experience of hope permitted by our merciful Heavenly Father (*e.g., see Glimpses, 8*). Typically, in the NDE, the spirit leaves the body (*see #112*) which may constitute death in the scriptural definition (*see #89*).

30. Do the scriptures contain examples of near-death experiences?

Yes. There are numerous examples in the scriptures where individuals have been brought back to life. These would be called near-death experiences today (*see #29*). Mark, Luke, and John reported on Jesus' raising three from the dead: Jairus' daughter (*Mark 5:22-42*); the widow of Nain's son (*Luke 7:11-15*); and Lazarus (*John 11:1-44*). Jesus demonstrated His power over death; and provided irrefutable evidence of the ability of the spirit to leave the body and then return. Apparently the spirit leaves the body in most NDEs (*see #112*); although experiencers are not typically dead for as long as Lazarus was (four days). Those Jesus brought back were not resurrected. They had died and were restored to life as mortals, meaning they would die again. Luke described Paul's resuscitation of Eutychus who had fallen asleep and then fell from the third story while listening to Paul's "long preaching." Eutychus was "taken up dead" but brought back to life (*Acts 20:9-12*). Elijah "cried unto the Lord" and raised the widow's son from the dead (*1 Kings 17:17-24*). A dead man was cast into Elisha's grave and then came back to life (*2 Kings 13:20-21*).

The scriptures relate several "nigh unto death" experiences that would also be defined as "near-death" in today's vernacular. For example, consider Alma's conversion story when an angel reprimanded him: "I fell to the earth and I did hear no more" and "it was for the space of three days and three nights that I could not open my mouth, neither had I the use of my limbs;" (*Alma 36:11,10*) and was "wading through much tribulation, repenting nigh unto death" (*Mosiah 27:28*).

Alma continued: "I was in the darkest abyss;" (*Mosiah 27:29*) "racked with eternal torment," being "encircled about by the everlasting chains of death" (*Alma 36:12, 18*). Alma's life passed before him: "I did remember all my sins and iniquities, for which I was tormented with the pains of hell" (*Alma 36: 13*). "Yea, methought I saw, even as our father Lehi saw, God sitting upon his throne, surrounded with numberless concourses of angels, in the attitude of singing and praising their God; yea, and my soul did long to be there" (*Alma 36:22*).

After this experience, Alma spoke with authority when he wrote about the spirit world (*see Alma 40*).

Other NDEs occurred to King Lamoni who "fell unto the earth, as if he were dead" (*Alma 18:42*), then rose on the third day to prophesy, prompting a similar experience for his wife (*see Alma 19:1-34*). Lamoni's father was struck "as if he were dead" before Aaron raised him (*see Alma 22:18-22*).

Jonah was in the belly of the fish three days, where he "fainted" and "remembered the Lord" (*Jonah 2:7*). Some scholars suggest he may have died and was raised, like Lazarus. Whatever happened to Jonah, we know he survived to give his remarkable nigh unto death report. Jesus himself referred to Jonah's experience (*Matthew 12:39-41; 16:4; Luke 11:29-30*).

When Jesus was crucified and came forth on the third day as the first to be resurrected, this monumental event culminated the type and shadow of others' three- day, nigh unto death experiences. Jesus was resurrected with an immortal body not subject to death.

31. Can LDS theology accommodate near-death accounts?

Yes. In general, most NDE reports are strikingly consistent with LDS revealed theology of the body and spirit, death, and the spirit world. For example, NDE studies show that most experience their spirit separated from the body while retaining their mind and identity. They are free of disability, pain, and illness, with feelings of peace and joy. Many are enveloped in a comforting light, meet deceased relatives, and see beautiful surroundings. Some encounter undesirable conditions, or what we would call hell. Whether the brief event is positive or negative, studies show experiencers almost always change in a positive way. They become kinder, happier, and better people suggesting the Lord's hand in these occurrences. The Lord reminds us: "whatsoever thing persuadeth men to do good is of me; for good cometh of none save it be of me" (*Ether 4:12*).

NDE researcher Dr. Raymond Moody recognized the similarity of LDS theology with NDE findings. He wrote: "the most prominent of the Western religions . . . to accept NDEs as a doorway to the spiritual world . . . is The Church of Jesus Christ of Latter-Day Saints" (*The Light Beyond, 88*). Latter-day Saints have been telling NDE stories for almost 200 years. Joseph Smith and other Apostles and prophets had visions and visits from angels that created an acceptance and understanding of spiritual manifestations among Latter-day Saints. NDEs were not popular with the general public until about thirty years ago perhaps because experiencers were often ridiculed or dismissed.

Many NDEs are experienced by children (*see* Melvin Morse MD, *Closer to the Light—Learning from the Near-death Experiences of Children*). We believe "little children are holy, being sanctified" (*D&C 74:7*); "children are alive in Christ" (*Moroni 8:22*); and "little children do have words given unto them" (*Alma 32:23*). These pure and undefiled children may have remarkable spiritual experiences that should not be easily dismissed.

A bibliographic search found hundreds of books published about NDEs, most of them in the past thirty years. Some focus on LDS NDEs. Many, including Latter-day Saints and others, find NDE stories to be uplifting and motivational.

32. Do NDEs contribute to our gospel understanding?

Yes. However, unless they are recorded in the scriptures, they are not part of our standard works. The study of NDEs should never substitute for one's study of the gospel of Jesus Christ. Non-scriptural NDE information is not required knowledge for individual salvation, but scriptural knowledge is. Since the 1800s, many faithful Saints have felt inspired to share their NDEs, and many have been published in the Church News and Church periodicals (*e.g. see Appendices* and *Sources*). Other NDEs have been recorded in family histories. Some of these accounts are retold in talks and writings by prophets, general authorities and LDS scholars as faith-promoting stories. Although NDEs may sometimes provide additional background information about the spirit world, our foundational understanding of the hereafter and the plan of salvation comes from the teachings of the prophets and the scriptures. The answers to the questions in this book come primarily from these teachings and are only augmented by NDEs throughout the book and in the appendices where deemed appropriate.

33. What other cautions are in order concerning NDEs?

Here are three other caveats to consider when discussing NDEs:

(a) ***NDEs are sacred and spiritual.*** We should use caution in relating and not sensationalizing the sacred nature of spiritual experiences. An NDE is an unusual and spiritual occurrence and therefore worthy of respect. Although it is estimated that millions have had an NDE experience, the vast majority of us have not. Researchers estimate that only ten to twenty percent of cardiac arrest patients who are medically dead and come back to life have recollection of an NDE (*see Evidence, 57*). A genuine, uninvited NDE constitutes a piercing of the veil, which may be a singular blessing allowed by Heavenly Father in his tender mercy. We don't know why some have the experience and some do not. Paul wrote: "God also bearing them witness, both with signs and wonders, and with divers miracles, and gifts of the Holy Ghost, according to his own will?" (*Hebrews 2:4*). NDE scholar and researcher Dr. Michael Sabom delineated why the NDE is fundamentally a spiritual experience:

> (1) it occurs in the realm of the spirit or soul and not in the physical realm; (2) it is essentially religious in nature and pertains to the things of religion that transcend the material world; (3) it is not amenable to scientific quantification—no instruments have ever detected or diagnosed an NDE; and (4) it is real, not imaginary or the product of an hallucination—experiencers strongly insist that NDEs are not just another dream (*Light & Death, 201*).

NDE researcher Kenneth Ring, PhD, observed that in his interviews of hundreds of experiencers over many years, they have almost always said: "This is the most profound, most secret, spiritual experience I have ever had." (The Light Beyond, 160).

Given the sacred nature, some may choose not to share it, share only certain things, or share only among family or close friends. However, some feel inspired that much good can come by sharing the experience for the benefit of any who can learn from it. We should not begrudge another's choice to share. Many faith-promoting NDEs both in the scriptures and outside of the scriptures have been appropriately shared and published for the edification of people from all walks of life.

(b) ***NDEs should be evaluated for credibility***. It is wise for us to consider the source and accuracy of reported NDEs. NDEs collected by research experts are screened. Because they have reviewed thousands of NDEs they have learned to detect inconsistent and dishonest stories. Compilers write that the vast majority of these NDEs are true as the experiencer can best describe it; although some have been shown to be false or embellished. Unfortunately some NDE stories seem to morph to satisfy an audience or agenda. Harold A. Widdison, PhD and NDE scholar, noted:

> I have no problem with the experience as originally reported by the experiencer. Where problems can and do arise is when the experiencer attempts to interpret and explain its meaning to others. This is where their cultural and personal beliefs, or suggestions by others as to their experience's true meaning . . . may distort the experience (Gibson, *They Saw Beyond Death, 281*).

(c) ***NDEs should not be induced or coaxed***. Because of the positive benefits of NDEs, some NDE researchers or others may try to induce near-death-like experiences. We should be careful to not want or cause them to happen. Spiritual experiences should not be coerced. The Holy Spirit can't be forced (*#82*). Such activities are contrary to the Lord's pattern (*see #83 and #166*).

The Apostle, Russell M. Nelson, MD, was once asked whether he would contribute NDE stories for a book. The compiler was gathering stories from patients who had come close enough to death to experience the other side and yet had survived to share those accounts. Elder Nelson said:

> When I considered that request, I remembered many such incidents which had been whispered in confidence to me over the years. But those seemed too sacred to share in a worldly way, especially to the benefit of a commercial venture. Besides, what would be the validity of isolated stories of life after life without supporting testimonies of witnesses? (*Ensign, May 1987*).

Perhaps for the aforementioned reasons, we don't see as many published NDEs in Church periodicals today as we did in the 1800s and early 1900s.

34. Do NDEs accurately describe the spirit world?

In general, NDE researchers and spirit world scholars think so, at least as experiencers can best describe it. As for the depictions of the spirit world in today's vast NDE library, undoubtedly, like the apocrypha, "there are many things contained therein that are true" and "there are many things contained therein that are not true" (*D&C 91:1-2*). Although there is amazing consistency among NDEs, they see what the Lord permits them to see, to be interpreted by the beholder, and primarily for the beholder's benefit. One's description of the extraordinary spirit world realm is limited by his earthly experience and perspective. The spirit world is so unusual, experiencers often say they don't have the words to describe it. Dr. Jeffrey Long explains how interpretations can differ:

> [A]lthough there may be some minor differences, in truth, looking at NDEs around the world is like showing a class of young, multinational students a photograph of the Eiffel Tower in France: some will know what it is, others will think it's scaffolding for a building in progress, and others will think it's a spaceship. All of the children are seeing the same

> thing; they are just interpreting and expressing it differently based on what they know of life (*Evidence, 157-158*).

To further illustrate, some may say they went to heaven, when in reality they went to the spirit world. They may say they saw the pearly gates of heaven, when they saw some beautiful gates. Or they may say they saw deity, when perhaps they really saw a spirit who had advanced with light and power in the spirit world. They may have assumed it was deity because they had never experienced a personage of such light. Researchers indicate it is rare in an NDE for a being of light to actually identify himself as deity. However, some have reported knowing a personage was Jesus because another spirit told them, or because they "just knew" with certainty.

Some of what one sees in an NDE or vision may be symbolic. For example, Isaiah and Ezekial saw visions of winged seraphim. Were their visions of symbolic creatures? Jesus said the winged beasts in John the Revelator's vision were figurative, the wings being a representation of power (*see D&C 77:2-4*). Consider that spirits, who are adults, may take on the form of a child in order to be recognized (*see #62*).

It is also possible that one's NDE could include a vision of another time, past or future, or even another place (*e.g., see A3*). Visions in the scriptures (which may or may not result from an NDE) are sometimes of the past, future, or different places.

Evidently, God has purposely limited our understanding of the spirit world, making it difficult to interpret the meaning or accuracy of some of the reports we read in NDEs. However, the general descriptions of the spirit world are amazingly similar given they come from adults and children of different faiths and culture.

35. Do NDEs provide evidence of life after death?

Yes. Dr. Jeffrey Long wrote: "By studying thousands of detailed accounts of NDErs, I found evidence that led to this astounding conclusion: *NDEs provide such powerful scientific evidence that it is reasonable to accept the existence of an afterlife.*" His evidences are summarized below:

(a) ***Lucid and clear consciousness.*** Those who are near death are generally unconscious or clinically dead. Yet they usually experience a "more heightened state of awareness than in everyday earthly life."

(b) ***Realistic out of body experiences.*** They describe events they "shouldn't be able to see" because they are unconscious. Many NDEs occur under general anesthesia. Sometimes the observations are of the room where their body lies, and their observations are almost always confirmed as completely accurate.[v]

(c) ***The blind have visual NDEs.*** "Individuals totally blind from birth are completely unable to perceive the visual world;" it's an abstract concept to them. "Their dreams do not include vision . . . Yet when a blind person has an NDE, the experience usually includes vision."

(d) ***Life Reviews restore memory.*** Real events in the experiencer's life are played back in amazing detail, "even if those events have been forgotten." The panoramic life reviews are very distinct and powerful.

(e) ***Seeing deceased relatives.*** "Virtually all beings encountered during NDEs are deceased at the time of the NDE, and most are deceased relatives." Sometimes the identity of the deceased is established by looking at old family photographs. "By contrast, in dreams or hallucinations the beings encountered are much more likely to be living."

(f) ***Children's experiences.*** "The striking similarity of content in NDEs among very young children and that of adults strongly suggests that the content of NDEs is not due to preexisting beliefs." This is strong evidence because very young children almost certainly have never heard of NDEs as adults often have. They become aware for the first time about typical NDE elements in their own NDE.

(g) ***Worldwide consistency.*** "The remarkable consistency of NDEs around the world is evidence that NDEs are real events." The only difference is the way the different cultures describe things.

(h) ***Aftereffects***. Near-death experiencers are transformed in many positive ways by their experience, often for life. They have a less fear of death, stronger belief in the afterlife, more love and compassion for others, and they become nicer (*see Evidence, 44-50*).

36. Do other spiritual experiences provide evidence of life after death?

Yes, some do. The test of whether a spiritual manifestation is of God is whether the light of Christ is present. The light or Holy Spirit is uplifting and edifying (*see #6*). Any such experience ratified by the Holy Spirit is evidence of God and His revealed plan of immortality and salvation for mankind. A remarkable spiritual manifestation may be enjoyed by those who are spiritually in tune, or it may be a gift from God bestowed to anyone as He sees fit to accomplish His purposes.

One need not be near death to have a near-death-like experience. In one NDE study 24% of respondents reported that their experience was connected with a non-life threatening situation (Migliore, *A Measure of Heaven, 19*). People report experiences that are similar to NDEs under various conditions, such as "non-life-threatening trauma, emotional and frightful events, and paranormal experiences growing out of prayer and meditation . . . serious depression, or without clear cause in fully conscious people" (Migliore, *A Measure of Heaven, 30*). In these experiences, the same evidences as described in NDEs above (*#35*) are noted.

The accomplished NDE researcher Dr. Kenneth Ring described the healing influence of one's encounter with spiritual light in a near-death or near-death-like experience:

> It is important to realize, however, that the healing balm of the Light is available not just to NDErs, of course, but to *anyone* who finds him—or herself in a deep spiritual crisis or on the verge of suicide. In my years of researching NDEs, I have in fact heard from many persons who, though they clearly were not physically near death, nevertheless had a kind of NDE, which in its properties *and* effects was indistinguishable from

> those that are triggered by an actual condition in which one's life is at risk. Thus, the Light seems to come to those who need it, *regardless* of the individual's physical state. Instead, it is the state of one's spiritual condition that appears to set the stage for the Light's salvational appearance in one's life (*Lessons from the Light, 229*).

There are many types of spiritual experiences, such as dreams, visions, feelings and impressions which evidence the hereafter and a caring God. He truly does love all His children of all faiths and culture; and he bears witness "both with signs and wonders . . . according to his own will" (*Hebrews 2:4*). The prophet Mormon wrote "there were divers ways that he did manifest things unto the children of men, which were good; and all things which are good cometh of Christ" (*Moroni 7:24*). One of the most convincing of these spiritual experiences in providing persuasive evidence of the afterlife is unexpected after-death communications (ADCs) from deceased loved-ones. A visitation from one who died years ago bringing timely comfort in a current trial is a compelling witness of the afterlife. Sometimes those who are approaching death receive such visitations (*see #107*). There are thousands of documented cases of unsolicited visitations from the spirit world (*see#85*). Dr. Kenneth Ring observed: "they seem to strongly suggest that *those dear to us who have died continue to exist after death, and that they can communicate to us in ways that help to heal us of our grief and enable us to let go*" (*Lessons from the Light, 266*). (*See also #83 for cautions about using mediums or chambers to communicate with the dead.*)

CHAPTER FIVE

NATURE OF A SPIRIT

Be still, my soul: The Lord is on thy side
—Katharina von Schlegel, Be Still, My Soul, Hymns, 124

37. What is a spirit?

A spirit is a child of Heavenly Parents born in the premortal existence of refined spirit matter that is not normally discerned by our mortal eyes. The spirit is a soul (*AD, Alma 40:15*), a person (*D&C 93:33*) with feelings and a mind to act. The spirit resembles the physical body. Here are some of the best descriptions of a spirit from inspired sources:

> Each person is literally a son or a daughter of God, having been born as a spirit to Heavenly Parents previous to being born to mortal parents on the earth. (*cf. Hebrews 12:9*). Thus each one of us is a dual being: an immortal spirit body, clothed with a body of flesh and bone . . . A spirit can live independent of a body, but the body cannot live without the spirit (*cf. James 2:26*) . . . all spirit is matter, but it is more refined and pure than mortal element (*D&C 131:7*) (*BD*, *776*).

> The spirit is a substance; that it is material, but it is more pure, elastic and refined matter than the body; that it existed before the body, can exist in the body; and will exist separate from the body, when the body will be mouldering in the dust; and will in the resurrection, be united again with it (Joseph Smith, *TPJS, 207*).

> The Father has a body of flesh and bones as tangible as man's; the Son also; but the Holy Ghost has not a body of flesh and bones, but is a personage of Spirit (*D&C 130:22*).

Prior to His mortal birth, the unembodied Jehovah showed His spirit because of the great faith of the brother of Jared: "Behold, this body, which ye now behold, is the body of my spirit; and even as I appear unto thee . . .will I appear unto my people in the flesh" (*Ether 3:16*).

38. Can a mortal see a spirit?

Generally not, unless the Lord allows it (*see #15*). The Lord said: "All spirit . . . can only be discerned by purer eyes; We cannot see it; but when our bodies are purified we shall see that it is all matter" (*D&C 131: 7-8*). There are unusual circumstances when the Lord enables a mortal to see a spirit. Brigham Young said the Lord can empower one to see a good or bad spirit, when "their spiritual eyes are touched by power of the Almighty" (*see JD 3:368*). Brigham Young asked:

> Can you see the spirits in this room? No. Suppose the Lord should touch your eyes that you might see, could you then see the spirits? Yes . . . If the Lord would permit it, and it was His will that it should be done, you could see the spirits that have departed from this world, as plainly as you now see bodies with your natural eyes (*JD 3:368*).

A spirit may or may not be sent from God. Sometimes unauthorized spirits manifest themselves in various ways (*see #44*). An unauthorized spirit may even try to imitate the light of a godly spirit. To detect the nature of a messenger from another realm Joseph Smith taught:

> When a messenger comes saying he has a message from God, offer him your hand and request him to shake hands with you. If he be an angel [a resurrected personage] he will do so, and you will feel his hand. If he be the spirit of a just man made perfect [a righteous disembodied spirit] he will come in his glory [light]; for that is the only way he can appear—Ask him to shake hands with you, but he will not move, because it is contrary to the order of heaven for a just man to deceive; but he will still deliver his message. If it be a devil as an angel of light, when you ask him

> to shake hands he will offer you his hand, and you will not feel anything; you may therefore detect him (*D&C 129:4-8*).

A spirit, though it may be visible, is not physically tangible. A spirit can pass through hands, other persons, walls, and other temporal objects. In general, mortals are oblivious to the actions of spirits. For example, it is not uncommon in an NDE for a spirit, having left the body, to be unable to grasp or hug mortals, to be seen, or to verbally get the attention of mortals.

As Joseph Smith and Brigham Young imply above, in special circumstances mortals may see or discern spirit world beings or resurrected angels without having to undergo an NDE. One may have a dream, where one communicates with a spirit, a dream which is vivid, clear, and real, unlike typical dreams. Or one may see a vision of a spirit being or spiritual things while in a heightened state of awareness, or as Paul said, "whether in the body, or out of the body, I cannot tell: God knoweth" (*2 Corinthians 12:3*). In the scriptures, we often read about prophets' dreams or visions, because God uses these methods to reveal truths. Parley P. Pratt described the clairvoyant state of vision in the body (flesh) as follows: "To discern beings or things in the spirit world, a person in the flesh must be quickened by spiritual element, the vail must be withdrawn, or the organs of sight, or of hearing, must be transformed, so as to be adapted to the spiritual sphere" (*KST, 130*).

Spirits can sometimes interact with mortals. Consider the vicious effect of evil spirits (*Matthew 8:28-32; Mark 9:25-26; Appendix B8*). Good spirits interact in positive ways. Mortals may sometimes sense, or in some delicate way feel the presence of the disembodied spirit of a ministering loved one, without actually seeing them. Sometimes words, sentences, or spiritual feelings come to mind, with the distinct impression the special message is being delivered by the deceased (*see #85 and Appendix B7 and B11*).

39. Do spirits see and feel spirits?

Yes. Brigham Young said: "Spirits are just as familiar with spirits as bodies are with bodies, though spirits are composed of matter so refined as not to be tangible to this coarser organization" (*DBY, 379*). Parley P. Pratt wrote: "The elements and beings in the spirit world are as real and tangible to spiritual organs, as things and beings of the temporal world are to beings of a temporal state" (*KST, 130*). Charles W. Penrose explained:

> Spirit is a substance, it is not immaterial . . . but it is a reality, a substantial reality. And spirit can understand spirit and grasp spirit. A spiritual person can take the hand of another spiritual person and it is substantial. A person in body could not grasp a spirit, for that spirit has different properties to those of our bodies, and it is governed by different laws to those that govern us in this sphere of mortality. A spiritual substance, organized into form, occupies room and space just as much in its sphere as these natural particles occupy in this sphere (*JD 26:22*).

Many near-death experiencers come to understand these concepts as spirits in their new spirit environment. It is not uncommon for disembodied spirits to see, communicate with, and embrace loved ones in the spirit world.

40. Do spirits have senses that mortals have?

Yes. Apparently spirits have many of the senses that mortals have; and expanded senses that mortals do not have (*see #122*). They can see, hear, touch, smell, talk, and walk. However, without a physical body, they can't have a "fulness of joy" (*D&C 93:34*), and they don't experience physical pain (*see #114*). Parley P. Pratt taught that the spirit body

> possesses every organ after the pattern, and in the likeness or similitude of the outward or fleshly tabernacle it is designed eventually to inhabit. Its organs of thought, speech, sight, hearing, tasting, smelling, feeling,

> etc., all exist in their order, as in the physical body; the one being the exact similitude of the other (*KST, 51*).

41. Can a spirit travel easily?

Yes. Parley P. Pratt taught that the spirit component facilitates what is considered supernatural movement to us (*see #123 and #138*):

> It is true that this subtle fluid or spiritual element is endowed with the powers of locomotion in a far greater degree than the more gross or solid elements of nature; that its refined particles penetrate amid the other elements with greater ease, and meet with less resistance from the air or other substances, than would the more gross elements. Hence its speed, or superior powers of motion (*JD 1:8*).

Spirits have enhanced capabilities beyond mortals. When a spirit enters a mortal body sometime before birth, these amazing spirit attributes become suppressed by the temporal body limitations. After the resurrection, the temporal limitations are removed even though the resurrected body has flesh and bones.

42. Can a spirit eat?

If a spirit can eat, then apparently not as a mortal or resurrected being with a body eats. There doesn't seem to be anything in the scriptures or other writings of the prophets to suggest that spirits eat mortal food, although some argue that the unembodied Jehovah ate with Abraham, and unembodied or disembodied angels ate with Lot. However, Joseph Fielding Smith explained that the three men who visited Abraham were mortals. "They had bodies and were able to eat, to bathe, and sit and rest from their weariness. Not one of these three was the *Lord*" (*DS 1:16*; *see Genesis 18: 1-8)*. The three angels (*see Genesis 19:1-3 JST)* who visited Lot and ate with him may have been translated beings or possibly mortals ministering as angels. They would not have been resurrected beings because Christ was the first one resurrected.

Jesus demonstrated that resurrected beings can eat mortal food when he dined with the disciples on bread and fish cooked on hot coals (*John 21: 9-15*).

It doesn't seem logical for a spirit to eat as mortals do because spirits do not have mortal bodies. "All spirit . . . can only be discerned by purer eyes; we cannot see it" (*D&C 131:7-8*). If a spirit could eat mortal food, would he suddenly become discernible? Is it possible that spirits eat pure and refined food (spirit food) consistent with the less-tangible material of the spirit? Jedediah M.Grant, who visited the spirit world, referred to spirit world "houses and gardens, fruit trees, and every other good thing there. The spirits of those things were made, as well as our spirits, and it follows that they can exist upon the same principle" (*JD 4:136*). Parley P. Pratt said spirits can taste (*see KST, 54*). Some reported NDEs suggest that spirits can eat (*e.g., see JNDS, Summer 1993, 236*). If spirits do indeed eat, is the food prepared like it is here? Because spirits are immortal, for what purpose would spirits eat? These are questions for which we do not have definitive answers yet.

43. What is the Spirit that is the influence of the Holy Ghost?

There are two types of spirit: (a) *a* spirit (or spirit body) which *acts* and is described in the answers above and (b) *the* Spirit which is *acted upon* by a person or spirit. This second Spirit is impersonal. "It is not an entity nor a person nor a personage. It has no agency, does not act independently, and exists not to act but to be acted upon" (Bruce R. McConkie, *Ensign, June 1989*). In its various levels of intensity and manifestation it constitutes the light of Christ, intelligence, glory, the Spirit of the Lord, the influence of the Holy Ghost, and the power of God. The second type is the capital "S" Spirit that is in and through all things, living and not living. The *Bible Dictionary* defines Spirit or light as:

> The light of Christ is just what the words imply: enlightenment, knowledge, and an uplifting, ennobling, persevering influence that comes upon mankind because of Jesus Christ. For instance, Christ is "the

> true light that lighteth every man that cometh into the world" (*D&C 93:2; John 1:9*). The light of Christ fills the "immensity of space" and is the means by which Christ is able to be "in all things, and is through all things, and is round about all things." It "giveth life to all things" and is "the law by which all things are governed." It is also "the light that quickeneth" man's understanding (*see D&C 88:6-13,41*). In this manner, the light of Christ is related to man's conscience and tells him right from wrong (*cf. Moroni 7:12-19*) (*BD, 725*).

God uses the Spirit to guide us in our lives. It is a compass to give us direction. We identify it by feelings of love, peace, comfort, and joy (*see #7*). The Spirit or light is "even the power God" (*D&C 88:13*). Parley P. Pratt explained how this can be:

> This divine element, or Spirit, is the immediate, active, controlling agent in all holy miraculous powers. Angels, and all holy men, perform all their miracles, simply, to use a modern magnetic term, by being in "*communication*" with this divine substance . . . [T]he holy fluid, or Spirit . . . goes forth to control the elements, and to execute all their mandates which are legally issued, and in accordance with the mind and wisdom of the Great Eloheim (*KST, 105*).

Evidently the two types of spirit (spirit and Spirit) are related because "the light which is in all things . . . giveth life to all things" (*D&C 88:13*) and "whatsoever is light is Spirit" (*D&C 84:45*). (*See also Chapter 16 Spirit World Light.*)

44. What is a ghost?

"The spirit of a dead person" (*AHD*). Bruce R. McConkie defined a ghost:

> Properly, a *ghost* is a spirit. In death the spirit leaves the body, or in other words the body gives up the ghost (*Gen. 49:33; Acts 5:10; Jacob 7:20-21*). Of our Lord's death, the scripture says he "yielded up the ghost" (*Matthew 27:50*). In referring to the third member of the God-

> head the terms *Holy Ghost* and *Holy Spirit* are used interchangeably (*MD, 312*).

Ghosts (disembodied spirits) may be of God or not. Parley P. Pratt said the spirits who have "departed this life, and have not yet been raised from the dead . . . include many grades of good and evil" (*KST, 117-118*). Good spirits "can appear unto men, when permitted" and have glory or light about them; while "spirits not worthy to be glorified will appear without this brilliant halo; and, although they often attempt to pass as angels of light, there is more or less of darkness about them" (*KST, 118; see #38, #218*). Many unholy spirits of the departed "are unhappy, linger in lonely wretchedness about the earth, and in the air, and especially about their ancient homesteads, and the places rendered dear to them by the memory of former scenes" (*KST, 118*). Apparently some are harmless but others inflict harm. "The more wicked of these are the kind spoken of in the scripture as "*foul spirits*" [*Mark 9:25*], "*unclean spirits*" [*Mark 3:11; Luke 6:18*], spirits who afflict persons in the flesh . . . They will sometimes enter human bodies . . ." (*KST, 118*). Joseph Smith said the "influence or the presence" of wicked spirits of the deceased may be "perceptibly felt" (*#165*).

Ghosts may sometimes be seen, felt or heard; manifesting themselves in different ways (*see KST 118-119*). "According to descriptions or depictions provided by believers, a ghost may appear as a living being or as a nebulous likeness of the deceased and, occasionally, in other forms" (*EB*). Heber Q. Hale, President of the Boise Stake, had a vision of the spirit world and noted that while righteous spirits may at times be given assignments to minister among mortals (*#219*); ungodly spirits have their agency and without authorization "seek pleasure about their old haunts" (*#165*).

A ghost could also mean a demon (*AHD*), an evil spirit who never had a body. Bruce R. McConkie wrote about these beings:

> [T]he true concept of *ghosts* was perverted so that disembodied spirits (ghosts) were conceived of as being hideous and horrible denizens of an

> unseen world who occasionally appeared in bodily likeness to torment and frighten mortals.
>
> Such appearances of spirit beings (supposed to be goblins, spooks . . . and the like) as have actually occurred, probably, have been appearances of devils who never had a body rather than of disembodied ghosts (*MD, 312*).

45. What gives life?

From modern revelation we learn what gives life. It is spirit or light: "The light which is in all things, which giveth life to all things" (*D&C 88:13*). The First Presidency, under Joseph F. Smith, stated that "life, or the vital force, may be infused into organized matter, though the details of the process have not been revealed unto man" (*Messages 5:26*). Abraham equated the spirit with the breath of life which makes man a living soul: "And the Gods formed man from the dust of the ground, and took his spirit (that is, the man's spirit), and put it into him; and breathed into his nostrils the breath of life, and man became a living soul" (*Abraham 5:7*). God also gave the breath of life to other living creatures (*see Moses 3:19*). In a phenomenon estimated to be repeated multiple times a second somewhere in the world, the miracle of life takes place when God puts an individual spirit, the breath of life, into a baby's physical body (*Abraham 5:7*; *see also #64*).

The physical body has no life or power by itself. The body is commanded and follows the direction of the spirit. Joseph Fielding Smith taught "the spirit which inhabits the body . . . is the *life*, for the spirit is life and is eternal, and when the spirit leaves the body, the body is dead . . . the real *substance*, the intelligent part, the part that made it think and exercise its intelligence, has departed" (*Man, His Origin and Destiny, 257-258*).

46. Where do our intellect and feelings reside?

Our intellect and feelings are in the spirit, or soul. The soul, in the most common definition, is equivalent to the spirit (*AD*). The "soul could never die" (*Alma 42:9*). It is the "spiritual, rational and immortal substance in man . . . that part of man which enables him to think and reason" (*AD*). The soul is the essence of a person. It is what constitutes one's identity or being. It is the soul that feels joy (*D&C 11:13*), hope (*Hebrews 6:19*), anguish (*Mormon 6:16*), and compassion (*2 Nephi 26:7*). It can be filled with the Spirit (*Jacob 7:8*), resulting in peace (*D&C 121:7*) and rest (*Enos 1:17*).

Joseph Fielding McConkie and Robert L. Millet explained: "The powers of intellect and the feelings of the heart reside within the spirit of man, or what is most frequently called the soul" (*The Life Beyond, 15*).

Parley P. Pratt wrote that one's spirit, or soul, is "the thinking being, the individual, active agent or identity . . . [which can] think, act, live, move . . . exercise sympathies, affections, hopes, and aspirations" (Parley P. Pratt, *JD 1:7*).

In the scriptures soul most often means the spirit (*e.g., see Abraham 3:23; Alma 40:11; Alma 40:23; 1Nephi 15:31; 1 Nephi 19:7; Mosiah 2:38; Matthew 10:28*). It is that part of us that can exert energy and effort to develop Christlike attributes (*Alma 5:43; D&C 30:11; D&C 31:5*).

Other scriptures speak of the soul as a mortal or resurrected being with a spirit and physical body (*Abraham 5:7; D&C 88:15*). A soul always has a spirit, even without a physical body. A physical body does not always have a soul, such as when it is dead. The spirit is what makes a person a soul.

47. Is the mind or consciousness able to exist outside the brain?

Yes. The mind or intellect is in the spirit that can survive outside the brain or body. Mainstream scientific opinion has historically dictated that human consciousness is nothing more than a byproduct of the brain and therefore can't extend beyond the head. This is called physicalism or materialism. A growing body of scientific researchers, however, point to well-documented paranormal activity, such as NDEs and out of body experiences as evidence of consciousness outside the brain. Such evidence reflects what the prophets and angels have told us all along; there is life after death, and consciousness does exist outside the brain.

Bruce R. McConkie explained that our mind exists independent of the brain:

> [T]o those who know about God and his eternal purposes, it is clear that the mind of man rests in the eternal spirit. The mind was present with the pre-existent spirit; it will be present with the disembodied spirit in the sphere immediately following mortality. Man's intelligence is in his spirit and not in the natural or mortal body (*MD, 501*).

Sir John Eccles, a Nobel-Prize winning neuroscientist, believed that consciousness exists apart from the brain:

> I maintain that the human mystery is incredibly demeaned by scientific reductionism, with its claim in promissory materialism to account eventually for all of the spiritual world in terms of patterns of neuronal activity. This belief must be classed as a superstition . . . We have to recognize that we are spiritual beings with souls existing in a spiritual world as well as material beings with bodies and brains existing in a material world (*cited in Evidence, 103*).

Hugh Nibley was familiar with Eccles' writings and noted:

> Eccles is the best and foremost authority on the biology of the brain. Eccles came to the conclusion that the consciousness has nothing to do with the body. It is not in the body. Eccles concludes that it is inescapable that consciousness exists outside of and independent of the body. It is not in the body (*CWHN 9:304*).

Eccles pondered the real questions: the meaning of life and death and what happens to the soul upon death. He was on the right track when he said: "We can regard the death of the body and brain as dissolution of our dualist existence. Hopefully, the liberated soul will find another future of even deeper meaning and more entrancing experiences, perhaps in some renewed embodied existence" (*cited in Evidence, 105*). Yes, indeed.

48. Surely the brain must have something to do with the mind?

Yes. In a mortal, the mind is channeled through the temporal brain. Joseph Fielding Smith elaborated:

> The mind is in the spirit which inhabits the body . . . It is not a part of the mortal body although the mortal body—brain—is the agency through which it works . . . The brain is merely . . . the vehicle, or medium of thinking . . . The mere combination of carbon, calcium, oxygen and any other physical elements, no matter how wonderfully they may be merged, can not have the power to make us think. They have no power to make us love or hate or perform any other function of the will . . . The mind is not the brain. No one has, by the aid of science ever been able to discover the mind, to circumscribe it, to declare its length or breadth, or to weigh it. It has been to all most elusive and yet they know it exists, and the brain is the seat of its operations (*Man, His Origin and Destiny, 255-257*).

49. Does the brain then affect the mind?

Yes. Obviously, in mortality we need to eat and sleep to think clearly. Further, when we properly care for our bodies (brain), keeping the Word of Wisdom, we are promised "wisdom and great treasures of knowledge" (*D&C 89:19*). To stay alert, we are counseled to "retire to thy bed early" and "arise early, that your bodies and your minds may be invigorated" (*D&C 88:124*). While the spirit is housed in a mortal body, the mind is impacted by mortal imperfections, limitations, and lack of care, "that which is spiritual being in the likeness of that which is temporal" (*D&C 77:2*).

The brain, by its temporal nature, places limitations on the mind to remember and learn (*see #50 and #81*). That comes with mortality. In addition, if there are birth defects, accidents, injuries, illnesses, or chemical imbalances, such can harm the brain resulting in further infirmities of mind during our mortal stay. Upon physical death, such infirmities of mind caused by a damaged brain will apparently be removed, just as all physical deformities will die with the body (*see GD, 28-29*). However, upon death, we understand that our imperfect knowledge, attitudes, and faith continue as our mind and spirit lives on. We will have ages to learn and correct personality faults and weaknesses in the hereafter. After the resurrection, the body including the brain will be perfected in due time which will greatly enhance our learning process.

50. Is a spirit capable of remembering everything?

Yes, except when the spirit is housed in a mortal body or when the Lord puts a veil over our memories. Orson Pratt said "the spirit has not lost its capacity for memory, but it is the organization of the tabernacle that prevents it from remembering" (*JD 2:239; see also #81*).

Daniel H. Ludlow elaborated on this concept:

> The spirit can remember everything it has learned. This characteristic might come as a surprise to those of us who have difficulty remembering our Social Security and home telephone numbers. Nevertheless, the ability of the spirit to remember everything it has learned is now accepted by many . . . However, we must recognize that our spirits presently are operating under the limitations of the 'veil of forgetfulness' that is part of our mortal probation. Many things we knew in our pre-earthly life are withheld from us. As Paul observed: "Now we see through a glass, darkly . . . now I know in part" (*1 Corinthians 13:12*). Also, our spirits may not be able to recall everything we have learned since our births into mortality because they are limited by our imperfect, mortal, physical bodies. Yet the information is still "stored" and available for recall and use (*SW, 380-381*).

Joseph F. Smith taught this same principle:

> May I say to you that in reality a man cannot forget anything? He may have a *lapse* of *memory*; he may not be able to recall at the moment a thing that he knows, or words that he has spoken; he may not have the power at his will to call up these events and words; but let God Almighty touch the mainspring of the *memory*, and awaken recollection, and you will find then that you have not even forgotten a single idle word that you have spoken! (*IE, May 1903*).

51. What is the potential of a human mind?

Omniscience. Man's spirit has the potential to become an exalted being like Abraham, Isaac and Jacob who, as gods, sit on thrones "where all things for their glory are manifest, past, present, and future" (*D&C 130:7*). Thus, man through righteousness and the grace of God can become omniscient through access to the Holy Spirit, because "the Spirit knoweth all things" (*Alma 7:13*).

To reflect on our potential, consider the late Kim Peek from Salt Lake City who died at age 58 in 2010. Kim was the inspiration for the movie, *Rain Man*. Kim had savant syndrome, defined by Dr. Darold Treffert as "a condition in which persons with a major mental illness or major intellectual handicap have spectacular islands of ability and brilliance that stand in stark, startling contrast to those handicaps" (*The Life and Message of The Real Rain Man, 15*). Dr. Treffert described Kim: "All savants have a remarkable memory, but Kim's memory is like no other person's memory . . . and I've looked into the literature in the past 145 years and there is no other case like his in history, either . . . It's the rapidity with which he stores information, the fidelity with which he stores it, and the magnitude with which he stores it is simply unprecedented" (*The Life and Message of The Real Rain Man, 30*).

His father, Fran Peek wrote about Kim's remarkable abilities, noting that "Kim has read over 12,000 books. Once he has read a book at lightning speed, he photographically retains the information and can recall and often recite it with 97% accuracy decades later." He could read two pages at a time in ten seconds; one page with one eye and the facing page with the other eye, "with almost total recall." Unlike those with normal brains, "Kim seems unable to forget things he has heard or read since he was two or three years old. And not only is the information retained in his brain, but it seems to be filed away for immediate recall." Kim's interests were "first manifest in rote memorization; however, unlike other savants, he has developed the capacity to comprehend much of the material he has committed to memory." He continued to grow and develop skills, learning to play the piano quickly as an adult, playing music he remembered from decades earlier. His cerebellum was malformed and, perhaps most crucial, he was missing the corpus callosum, the sheaf of nerve tissue that connects the brain's hemispheres. Physicians almost expected to find something extra in the MRI scans of his brain; something that would give him this extra talent or memory; but what they found was missing parts of the brain. It has been theorized by physicians that some of his talents might be attributed to this brain abnormality. Though physically and socially handicapped, Kim was "a unique, loving, totally innocent and honest human being. He is the brightest, warmest, most amazing person I have ever known" (*The Life and Message of The Real Rain Man, iv, 13, 14, 25, 69, 110*).

His life was a wonderful example of the potential of the human mind to retain facts and continue to learn. His intellect and goodness glorified God because "the works of God" were "manifest in him" (*John 9:*3). Kim was commonly described as an inspiration, broadening our perspective of what God has in store for us in the hereafter. Because our mortal brains restrict our memories and the learning faculty of the spirit when housed in a temporal tabernacle, our educational capabilities will be greatly enhanced in the spirit world without the mortal limitations (*see #81 and #122*). Perhaps Peek's incomplete brain did not restrict his memory to the extent a complete brain does in others, although it left him with limited social and motor skills. Imagine the potential of the spirit without any mortal restrictions or impairments.

52. Besides omniscience, what potential does the human mind have?

Although physical and spirit bodies can only be in one place at a time, worthy spirits can communicate with, speak to, and hear others through the Holy Spirit without limitations in distance or number. This is how God hears and answers so many prayers simultaneously (*see D&C 88:13*). Through the Spirit, God is omnipresent. Parley P. Pratt explained that through the spiritual substance of the Spirit, holy beings can communicate: "Two beings, or two millions—any number thus placed in '*communication*'—all possess one mind" (*KST, 105*). Thus, the desires and influence of the human mind has the potential to be manifest beyond the spirit body throughout space.

Further, through that Holy Spirit one can detect the thoughts of others, such as Alma who knew the thoughts of Zeezrom (*see Alma 12:3,7*). The Lord admonished: "open ye your ears and hearken to the voice of the Lord your God . . . [who] is a discerner of the thoughts and intents of the heart" (*D&C 33:1*). Mankind has the potential with the power of God, to become like God (*see #59*) and obtain the gift of mental telepathy. Many NDEs in the spirit world describe this ability to communicate without words.

The powers of the Holy Spirit are important in the spirit world just as they are here. So it is understandable that many in the spirit world are anxious to have the baptism and confirmation ordinances done on their behalf in the temples of the Lord in order to receive the gift of the Holy Ghost and obtain the enhanced influence of the Spirit.

53. Is a spirit able to communicate with God in mortality?

Yes. Even when clothed with a mortal body, man's spirit can transmit thoughts and words heavenward through prayer and receive inspiration back. Inspiration from above can be in many different forms, such as enticings to do good, words which come to mind, feelings, ideas, impressions, and dreams. With the power of the Holy Ghost, our Heavenly Father guides us using these quiet forms of inspiration. For example, scripture "has been spoken by the manifestation of my Spirit" (*D&C 8:1*). Scripture is for the benefit of all mankind but inspiration is not limited to scripture. When we need individual knowledge for our own unique circumstances, the Lord promised: "I will tell you in your mind and in your heart, by the Holy Ghost, which shall come upon you and which shall dwell in your heart. Now behold, this is the spirit of revelation" (*D&C 8:2-3*) and "whatsoever you shall ask me to tell you by that means, that will I grant unto you, and you shall have knowledge concerning it" (*D&C 8:9*). Joseph Smith taught that God reveals things directly to one's spirit or soul as if we had no body:

> All things whatsoever God in his infinite wisdom has seen fit and proper to reveal to us, while we are dwelling in mortality, in regard to our mortal bodies, are revealed to us in the abstract, and independent of affinity of this mortal tabernacle, but are revealed to our spirits precisely as though we had no bodies at all (*TPJS, 533*).

CHAPTER SIX

OUR DIVINE GENEALOGY

But trailing clouds of glory do we come
From God, who is our home
—William Wordsworth, Ode: Intimations of Immortality

54. Who is Heavenly Father?

He is God. His and the Son's names "are the most sacred and holy words that can be spoken on earth or in heaven" (*NW, 43*). He is Ahman (*WJS, 64; D&C 95:17*), Abba (*Mark 14:36*), Eloi (*Mark 15:34*), Elohim (*BD, 681*), or Man of Holiness (*Moses 7:35*). He is proclaimed as merciful, gracious, long-suffering, ready to pardon, slow to anger, and of great kindness (*see Exodus 34:6-7; 2 Nephi 9:8; Psalms 116:5; James 5:11*). He loves and understands us perfectly. He cares deeply for each of us, and we can trust Him completely. "[A]s a person, he can only be one place at a time" (*NW, 53*), but by the "power of his Spirit, God is everywhere present at one and the same time" (*NW, 53*). The *Bible Dictionary* describes him as:

> The supreme Governor of the universe and the Father of mankind. God . . . [is] omnipotent, omniscient, and omnipresent (through his Spirit). Mankind has a special relationship to him that differentiates man from all other created things: man is literally God's offspring, made in his image, whereas all other things are but the work of his hands (*cf. Acts 17:28-29*). The God of the scriptures is a holy being . . . who is concerned for the welfare of mankind, and a Personage who hears and answers prayers (*BD, 681-682*).

President Gordon B. Hinckley said: "I challenge every one of you who can hear me to rise to the divinity within you. Do we really realize what it means to be a child of God, to have within us something of the divine nature? (*Ensign, November 2002*).

55. Do we have a Heavenly Mother?

Yes. The *Encyclopedia of Mormonism* summarizes the support for this teaching:

> Though the scriptures contain only hints [*e.g., see 1 Nephi 11:18*], statements from presidents of the Church over the years indicate that human beings have a Heavenly Mother as well as a Heavenly Father. In this perspective parenthood requires both father and mother, whether for the creation of spirits in the premortal life or of physical tabernacles on earth (*EM, 961*).

The First Presidency and Quorum of Twelve Apostles of the Church of Jesus Christ of Latter-day Saints proclaimed:

> ALL HUMAN BEINGS—male and female—are created in the image of God. Each is a beloved spirit son or daughter of heavenly parents, and, as such, each has a divine nature and destiny. Gender is an essential characteristic of individual premortal, mortal, and eternal identity and purpose (*The Family: A Proclamation to the World, 1995*).

Male and female spirits were born in the premortal existence in the image and likeness of our heavenly parents; and were born in mortality in the likeness of both our heavenly and earthly parents (*see Gen 1:26-27; Moses 3:4-7; Abraham 3:18-23*).

Joseph Smith consoled Zina D. Young, who was a girl when she lost her mother, telling her she would not only see her earthly mother again, but also her Heavenly Mother. Zina had not known about a Heavenly Mother and Joseph Smith responded: "How could a Father claim His title unless there were also a Mother to share that parenthood?" (Susa Gates Young, *History of the Young Ladies Mutual Improvement Association, 16*).

56. Were we reared to maturity in heaven before we were born?

Yes. The First Presidency, in 1909, under Joseph F. Smith issued a statement on the origin of man declaring that: "man, as a spirit, was begotten and born of heavenly parents, and reared to maturity in the eternal mansions of the Father . . . All men and women are in similitude of the universal Father and Mother, and are literally the sons and daughters of Deity" (*Messages 4:203, 205*).

57. Did we actually live with God and know Him?

Yes. Brigham Young emphasized this fact:

> Father actually begat the spirits and they were brought forth and lived with him . . . I want to tell you, each and every one of you, that you are well acquainted with God our Heavenly Father, or the great Elohim. You are well acquainted with him, for there is not a soul of you but what has lived in His house and dwelt with Him year after year; and yet you are seeking to become acquainted with Him, when the fact is, you have merely forgotten what you did know . . . We are the sons and daughters of celestial Beings, and the germ of Deity dwells within us (*DBY, 50*).

Parley P. Pratt said the spirit body was "born and matured in the heavenly mansions, trained in the school of love in the family circle, and amid the most tender embraces of parental and fraternal affection" (*KST, 51*).

58. How many at a time were reared to maturity in the family circle of His heavenly mansions?

We don't know the details of our premortal life such as the number of children, family size, timelines, and heavenly location of our upbringing and growth during the ages in the first estate spirit world, which could refer to one or more spheres. We do know that we were not all born at once. The First Presidency declared: "Among the spirit children of Elohim the firstborn was and is Jehovah or Jesus Christ to whom all others are juniors" (*Messages 5:33*).

Bruce R. McConkie taught that our Heavenly Father "has presided in our universe for almost 2,555,000,000 years" (*BYU Speeches, June 1, 1980; refers to letter from W.W. Phelps to William Smith, Times and Seasons 5:757-758*).

Whatever the span of ages our Heavenly parents had children destined for this earth (it's hard to imagine), there must have been time for each of His children to be tutored tenderly.

Eliza R. Snow's powerful and inspired hymn, *O My Father* (*Hymns, 292*) paints a picture of what might have been:

O My Father, thou that dwellest In the high and glorious place,
When shall I regain thy presence, And again behold thy face?
In thy holy habitation, Did my spirit once reside!
In my first primeval childhood, Was I nurtured near thy side?
For a wise and glorious purpose Thou hast placed me here on earth,
And withheld the recollection Of my former friends and birth;
Yet oftimes a secret something Whispered, "You're a stranger here;"
And I felt that I had wandered From a more exalted sphere.
I had learned to call thee Father, Through the Spirit from on high;
But until the Key of Knowledge Was restored, I knew not why.
In the heavens are parents single? No; the thought makes reason stare!
Truth is reason, truth eternal Tells me I've a Mother there.
When I leave this frail existence, When I lay this mortal by,
Father, Mother, may I meet you In your royal courts on high?
Then, at length, when I've completed All you sent me forth to do,
With your mutual approbation Let me come and dwell with you.

59. Was God once a mortal who died and was resurrected?

Yes. In what some call the greatest exhortation of Joseph Smith, the magnificent King Follett sermon, he gave this revelation:

> God himself was once as we are now, and is an exalted man, and sits enthroned in yonder heavens! That is the great secret. If the veil were

> rent today, and the great God who holds this world in its orbit, and who upholds all worlds and all things by his power, was to make himself visible—I say, if you were to see him today, you would see him like a man in form—like yourselves in all the person, image, and very form as a man; for Adam was created in the very fashion, image and likeness of God, and received instruction from, and walked, talked and conversed with him, as one man talks and communes with another . . . It is the first principle of the Gospel to know for a certainty the Character of God, and to know that we may converse with him as one man converses with another, and that he once was a man like us; yea, that God himself, the Father of us all, dwelt on an earth, the same as Jesus Christ himself did; and I will show it from the Bible (*TPJS, 345-346*).

Robert J. Matthews succinctly explained:

> Our heavenly parents, our Eternal Father and Mother, were once spirits, children of an earlier generation of gods who were born into a world (not this world) and lived as mortals, then died, and later received their bodies again in a resurrection. Because they were obedient to the plan of salvation (the same plan that we have been taught), they were exalted to become gods. They are now giving us the same chances for progress that they have experienced and the opportunity to become gods, even as they are gods (*Selected Writings of Robert J. Matthews, 496*). [vi]

The Lord said: "Ye are gods; and all of you are children of the most High" (*Psalm 82:6*) C.S. Lewis understood our potential to become gods:

> The command *Be ye perfect* is not idealistic gas. Nor is it a command to do the impossible. He is going to make us into creatures that can obey that command. He said (in the Bible) that we were "gods" and He is going to make good His words. If we let Him—for we can prevent Him, if we choose—He will make the feeblest and filthiest of us into a god or goddess, dazzling, radiant, immortal creature, pulsating all through with such energy and joy and wisdom and love as we cannot now imagine . . . The process will be long and in parts very painful; but that is what we are in for. Nothing less. He meant what He said (*Mere Christianity, 174-175*).

60. Why is mankind born upon this earth?

God's work is to "bring to pass the immortality and eternal life [exaltation] of man" (*Moses 1:39*). To accomplish that end, His plan of salvation prescribed that we come to this earth as a mortal for these purposes:

(a) ***To get a body.*** Joseph Smith said we are here to obtain a physical "body and present it pure before God in the Celestial Kingdom" (*WJS, 60*). Before we can be resurrected and progress further, we must obtain a body. Bruce R. McConkie explained:

> We come here to gain bodies . . . which—following the natural death—we will receive back again in immortality. Those of us who arrive at the years of accountability [age eight] are here to develop and to be tried and tested, to see if we can so live as to regain the state of innocence and purity which we enjoyed as children, and thereby be qualified to go where God and Christ are (*Ensign, April 1977*).

(b) ***To be tried and tested and gain experience.*** Men are brought to earth "for a trial of their faith" (*D&C 105:19*). "We will prove them herewith, to see if they will do all things whatsoever the Lord their God shall command them" (*Abraham 3:25*).

(c) ***To help others progress by bearing children and nurturing others.*** The Lord allows us to help in a vital way with the progression of His children. He commanded and then gave mankind the procreation power to "be fruitful and multiply" (*Moses 2:22),* and then "teach them the good way" (*1 Kings 8:36*).

61. Are spirits full-grown before birth in the world and after death as a child?

Yes. Our spirits lived premortally and were full-grown and mature before experiencing mortality. Upon death, a spirit will enter the spirit world as a full-grown and mature spirit even if death occurs as a child. A child who dies will be resurrected as a child. Joseph F. Smith explained:

> The spirits of our children are immortal before they come to us, and their spirits, after bodily death, are like they were before they came . . . Our children were full-grown and possessed their full stature in the spirit, before they entered mortality, the same stature they will possess after they have passed away from mortality... Joseph Smith taught the doctrine that the infant child that was laid away in death would come up in the resurrection as a child; and pointing to the mother of a lifeless child, he said to her: "You will have the joy, the pleasure, and satisfaction of nurturing this child, after the resurrection, until it reaches the full stature of its spirit" (*GD, 574-575*).

62. Does that mean there are no children in the spirit world?

Because children who die resume their former adult state upon entering the spirit world, the inference is that there are no infants or children in the spirit world. It is uncommon to hear of children in the spirit world from those who have been there. Dr. Raymond Moody started asking children how old they are during the NDE: "A surprising number of them say that they are adults during the episode, although they can't say how they knew this" (*The Light Beyond, 74*). Heber Q. Hale noted an absence of small children in the spirit world (*see HQH, 2*). From their NDE research, Brent and Wendy Top wrote: "the relative absence of accounts involving children in the afterlife seems conspicuous, especially when so many conditions there reflect and magnify the same conditions found in earth life" (*Glimpses, 212*).

There are, however, some NDE accounts that describe children (*e.g., see Glimpses, 212*). What is the explanation? In some cases (*see #63 below and #135*), the adult spirits take on the form of a child to be recognized. There are other possible explanations. Could the NDE include a vision of another time and place? (*e.g., see A3*). NDEs are generally experienced for the benefit of that person alone, and we are not given to know all the Lord's purposes and ways of spiritually communicating to individuals. Could the children be figurative? Could premortal, resurrected or translated children visit the spirit world? The Lord has not revealed the details of children demographics in the spirit world, so we can not positively answer these questions.

63. Would one recognize a son or daughter in the spirit world who died in infancy?

Not necessarily, unless the disembodied spirit took on the infant form. Joseph F. Smith explained:

> If you see one of your children that has passed away it may appear to you in the form in which you would recognize it, the form of childhood; but if it came to you as a messenger bearing some important truth, it would perhaps come as the spirit of Bishop Edward Hunter's son (who died when a little child) came to him, in the stature of full-grown manhood, and revealed himself to his father, and said: "I am your son." Bishop Hunter did not understand it. He went to my father and said: "Hyrum, what does it mean? I buried my son—when only a little boy, but he has come to me as a full-grown man—a noble, glorious, young man, and declared himself my son. What does it mean?" Father (Hyrum Smith, the Patriarch) [older brother of Joseph Smith] told him that the Spirit of Jesus Christ was full-grown before he was born into the world; and so our children were full-grown and possessed their full stature in the spirit, before they entered mortality, the same stature that they will possess after they have passed away from mortality, and as they will also appear after the resurrection, when they shall have completed their mission (*GD, 574-575*) (*see also #135*).

64. What is the nature of the spirit in a baby?

At some point before birth—there is no direct revelation on when—God places the person's premortal spirit into the baby's physical body. Therefore, we understand that a baby is alive with a spirit before birth (*see also #45*). Parley P. Pratt wrote:

> The entrance of this spirit into its embryo tabernacle of flesh is called quickening. The infallible evidence of its presence is voluntary motion,

> which implies a degree of independent agency, or inherent will, which individual identity alone possesses (*KST, 128-29*).

Joseph Smith taught that spirit matter has elasticity (*TPJS, 207*) which apparently enables a full-grown premortal spirit to be reduced to the size of a tiny baby before birth. Then the spirit expands as the child grows. "The spirit is in the likeness of the physical body, as demonstrated in *Gen 2:5; 1 Ne 11:11; Ether 3:15-16; D&C 77:2; Moses 3:4-7*" (*BD, 776*). Joseph Smith explained: "the spirit of man in the likeness of his person, as also the spirit of the beast, and every other creature which God has created" (*D&C 77:2*). Upon death, the immortal spirit leaves as a full-grown person, whether death occurs as a baby, toddler, teenager, or adult.

Oscar W. McConkie wrote: "The spirit form and appearance are similar to the temporal form or appearance. This is true of each particular form of life" (*Aaronic Priesthood, 93*).

65. Can a spirit bear children?

No, not as we currently understand. Only resurrected and exalted beings can "have an increase" (*see D&C 131:1-4*). The First Presidency under Joseph F. Smith declared:

> So far as the stages of eternal progression and attainment have been made known through divine revelation, we are to understand that only resurrected and glorified beings can become parents of spirit offspring. Only such exalted souls have reached maturity in the appointed course of eternal life; and the spirits born to them in the eternal worlds will pass in due sequence through the several stages or estates by which the glorified parents have attained exaltation (*Messages 5:34*).

66. Do resurrected beings have blood?

No. Resurrected beings have flesh and bones but not blood. Joseph Smith taught that resurrected beings have "spirit in their [veins] and not blood" (*WJS,* 270). Joseph Fielding Smith explained that a resurrected body "when raised to *immortality* shall be *quickened by the spirit* and not the blood" (*DS 2:284*).

Spirit is born of spirit and blood is born of blood. Melvin J. Ballard suggested it's all quite logical: "I don't think that is very difficult to comprehend and understand. The nature of the offspring is determined by the nature of the substance that flows in the veins of the being" (Hinckley, *Sermons and Missionary Services of Melvin Joseph Ballard, 239*).

67. Can a resurrected being bear physical children with flesh and bones?

Yes. Our Heavenly Parents are resurrected beings. They begat the physical-spiritual, but non-mortal "Adam, who was the son of God" (*Moses 6:22*) and Eve, both with flesh and bones, who lived in the terrestrial Eden until the fall when they became mortal and spirit was replaced with blood (*see #75*).

Heavenly Father also begat "Jesus, who is called Christ, [who] is the firstborn of the Father in the spirit and the Only Begotten of the Father in the flesh" (*BD, 633*). Jesus, whose mother was Mary, was born as a mortal, in the flesh, with blood, and subject to death. We have no other record of physical children of resurrected beings. Of course, we know of billions of spirit children born of our Heavenly Parents who have come to this earth. We believe resurrected and exalted beings can become like God and therefore, like God, it would seem they could have physical children (*see #59*).

68. What does *in the flesh* mean?

In the scriptures *in the flesh* often refers to mortality. The *Bible Dictionary* clarifies:

> The flesh is often spoken of as being a part of our mortal or fallen nature . . . Since flesh often means mortality, Adam is spoken of as the "first flesh" upon the earth, meaning he was the first mortal on the earth, all things being created in a non-mortal condition, and becoming mortal through the fall of Adam. Jesus is the "Only Begotten of the Father" in the flesh, meaning he is the only one begotten of the Father into mortality (*Moses 3:7*) (*BD, 675*).

69. If God begat Adam, are we then physically direct descendants of God, the Father?

Yes. That is what the scriptures tell us. Adam "was the son of God" (*Moses 6:22*) and the "firstborn" (*Abraham 1:3*) in our divine physical body pedigree which extends back some 6000 years to Adam and Eve's birth from our Heavenly Parents. Children are begotten by birth. That is logical and makes sense. Joseph Fielding McConkie explained: "Be it Adam, Christ, or any other human being, the process of birth is the same" (*Answers, 160*).

Our immortal spirit body pedigree is much shorter. We are first generation children of our Heavenly Parents (*see #57*). Joseph F. Smith and the First Presidency wrote that just as we were born as spirit children in heaven, "all who have inhabited the earth since Adam have taken bodies and become souls in like manner" (*Messages 4:205*).

Benjamin F. Johnson said Joseph Smith "taught us that God was the great head of human procreation—was really and truly the father of both our spirits and our bodies" (LeBaron, *Benjamin Franklin Johnson, 340*).

70. In what sense can we become sons and daughters of Christ?

We are all begotten spirit sons and daughters of God, the Father. However, by faithful obedience and through the atoning sacrifice of Jesus Christ, we can become God's children in a much more expansive sense. We can become His heirs, with the potential of inheriting the divine powers that God has (*D&C 84:33-38*). To receive this, the greatest of all gifts, one must accept Jesus Christ as the Savior, repent, and make and obey certain covenants. The willing are to "take upon you the name of Christ" (*Mosiah 5:8*) and be "born again" (*Alma 7:14*), meaning they are changed from their "carnal and fallen state, to a state of righteousness" (*Mosiah 27:25*), with "no more disposition to do evil" (*Mosiah 5:2*). Because of Christ's pivotal role, qualifying persons are "called the children of Christ, his sons, and his daughters; for behold, this day he hath spiritually begotten you; for ye say that your hearts are changed through faith on his name; therefore, ye are born of him and have become his sons and his daughters" (*Mosiah 5:7*). Through the grace of Jesus Christ, one can be redeemed and sanctified, qualify for exaltation and become joint-heirs with Jesus Christ of all that the Father has.

The First Presidency and twelve Apostles under Joseph F. Smith wrote: "Jesus Christ is regarded as the Father" when we "accept His Gospel and thereby become heirs of eternal life" (*Messages 5:27*). "It is consistently proper to speak of Jesus Christ as the Father of the righteous, they having become His children and He having been made their Father though the second birth—the baptismal regeneration" (*Messages 5:31*).

In 1830, Jesus taught Orson Pratt, "that as many as would believe might become the sons of God. Wherefore you are my son" (*D&C 34:3*). Women are included. In 1831 Jesus told Emma Smith: "all those who receive my gospel are sons and daughters in my kingdom" (*D&C 25:1*). Finally, in 1851 Jesus declared: "Fear not, little children; for you are mine, and I have overcome the world, and you are of them that my Father hath given me" (*D&C 50:41*).

CHAPTER SEVEN

HEAVENS

We believe in the Great Elohim who sits enthroned in yonder heavens.
—Joseph Smith, TPJS, 313

71. What is heaven?

Scripturally there are several meanings for heaven.

(a) ***First and foremost, it is the home of God***, "thou in heaven thy dwelling place" (1 *Kings 8:30*). We accordingly pray to: "Our Father which art in heaven" (*Matthew 6:9*). Heaven is the "celestial, or the residence of God . . . or the place where God resides" (*Abraham, Facsimile No. 2, Figures 1 and 2)*. We don't have a more specific name, but we know heaven is an exalted, celestial sphere. The nearest planet is Kolob (*Figure 1; see also #79*). Next to Kolob is Oliblish (*Figure 2*), another grand governing planet near heaven. In the scriptures, *heavens* often refers to God's realms which are "higher than the earth" (*Isaiah 55:9; see also Moses 1:37*). "The heavens is a place where God dwells and all his holy angels" (*Alma 18:30*).

(b) ***Heaven often means the "future home of the saints,"*** the celestial or highest realm, after the resurrection (*see BD, 699*). The faithful "are received into heaven, that thereby they may dwell with God in a state of neverending happiness" (*Mosiah 2:41*).

(c) ***Heaven can also refer to other kingdoms of glory after the resurrection***. All but the most deliberate followers of Satan will eventually go to one of the three primary kingdoms: celestial, terrestrial, and telestial (*see D&C 76*), with multiple levels or heavens within these kingdoms (*see D&C 76:98 and D&C 131:3-4*). In these revelations in the *Doctrine & Covenants* Joseph Smith restored Jesus' teaching of "many mansions" that he will prepare for us (*John 14:2*) and Paul's teaching of multiple heavens (*see 1 Corinthians 15:40-41 and 2 Corinthians 12:2*). Although each of the kingdoms and multiple levels within are distinct in glory, all are a state of ecstasy and bliss. Interestingly, an enhanced state of happiness is sometimes called "cloud nine" or "seventh heaven."

(d) ***Heaven "also means the expanse around the earth, as the heavens"*** (BD, 699; see Genesis 1:1,17; Exodus 24:10).

(e) ***Finally, heaven can also mean paradise, the abiding place of the righteous dead in the spirit world*** (*see D&C 129:1-3*); although Latter-day Saints clearly distinguish God's home from paradise. As an illustration of this differentiation, "Jesus visited paradise after his death on the cross, but on the third day thereafter, he informed Mary that he had not yet been to the Father" (*BD, 699; see Luke 23:39-44; John 20:17*).

72. Do we have a description of heaven, the residence of God?

Yes. "The place where God resides is a great Urim and Thummin . . . Angels . . . reside in the presence of God, on a globe like a sea of glass and fire, where all things for their glory are manifest, past, present, and future, and are continually before the Lord" (*D&C 130:6-8*). Joseph Smith said:

> The past, the present, and the future were and are, with Him, one eternal "now" (*TPJS, 220*). God Almighty Himself dwells in eternal fire; flesh and blood cannot go there for all corruption is devoured by the fire. "Our God is a consuming fire." When our flesh is quickened by the Spirit [resurrection], there will be no blood in this tabernacle (*HC 6:*366).

The transparency of glass conjures a metaphor of the crystal clear perspective of eternal truths and omniscience in heaven. Perhaps the powerful fire of the Spirit conveys His Holy omnipotence.

Apparently heaven, where God lives, is a model of the future heaven, the celestialized earth, where the saints will dwell after the resurrection. "This earth, in its sanctified and immortal state, will be made like unto crystal and will be a Urim and Thummin to the inhabitants who dwell thereon . . . and this earth will be Christ's" (*D&C 130:9*).

At the beginning of the millennium, the "earth will be renewed and receive its paradisiacal glory" (*Tenth Article of Faith*) which is the glory of the former Edenic state (*see NW, 648*). After the millennium, the earth will die and be resurrected (*D&C 88:*26) and become the celestial kingdom (*D&C 130:9-11*).

73. Upon death, do the righteous immediately go to heaven?

No. Heaven generally refers to the place where God lives or where resurrected beings go. Spirits of the dead go to the spirit world until their resurrection (*see also #19*).

Alma wrote that upon death, the spirits of all men "are taken home to that God who gave them life" (*Alma 40:11*); "meaning that it returns to live in the realm of spiritual existence (*Ecclesiastes 12:7*)" (Bruce R. McConkie, *MD, 402*). In other words, our existence continues in the same God-given spirit form as before birth. It does not mean that spirits bypass the spirit world and go directly to Heaven to be with God, the Father.

Heber C. Kimball taught the same principle:

> As for my going into the immediate presence of God when I die, I do not expect it, but I expect to go into the world of spirits and associate with my brethren, and preach the Gospel in the spiritual world, and prepare myself in every necessary way to receive my body again, and then enter through the wall into the celestial world. I never shall come into the presence of my Father and God until I have received my resurrected body, neither will any other person (*JD 3:112-113*).

We will follow the pattern Jesus set by going to the spirit world after death. Following the crucifixion, Christ preached to the spirits in prison (*1 Peter 3:18-19*). After His resurrection He "appeared first to Mary Magdalene" (*Mark 16:9*), telling her: "Touch me not; for I am not yet ascended to my Father . . . and your Father; and *to* my God, and your God" (*John 20:17*). Like Jesus, we will not ascend to heaven, *to our God*, until after we are resurrected.

74. Where was the earth formed?

Near heaven. Brigham Young said:

> When the earth was framed and brought into existence and man was placed upon it, it was near the throne of our Father in heaven. And when man fell . . . the earth fell into space, and took up its abode in this planetary system, and the sun became our light . . . This is the glory the earth came from, and when it is glorified it will return again unto the presence of the Father, and it will dwell there, and these intelligent beings that I am looking at, if they live worthy of it, will dwell upon this earth (*JD 17:143*).

> This earthly ball, this little opake [opaque] substance thrown off into space, is only a speck in the great universe; and when it is celestialized it will go back into the presence of God, where it was first framed (*JD 9:317*).

John Taylor taught that the earth was formed near Kolob which is near heaven (*see #79*). Joseph Smith taught that when the earth is made into a celestial sphere, "it will be rolled back into the presence of God" (*TPJS, 181*).

75. What steps were involved in the creation of the earth and the spirit world?

Robert J. Matthews clarified the creation process by breaking it down into three steps as summarized below. It is important to differentiate among all three. All took place in the heavens near Kolob:

Step 1: ***Spirit Creation.*** The earth, plants, animals, and mankind were all created as spirits in heaven before any physical creation. "This would be properly spoken of as the *spirit* creation."

Step 2: ***Physical-Spiritual Creation.*** "Then God created all things physically, but there was no death and no sin attached. Therefore the physical creation was tangible in nature, but *spiritual* in its conditions." There are six creative periods. "Animals and plants [were] created and placed on earth prior to man. Accounts [are] given in *Genesis 1-2; Moses 2-3; and Abraham 4-5.*"

Step 3: ***The Mortal, Temporal, Fallen World.*** "Accounts of the fall . . . [which brought] blood, death, reproduction, and sin . . . [are] given in *Genesis 3 and Moses 4-5*" (Robert J. Matthews**,** *The Man Adam,* ed. by Joseph Fielding McConkie and Robert Millet, *47-49*).

Step 1 refers to our spirit births in heaven. "I am God; I made the world, and men before they were in the flesh" (*Moses 6:51*). Apparently the postmortal spirit world was created in the heavens as part of the *spirit* creation, and not the physical-spiritual creation. Just as mankind has a spirit, the earth is alive with a spirit. The *Encyclopedia of Mormonism* explains:

> The earth itself and the living things on the earth have spirit counterparts that existed before the physical creation . . . This spirit existence, where living things are composed of organized, refined spirit matter, extends beyond the human family and includes animals and plants (*EM, 1408*).

Step 2 is the traditional creation story. It describes the physical creation of the earth in its paradisiacal or terrestrial glory. It's called a *spiritual* (*not spirit*) creation because there was no death (*see 2 Ne. 2:22*); and no reproduction (*see 2 Ne: 2:23; Moses 5:11*); no blood (*BD, 670*); and no sin (*see 2 Ne 2:23*).

Step 3 refers to the fall. Man was the first to fall and become mortal, and then other forms of life became mortal. After the fall, the earth assumed its place in the current geography of the solar system (*see #74*).

76. What elements were used to form the earth and spirit world?

Joseph Smith explained how unorganized matter was used to form the world:

> This earth was organized or forged out of other planets which were broke up and remodeled and made into the one on which we live (*WJS, 60*). God had materials to organize the world out of chaos . . . [which] may be organized and re-organized, but not destroyed (*TPJS, 351-352*).

The prophet Joseph gave us only this limited information about the original elements. We know even less about the materials used to form the spirit world, except that it is "all matter" (*see D&C 131:7-8*) and must have been formed from refined, but existing materials.

Consider the creation's complexity from man's limited perspective for a moment. The earth was created from *used* matter which has *always* existed. The physical earth was created as a spiritual, *paradisiacal* (terrestrial) sphere (*NW, 649*), a system of glory we know precious little about; in yonder heavens far beyond our solar system. It was created in a time frame unfamiliar to us: "it was after the Lord's time . . . for as yet the Gods had not appointed unto Adam his reckoning" (*Abraham 5:13*). When Adam fell, man became mortal and the earth became telestialized, leaving only telestial evidence. So, the earth was created with used, paradisiacal matter under unknown uncircumstances; and all the original evidence has completely changed. No wonder we don't understand much about the creation beyond what the Lord has told us! What's more, those "hidden things which no man knew, things of the earth, by which it was made" will not be revealed until "that day when the Lord shall come" (*D&C 101:32-33*).

77. Will the righteous eventually return home to Heavenly Father?

Yes. As Brigham Young said "those who keep his celestial law will return to him" (*JD 9:317*). Neal A. Maxwell eloquently described this anticipated event:

> Even now as Latter-day Saints, we know whose we are, whence we came, why we are here, and what manner of men and women we are meant to become (*see 2 Peter 3:11; 3 Nephi 27:27*). Still like Alma, we will "long to be there" (*Alma 36:22*), in the "royal courts on high." It is the only destination that really matters. Resplendent reunion awaits us! What is more reasonable and more wonderful than children going home? Especially to a home where the past, the present, and the future form an everlasting and eternal now! (*see D&C 130:7; 38:2*; *TPJS, 220*) (*Men and Women of Christ, 51*).

78. Are individuals who have already been resurrected now in heaven?

Yes. Heaven is not only where God lives, but it can also refer to the "future home of the saints" after the resurrection (*BD, 699*). Apparently there is place for resurrected beings (which may be heaven where God lives or other glorified sphere in yonder heavens). These righteous saints have already been resurrected and are awaiting the earth's millennial renewal of paradisiacal glory and subsequent celestialization. Joseph Smith said that after Jesus' resurrection, Jesus went to "minister to resurrected bodies" (*HC 4:425*). Parley P. Pratt wrote: "In the former resurrection, those raised left the earth and ascended, or, were transplanted far on high, with the risen Jesus, to the glorified mansions of his Father, or to some planetary system already redeemed and glorified" (*KST, 136*).

Just because resurrected beings qualify for a heavenly home does not mean they won't visit other realms to advance the Lord's purposes. For example, resurrected beings may minister as angels on the earth. If the Lord requires, resurrected beings could also teach and minister in the spirit world. Who was better qualified to take the gospel to the spirit prison immediately after Christ opened it for missionary work after his death than the righteous saints that were resurrected with Christ? Indeed, "our Redeemer spent his time during his sojourn in the world of spirits, instructing and preparing the faithful spirits of the prophets who had testified of him in the flesh; That they might carry the message of redemption unto all the dead" (*D&C 138:36-37*).

Resurrected beings may also minister as necessary on the earth during the millennium. Parley P. Pratt suggested that resurrected beings from the time of Christ and also at His second coming will "receive an inheritance on the earth, and will build upon and improve the same for a thousand years" (*KST, 137*). During the millennium: "People who have been resurrected will help the people living on earth to find the names of their dead relatives and correct any mistakes in the records" (*Gospel Fundamentals, 189*).

79. What is Kolob?

Kolob, the first creation, is the grand governing planet or star nearest to God (*see Abraham 3:3,16; Facsimile No. 2 figure 1; see also #71*). The Lord said: "I have set this one to govern all those which belong to the same order as that upon which thou standest" (*Abraham 3:3*). In the poetic rendition of *D&C 76* from Joseph Smith, "reference is made to 'the council in Kolob,' implying that at least part of our premortal experience took place on that planet nearest to where God dwells (*Abraham 3:3*)" (Lawrence R. Flake, *Three Degrees of Glory, 27*). John Taylor taught that the earth "fled and fell from where it was first was organized, near the planet Kolob" (*The Mormon, August 1857*). This is consistent with Brigham Young's statement that the earth was formed near the throne of God (*see #74*). We don't know much about Kolob, heaven, or our premortal life, because the veil of forgetfulness has removed this memory, and the Lord has only revealed limited information to the prophets.

CHAPTER EIGHT

THE VEIL

The visions and blessings of old are returning,
And angels are coming to visit the earth
The knowledge and power of God are expanding;
The veil o'er the earth is beginning to burst.
—William W. Phelps, The Spirit of God, Hymns, 2

80. What is the *veil*?

The veil has many different meanings, which Neal A. Maxwell boiled down to this nutshell definition: "We define the veil as the border between mortality and eternity; it is also a film of forgetting which covers the memories of earlier experiences" (*Ensign, October 1980*). N.L. Nelson poignantly defined it as "that mysterious curtain which confines our perceptions to the natural world; limits our eyes, our ears, and all our other senses to the sphere of the here and now" (*IE, March 1929*). The veil in general describes the separation between God and man, the temporal and spiritual, or the natural and ethereal. It limits our contact with spiritual things, and our memories of our premortal spirit state.

The veil becomes thinner when one receives inspiration from God (*see #85*). Such inspiration usually comes as a spiritual or uplifting feeling to our heart, a metaphor for the soul (*see #53*). Such enlightenment can be common for one undergoing the process of being born again and overcoming the natural man resulting in a spiritual heart with no desire to do evil (*see #70; 1 Corinthians 2:14*). To those who seek and receive the Spirit over time it "shall distill upon thy soul as the dews from heaven" (*D&C 121:45*), resulting in a testimony and conviction of the things of God, and a closeness to God that makes the veil sometimes seem thin. The Lord said "Draw near unto me and I will draw near unto you" (*D&C 88:63*).

The veil may be lifted or parted to a greater degree when extraordinary events happen, such as a vision, a powerful dream, an out of body or near-death experience, or conversations with heavenly messengers (*see #31, #36, #85, #218, #219*). When we talk of veil-rending experiences we are normally referring to these extraordinary events that are uncommon for most people.

81. Where is the veil and how is it regulated?

God has not revealed all the details about the veil and how it is regulated. Certainly He has all the eternal laws at His disposal to control the nature and location of the veil. However, from the scriptures and prophets, we have some clues about the veil. There are at least three types of veils:

(a) ***Internal veil—within the mind and spirit.*** In this context, the veil is within one's mind, the intellect of the individual spirit or soul. God can control the veil in our minds, allowing us to see and understand spiritual things. For example in 1836, Joseph Smith and Oliver Cowdery had a "vision opened to both of us" (*HC 2:435*): "The veil was taken from our minds, and the eyes of our understanding were opened. We saw the Lord standing upon the breastwork of the pulpit, before us" (*D&C 110: 1-2*). Prior to this manifestation, the Lord had promised the "veil of darkness" would be rent and the "purified" would see him (*D&C 38:8*).

It is through the Spirit that God can open our minds and eyes. While "in the Spirit" (*D&C 76:113*) Joseph Smith and Sidney Rigdon saw the Savior in vision: "By the power of the Spirit our eyes were opened and our understandings were enlightened, so as to see and understand the things of God" (*D&C 76:12*). The Spirit is necessary for a mortal being to see God: "For no man has seen God at any time in the flesh, except quickened by the Spirit of God" (*D&C 67:11*). Mortals can experience spiritual things while still in the physical body: "That through the power and manifestation of the Spirit, while in the flesh, they may be able to bear his presence in the world of glory" (*D&C 76:118*).

God regulates the veil through the Spirit. Paul said "the things of God knoweth no man, except he has the Spirit of God" (*1 Corinthians 2:11*); "God hath revealed them unto us by his Spirit" (*1 Corinthians 2:10*). Nephi said "for by the Spirit are all things made known unto the prophets" (*1 Nephi 22:2*). John was "in the Spirit on the Lord's day" when he had his marvelous vision (*Revelation 1:10*). Through the influence of the Holy Spirit to the spirit of man, the Lord can reveal things in many different ways such as through dreams, visions, words, feelings, and impressions (*e.g. see Ezekial 37-39; 1 Nephi 8, 10-14; Moses 6-7*).

The Spirit may have enough intensity to cause a transfiguration, an illumination of countenance. Such was the case with Moses on Mt. Sinai (*Moses 1:11; Exodus 34:29-35*); Jesus, Peter, James and John on the Mount of Transfiguration (*TPJS, 158*); Stephen (*Acts 6:15; DNTC 2:67*); Abinadi (*Mosiah 13:*5); and Joseph Smith (*Revelations of the Restoration, 513*). Transfiguration is a "special change" to a "higher state" by the "power of the Holy Ghost" (*MD, 803*). In order to see God with his "spiritual eyes" Moses "was transfigured before him" because "my natural eyes could not have beheld" (*Moses 1:11*).

The scriptures suggest that the Spirit may actually carry a mortal being to another place. Nephi said: "I was caught away in the Spirit of the Lord, yea, into an exceedingly high mountain, which I never had before seen, and upon which I never had before set my foot" (*1 Nephi 11:1*); "upon the wings of his Spirit hath my body been carried away upon exceedingly high mountains" (*2 Nephi 4:25*). Nephi, the son of Helaman, escaped from prison when he was physically "taken by the Spirit and conveyed away out of the midst of them" (*Helaman 10:16*). When Adam was baptized he "was caught away by the Spirit of the Lord, and was carried down into the water" (*Moses 6:64*). Enoch's people "were caught up by the powers of heaven into Zion" (*Moses 7:27*).

(b) ***Mortal body as a veil.*** Wilford Woodruff said "our veil is our bodies" (*JD 21:194; see also #50*). The mortal body separates us from the spirit realm. When the spirit is separated from the body, which is an out of body experience, the veil is rent. Sometimes the veil-rending experience transcends our mortal frame of reference making it difficult to describe. It may not be obvious whether the crossed veil is internal or external, in the body or out of the body. For example, the Three Nephites were:

> caught up into heaven, and saw and heard unspeakable things . . . And whether they were in the body or out of the body, they could not tell; for it did seem unto them like a transfiguration of them, that they were changed from this body of flesh into an immortal state, that they could behold the things of God (*3 Nephi 28:13,15*).

Paul had a comparable experience: "whether in the body . . . or out of the body, I cannot tell" (*see 2 Corinthians 12:1-4*). Joseph Smith had a vision of the future when he "beheld the celestial kingdom of God, and the glory thereof, whether in the body or out I cannot tell" (*D&C 137:1*). Alma was so filled with joy that "my soul is carried away, even to the separation of it from the body, as it were, so great is my joy" (*Alma 29:16*). Ammon noted that King Lamoni was "under the power of God . . . the light of the glory of God . . . had infused such joy into his soul . . . that this had overcome his natural frame, and he was carried away in God" (*Alma 19:6*).

Sometimes individuals other than prophets also have out of body experiences. Approximately 75% of NDEs report an out of body experience (*see #112*). Some have visions or spiritual epiphanies where there is uncertainty about whether they were in or out of body. What they do know is they experienced an unforgettable veil-rending phenomenon as real as anything that has ever happened to them.

(c) ***External veils***. There are external veils or curtains that separate spheres. These veils characterize the boundaries between actual places such as the premortal spirit world, the mortal earth, the postmortal spirit world, other worlds and heaven. The veils restrict contact and the Spirit among these spheres. Hugh Nibley wrote:

> The purpose of numerous curtains or veils is to apportion to each world the light it is ready to receive. When Moses asked about the other worlds, the Lord informed him that he was not to know about them at the present and Moses agreed to be satisfied with learning "concerning this earth, and the inhabitants thereof, and also the heavens, and then thy servant will be content" (*Moses 1:36*). Numerous ancient documents attest to the curtains' existence (*Ensign, April 1977*).

Apparently there is a border or a boundary between mortality on earth and the spirit world. When one dies, the spirit leaves the body and crosses to the other side of the veil or, as we sometimes say, passes through the veil. The spirit, which includes the soul and mind of man never dies; it goes into the spirit world. NDE reports often mention some kind of film, tunnel, or other border separating mortality and the spirit world. Sometimes near-death experiencers mention a second boundary in the spirit world like a fence, curtain, door or natural barrier like a stream or hedge (*see Evidence, 16*). This is another type of veil, which spirits understand they must not cross if they want to return to mortality.

82. Can we break through the veil?

"Spiritual things cannot be forced," taught Boyd K. Packer (*That All May Be Edified, 13*). Light is the power and the "law by which all things [including the veil] are governed" (*D&C 88:13*). According to his will and purposes, special spiritual manifestations, dreams, and visions may take place. This can happen based on one's spiritual readiness, a gift from God, or a need: "God also bearing them witness, both with signs and wonders, and with divers miracles, and gifts of the Holy Ghost, according to his own will?"(*Hebrews 2:4*).

The Lord can remove or partially remove the veil. He can open our eyes spiritually through the Holy Ghost. We need not presume the extent of the veil is the same for all. The piercing of the veil is available to all righteous people, and some not so righteous (*e.g., Paul* and *Alma*), according to the Lord's purposes. Joseph Smith pointed to our potential: "Could we all come together with one heart and one mind in perfect faith the veil might as well be rent today as next week, or any other time" (*TPJS, 9*). Bruce R. McConkie echoed this view: "The Lord wants all his children to gain light and truth and knowledge from on high. It is his will that we pierce the veil and rend the heavens and see the visions of eternity" (*Ensign, November 1978*).[vii]

The prophet Ether taught that faith may be a factor in piercing the veil: "And there were many whose faith was so exceedingly strong, even before Christ came, who could not be kept from within the veil, but truly saw with their eyes the things which they had beheld with an eye of faith, and they were glad" (*Ether 12:19*). The prophet Moroni admonished us to "rend that veil of unbelief" to unfold "great and marvelous things" and "revelations" (*Ether 4:15,16*).

As N.L. Nelson suggested:

> Growth in spiritual discernment implies exercise, as in the case of any natural faculty, and exercise implies faith. Skepticism is ever the snow and frost above the soil of any faculty otherwise ready to sprout and grow . . . [However] nearly transparent the spirit Veil becomes, it still remains a veil. Actually to see a heavenly being, or hear an articulated spirit voice, as the Prophet Joseph did, implies the lifting or taking away of the Veil; and this is always an *event* rather than a soul *status* (*IE, March 1929*).

Veil-piercing experiences can be wonderful, indeed the very signature of God. But they are not necessary for our salvation. Paul taught that our mortal perspective is limited: "For now we see through a glass, darkly"

(*1Corinthians 13:12*); but if we exercise faith in "things not seen," (*Hebrews 11:1*) at length, "then shall I know even as also I am known" (*1 Corinthians 13:12*).

83. Are there unauthorized communications through the veil?

Mortals and spirits are free to obey or disobey the Lord's commandments. With their God-given agency (*see #44, #117, #165, #166*), they may try to communicate with each other. But without authorization and the Spirit of the Lord, such attempts from both mortals and spirits are forbidden (*see #218*). Joseph Fielding Smith quoted President Charles W. Penrose who wrote: "By permission of the Lord, persons on either side of the veil may be manifest to those on the other, but this will certainly be by law and according to the order which God has established" (*AGQ, 4:110*).

Illicit communication and tampering with the veil through spirit-mediums is contrary to the Lord's pattern of righteousness. Pursuit of such unauthorized communications results in evil degeneracy, unhappiness and deep sorrow. No good can come of it. Abuse of the veil can be catastrophic, and destroy our faith. Faith is a spiritual gift from God that grows through obedience and divine light, not signs from evil means and realms. Satan's counterfeit for spirituality is spiritualism, which is attempting to communicate with the dead through a medium. (*See also #33, #166.*)

In a similar vein, Latter-day Saints and others sometimes mistake the source of their inspiration. Satan is crafty and can fool us. We must measure inspiration against God's revealed word, His protocol, and the proper Spirit.

N.L. Nelson concludes on the answer to our question:

> Latter-day Saints have therefore everything to lose and nothing to gain by giving attention to spirit-seances or promoting their teachings in any way. Nay, let us rather dedicate our homes, and pray for special protec-

tion against all influences that come to man through a violated Veil! (*IE, April 1929*).

84. Why is a veil of forgetfulness necessary at the time of our physical birth?

So that we can exercise faith and grow towards exaltation. Brigham Young declared:

> It has also been decreed by the Almighty that spirits, upon taking bodies, shall forget all they had known previously, or they could not have a day of trial—could not have an opportunity for proving themselves in darkness and temptation, in unbelief and wickedness, to prove themselves worthy of eternal existence (*JD 6:333*).

Neal A. Maxwell explains why we should appreciate the veil:

> Without the veil, for instance, we would lose that precious insulation which keeps us from a profound and disabling homesickness that would interfere with our mortal probation and maturation. Without the veil, our brief, mortal walk in a darkening world would lose its meaning . . . The veil (which is both the film of forgetting and the border between mortality and eternity) will, one day, be shown to have been a succoring screen for us earthlings. Were it possible to breach it on the wrong terms, we would see and experience, before we are ready, things that would moot much of the value in this mortal experience . . . Fortunately, the veil keeps the first, second, and third estates separate, hence our sense of separateness. The veil insures the avoidance of having things "compound in one" (*2 Nephi 2:11*)—to our everlasting detriment (*All These Things Shall Give Thee Experience, 10-11*).

85. Is the veil between this life and the spirit world thin?

Yes. President Ezra Taft Benson taught: "The spirit world is not far away. Sometimes the veil between this life and the life beyond becomes very thin. Our loved ones who have passed on are not far from us" (*Ensign, June 1971*).

Elder Charles A. Callis said sometimes we are not even aware: "Death does not congeal the lips of those who go before us; they are not far from us and they help us more than we know" (*CR, October 1939*).

There are many documented, inspirational stories establishing that authorized visits, visions and communications from the spirit world occur. Our deceased loved ones have experienced the difficulty of mortality. Their empathy is real. They have progressed, and their love has grown even more powerful. They are pulling for us, they pray for us, and they want to help us as they are allowed (*see #218*).

Joseph F. Smith commented on how disembodied spirits can see us and visit us more than we visit or see them:

> [O]ur fathers and mothers, brothers, sisters and friends who have passed away from this earth, having been faithful, and worthy to enjoy these rights and privileges, may have a mission given them to visit their relatives and friends upon the earth again, bringing from the divine Presence messages of love, of warning, of reproof and instruction to those whom they had learned to love in the flesh (*JD 22:351*).

> If we can see, by the enlightening influence of the Spirit of God . . . beyond the veil that separates us from the spirit world, surely those who have passed beyond, can see more clearly through the veil back here to us than it is possible for us to see them from our sphere of action . . . We can not forget them; we do not cease to love them; we always hold them in our hearts, in memory . . . If this is the case with us in our finite condition, surrounded by our mortal weaknesses, short-sightedness . . . how much more certain it is and reasonable and consistent to believe that those who have been faithful, who have gone beyond . . . can see us better than we can see them; that they know us better than we know them. They have advanced . . . we live in their presence, they see us, they are solicitous for our welfare, they love us now more than ever (*Messages 5:6-7*).

Speaking at funerals, Harold B. Lee taught that the presence of deceased loved ones may one day be felt:

> [I]n the quiet loneliness of your home, in a day not too intense because of the motherhood requirements, there will come times when you will say, "My, he seemed to be so close to me. I seem to have felt his nearness." And it will be real. It will be something you can't deny.
>
> [R]ealize that your father might return to you as your holy guardian, limited in his scope but there when you need him the most. How do you know but that he may be very close and very near on occasions when such a messenger would be very valuable? (*The Teachings of Harold B. Lee, 60*).

Researchers report that stories of communications from deceased loved ones, called *after-death communications* or *ADCs* are "astonishingly common, even if, until recently, not commonly talked about" (Kenneth Ring, PhD, *Lessons from the Light, 269*). ADCs as defined occur when someone is contacted unexpectedly by a deceased family member or friend. Mediums are not involved. Bill and Judy Guggenheim amassed more than 3300 of such accounts and presented 350 of the stories in a book titled *Hello from Heaven!* In spite of the tabloidal title, the research is comprehensive. (*See also #36, #38, #218 and #219, #B2, #B11, #B12.*)

86. If a person is permitted to see a deceased family member or acquaintance, how can they recognize them?

Spirits resemble the physical body (*see #37*), apparently at least enough for beholders to recognize a loved one (*see #35 and Appendix B*). If necessary, the elasticity of the spirit (*see #37*) seemingly enables spirits to change their size, dress, and appearance for purposes of recognition by mortals. Numerous reported NDEs suggest this is the case.

N.L. Nelson explained his view:

> On the earth-plane, our rigid garment of clay makes it fairly difficult for us to change our appearance very greatly; but in the after-world, a spirit may, so it would seem, assume at will any stage of its previous earth life, with the very appearance of clothes worn at the time, including the peculiarities of personal bearing and mental traits (*IE, April 1929*).

87. Have deceased Church leaders been seen in the spirit world?

Yes. Some have reported seeing Jesus Christ, Joseph Smith, Hyrum Smith, Brigham Young, John Taylor, Wilford Woodruff, Joseph F. Smith, Spencer W. Kimball and other Church leaders (*e.g., see below, #135, #136, D&C 138*).

Mortals, empowered by God, may see spirits in the spirit world or in earthly surroundings. Wilford Woodruff delivered these remarks at General Conference in 1880:

> After the death of Joseph Smith I saw and conversed with him many times in my dreams in the night season. On one occasion he and his brother Hyrum, met me when on the sea, going on a mission to England. I had Dan Jones with me. He received his mission from Joseph before his death; and the prophet talked freely to me about the mission I was then going to perform. And he also talked to me with regard to the mission of the Twelve Apostles in the flesh, and he laid before.me the work they had to perform; and he also spoke of the reward they would receive after death. And there were many other things he laid before me in his interview on that occasion. And when I awoke many of the things he had told me were taken from me, I could not comprehend them. I have had many interviews with Brother Joseph until the last 15 or 20 years of my life; I have not seen him for that length of time. But during my travels in the southern country last winter I had many interviews with President Young, and with Heber C. Kimball, and George A. Smith, and Jedediah M.Grant, and many others who are dead. They attended our conference, they attended our meetings. And on one occasion, I saw Brother Brigham and Brother Heber ride in carriage ahead of the carriage in which I rode when I was on my way to attend conference; and they were

dressed in the most priestly robes. When we arrived at our destination I asked President Young if he would preach to us. He said, "No, I have finished my testimony in the flesh; I shall not talk to this people any more. But I have come to see you; I have come to watch over you, and to see what the people are doing. Then I want you to teach the people—and I want you to follow this counsel yourself—that they must labor and so live as to obtain the Holy Spirit, for without this you cannot build up the kingdom . . ." (*Temples of the Most High, 280*).

88. If Jesus dwells in heaven, why would He be seen in the spirit world?

God the Father and Jesus Christ can visit all their creations and realms as they see fit.

They have visited earth (*e.g., JS-History 1:17*; *see #19*).

CHAPTER NINE

PHYSICAL DEATH

There is no end to glory
There is no end to love
There is no end to being
There is no death above
—William W. Phelps, If You Could Hie to Kolob, Hymns, 284

89. What is physical death?

The separation of the spirit from the physical body. The Apostle James wrote: "the body without the spirit is dead" (*James 2:26*).

Robert L. Millet put this uplifting spin on death:

> Strictly speaking, there is no death and there are no dead. When things die, they do not cease to be; they merely cease to be in this world. Life goes on. Death is a transition, a change in assignment, a transfer to another realm. When we die, the spirit continues to see and act and feel and associate; only the physical body becomes inactive and lifeless for a season. And so the term death describes what we perceive from our limited perspective. From an eternal vantage point, however, there is only life (*Life After Death, 6*).

Job understood that the spirit doesn't die. He was talking about the resurrection of the body (flesh) and not the cessation of existence when he answered his own question, "If a man die, shall he live again?":

> For I know that my redeemer liveth, and that he shall stand at the latter day upon the earth. And though after my skin worms destroy this body,

> yet in my flesh shall I see God: Whom I shall see for myself, and mine eyes shall behold (*Job 19:25-27*).

90. Why is death necessary?

Death is a consequence of the fall of Adam (*see BD, 655*). The scriptures are clear: "For as in Adam all die (*1 Corinthians 15:21*), and "by reason of transgression cometh the fall, which fall bringeth death" (*Moses 6:59*). We do not condemn Adam and Eve because death is not a bad thing for mankind. God planned it this way: "all things have been done in the wisdom of him who knoweth all things" (*2 Nephi 2:24*). Death is necessary to be resurrected and obtain a fulness of joy. Russell M. Nelson said "We live to die, and we die to live again" (*CR, April 3, 2011*). Dallin H. Oaks explained that Adam and Eve "understood the necessity of the Fall" (*CR, October 1993; see 2 Nephi 2:25 and Moses 5:10*).

91. If the spirit has left the body can the body still show signs of life?

Yes. President David O. McKay explained that one's spirit may leave, while the body may briefly still have some animation. He saw one young man who was evidently responding in the spirit world to his deceased Father. When President McKay was asked by a loved one to administer to the young man, he explained:

> I said, "It is too late, he is gone," But yet his heart was beating, his vocal chords were expressing words, but I was conscious and sure as that I am standing here, that he was unresponsive to us. He was responding to another environment to which we were unresponsive, to which we were dead. Not five minutes passed before his heartbeat stopped, and then we said he was dead. His spirit was free, even before the heartbeat stopped (*Gospel Ideals, 54-55*).

Evidently one could be dead according to the scriptural definition of separation of spirit from body, yet still be clinically or medically alive. Some near-death experiencers have reported this phenomenon of observing their body function from their spirit which has separated and lingers above the body. So, even though one's spirit may leave the body, there may be momentary outward signs of life in the body.

92. What is the medical definition of death?

The medical profession has struggled with this question for centuries. There is no consensus. The definition varies among institutions. The *American Heritage Medical Dictionary* defines death in 2010 as: "The end of life; the permanent cessation of vital bodily functions, as manifested in humans by the loss of heartbeat, the absence of spontaneous breathing, and brain death." So, technically, under this medical definition, one who "dies" and comes back to life didn't really die because death is permanent. Determining "permanent cessation" can be difficult. With advancing technology it's harder to define when life ends. For example, death used to be defined as the cessation of a heartbeat and breathing, but modern resuscitation techniques can sometimes restart these functions. Even brain death is apparently not always obvious to physicians because cessation of brain activity caused by certain drugs or hypothermic conditions can sometimes be reversed (*see also #29*). If death is the "end of life," just what is life? (*see also #45*). There is no consensus on the scientific and medical definition of life either.

Jeffrey Long, MD, wrote: "when the heart stops beating, blood immediately stops flowing to the brain. Approximately ten to twenty seconds after blood stops flowing to the brain, the electroencephalogram (EEG), which measures brain electrical activity, goes flat" (*Evidence, 57*). Long, who has researched thousands of NDEs, believes most NDEs occur when the body is unconscious but not EEG flatlining, although some occur when flatlining (*correspondence with the author*).

Prophets and angels speaking under the inspiration of God in the scriptures give the best answers about what constitutes death and life. It is all about the spirit (*see #45 and #89*).

93. What does the scripture "those that die in me shall not taste of death" mean?

It means the death of the righteous shall not be bitter. The sting in death is the regret of unrepentant sin. The Lord said: "those that die in me shall not taste of death, for it shall be sweet unto them; And they that die not in me, wo unto them, for their death is bitter" (*D&C 42:46-47*); "blessed are the dead that die in the Lord, [for they] shall receive an inheritance before the Lord, in the holy city" (*D&C 63:49*); "O death, where is thy sting? O grave, where is thy victory? The sting of death is sin" (*1 Corinthians 15:55-56*).

94. Why do we shun death?

Joseph Smith reportedly explained that "the Lord in his wisdom had implanted the fear of death in every person that they might cling to life and thus accomplish the designs of their creator" (*Diary of Charles Lowell Walker 1:465-66*).

95. Should we have no anxieties over death?

Surely a little apprehension is acceptable. Neal A. Maxwell poetically penned this refreshing perspective:

> Some anxieties are understandably common to life's exit routes leading to death. Later, when we look back after the trip through the veil, our anxieties will turn out to be naïve and perhaps even amusing. After all, in gospel grammar, death is not an exclamation point, merely a comma. Nevertheless, dying is a new, individual experience. For those paradise-bound, what seemed to be the grim ballet of separation, with but one pirouette, turns out to be a resplendent reunion (*Moving in His Majesty and Power, 91*).

Interestingly, most who have encountered an NDE have no anxieties over death. They realize that death is a favorable transition and not something to fear (*see # 35*).

96. Should we mourn for those who die?

Daniel H. Ludlow answered: "Yes. However, for the righteous who die we should mourn only because we are temporarily separated from them" (*SW, 286*). Mourning is an acceptable response to the passing of a loved one. The Lord said: "Thou shalt live together in love, insomuch that thou shalt weep for the loss of them that die, and more especially for those that have not hope of a glorious resurrection" (*D&C 42:45*).

Spencer W. Kimball reasoned:

> If we say that early death is a calamity, disaster, or tragedy, would it not be saying that mortality is preferable to earlier entrance into the spirit world and to eventual salvation and exaltation? If mortality be the perfect state, then death would be frustration, but the gospel teaches us there is no tragedy in death, but only in sin, "blessed are the dead that die in the Lord" (*D&C 63:49*) (*TD,6*).

Russell M. Nelson said: "From an eternal perspective, the only death that is truly premature is the death of one who is not prepared to meet God" (*CR, April 3, 2011*).

97. Why do innocent tragedies of death happen? Why doesn't the Lord protect such victims? Why is a young mother, a father providing for a family, a child, or a missionary taken?

Spencer W. Kimball, in his well-known *Tragedy or Destiny* talk at BYU in 1955, responded insightfully to these questions:

> Answer, if you can. I cannot, for though I know God has a major role in our lives, I do not know how much he causes to happen and how much he merely permits. Whatever the answer to this question, there is another I feel sure about. Could the Lord have prevented these tragedies? The answer is, Yes. The Lord is omnipotent, with all power to control our lives, save us pain, prevent all accidents, drive all planes and cars, feed us, protect us, save us from labor, effort, sickness, even from death, if he will. But he will not. We should be able to understand this,

because we can realize how unwise it would be for us to shield our children from all effort, from disappointments, temptations, sorrows, and suffering (*TD, 2*).

98. In death is one called home by God?

Sometimes. Joseph Fielding Smith responded:

> One of the greatest blessings given to mankind is the gift of free agency. Even good, faithful persons, who disregard the laws of health, may shorten the life span which otherwise could have been theirs. Moreover, we are all subject to the ravages of disease, disaster, accidents that could, and often do, shorten life. Nearly every day we read of innocent persons dying in automobile accidents, by drowning...or other danger, death has overtaken them, and it was no fault of their own. We are all subject to the various vicissitudes and conditions in life which confront us which could not be foreseen. It would be contrary to sound thinking to assume that the Lord has decreed that these individuals had been called home by such accidents or calamities, and that "fate" had ordered it so.
>
> It is true that some have been "called home" by sudden death. This was the case with the Prophet Joseph Smith and his brother Hyrum. They had finished their work and the keys of authority, by divine revelation, had been lawfully bestowed upon the twelve. Joseph and Hyrum were in the vigor of their manhood, but the time had come for them to lay down their lives, for it was decreed in the heavens that their passing from this world should be by martyrdom. They had to seal their testimony with their blood and make that testimony binding upon an unbelieving world. No one in reason would deny the right of our Eternal Father to call an individual home, should he will it. Nor would he argue that to take a person from the mortal life in his youth or early childhood, would be unjust, because it deprived the individual of the pleasures and sorrows of mortality, and the experiences to be gained here. He may call any person "home" at any time he chooses, whether in infancy, childhood, youth, or old age. We are all subject to the will of our Heavenly

> Father, but we cannot in truth declare that all the righteous dead were "called home" by divine decree (*AGQ 3:46-48*).

Spencer W. Kimball echoed Joseph Fielding Smith's sentiments:

> I spoke at the funeral service of a young Brigham Young University student who died during World War II. There had been hundreds of thousands of young men rushed prematurely into eternity through the ravages of that war, and I made the statement that I believed this righteous youth had been called to the spirit world to preach the gospel to these deprived souls. This may not be true of all who die, but I felt it true of him (*TD, 6-7*).

99. We are commanded to acknowledge or confess "his hand in all things" (*D&C 59:21*). Does God have a hand in all things, even deaths?

Neal A. Maxwell wrote about the concept of confessing His hand in all things by referring to President Joseph F. Smith's interpretation:

> Confessing or acknowledging God's hand also involves allowing for how deeply God is committed to our "moral agency" (*D&C 101:78*). It was in this connection that President Joseph F. Smith forthrightly disclosed his feelings about the verse we are discussing: "The Lord is greatly displeased only with those who do not confess or acknowledge 'his hand in all things, and obey not his commandments.' Many things occur in the world in which it seems very difficult for most of us to find a solid reason for the acknowledgment of the hand of the Lord. [The only thing] I have been able to discover by which we should acknowledge the hand of God in some occurrences is the fact that the thing which has occurred has been permitted of the Lord." God's commitment to our moral agency is so much higher than, given our lower ways, we can even imagine! Some things clearly are permitted of God which are not approved of God (*That Ye May Believe, 28*).

In a similar vein, some things clearly are permitted of God and approved by God, but not caused by God, such as accidental deaths.

100. What does Ecclesiastes 3:2, "A time to be born, and a time to die" mean?

Often scriptures provide the best explanation for scriptures. The following scriptures frame the question quite well:

"God knoweth all the times which are appointed unto man" (*Alma 40:10*);

"thus did I, the Lord God, appoint unto man the days of his probation" (*D&C 29:43*). He knows when we will be born and when we will die.

"God that made the world and all things therein . . . and hath determined the times before appointed, and the bounds of their habitation" (*Acts 17:24,26*).

Spencer W. Kimball elaborated:

> Just as *Ecclesiastes (3:2)* says, I am confident that there is a time to die, but I believe also that many people die before "their time" because they are careless, abuse their bodies, take unnecessary chances, or expose themselves to hazards, accidents, and sickness (*TD, 9*).

101. Do the righteous die before their time?

No. The righteous person (assuming they are not careless as Spencer W. Kimball mentions above) can expect to complete his or her life's mission. Numerous Apostles and prophets have made this observation. Here's one of the quotes from Joseph Fielding Smith:

> May I say for the consolation of those who mourn, and for the comfort and guidance of all of us, that no righteous man is ever taken before his time. In the case of faithful saints, they are simply transferred to other fields of labor. The Lord's work goes on in this life, in the world of

> spirits, and in the kingdoms of glory where men go after their resurrection (*Funeral service for Richard L. Evans, November 4, 1971, typescript, cited by Robert L. Millet, Life After Death, 7*).

At the funeral of S. Dilworth Young, Bruce R. McConkie said: "It is with him as President [J. Reuben] Clark expressed it at the funeral of Brother Matthew Cowley: 'No righteous man is ever taken before his time'" (*Funeral Service for Elder S. Dilworth Young, July 13, 1981, cited in Horne, Faith to Heal, 43*).

Dallin H. Oaks quoted his cousin who spoke at the funeral of a teenage girl who had died of a serious illness. The words first "astonished" him and then "edified" him:

> I know it was the will of the Lord that she die. She had good medical care. She was given priesthood blessings. Her name was on the prayer roll in the temple. She was the subject of hundreds of prayers for her restoration to health. And I know that there is enough faith in this family that she would have been healed unless it was the will of the Lord to take her home at this time (*CR, April 2010*).

Numerous near-death reports indicate that spirit world greeters commonly hail near-death experiencers with a message such as: "It's not your time." Sometimes the greeters state: "you have a job to do," or they specify a mission to be performed. Survivers return with an understanding that life is a precious gift with a purpose. The author Richard Bach said: "Here is a test to find whether your mission on earth is finished: if you're alive, it isn't."

102. Does agency play a role in the timing of one's death?

Yes. Although "God knoweth all the times which are appointed unto man" (*Alma 40:10*) it doesn't mean He always influences the time of death. As discussed in previous questions and answers, we can't assume the Lord always calls home the deceased. God's gift of agency is inextricably linked to chance and misfortune. Happenstance is often a factor determining the timing of death for many. Unpredictable fatal accidents occur, and terminal diseases are contracted by chance, thereby ending one's life by a fluke when that life might otherwise have been extended. A person could be a victim of circumstance. Once a righteous individual has satisfied the mortal purposes for which he was foreordained (or she was predesignated) in the pre-earth life, one's death may occur at any time. So it seems that one's time to die may sometimes be a range rather than a specific point in time. Everyone will die from something. Because agency is so important to God, it's reasonable that agency would often play a role in the timing. It might be said on one's accidental death that both: (a) He just happened to be in the wrong place at the wrong time, a victim of circumstance; and (b) He didn't die before his time. In the gospel perspective, death is not necessarily unfortunate, even if it did happen by chance.

103. Should survivors feel guilty upon the death of a loved one?

No. Regardless of whether death is from old age or an unforeseen occurrence, when one's time has come, one is *appointed unto death*, because God has not chosen to delay it further. All must die, and it's not productive to belabor the cause. Robert D. Hales wrote about the pointlessness of survivor's guilt:

> Besides sorrowing for the passing of loved ones, sometimes we experience the sorrow of guilt for what we might have done to prevent death or better support and comfort the dying in the twilight of their lives. Some may even wonder whether they might have saved their family member or friend if they had only been more diligent or exercised more faith in their behalf. We should not blame ourselves or let guilt compound our grief when a loved one passes away . . . There is a time appointed for each of us to leave this world (*see D&C 42:48*), which means that as long as there is no unrighteousness involved, there is nothing we can do to prevent death or forestall it when the appointed time has come. We should leave the burden of such groundless guilt at the feet of the Savior and "bear a song away," focusing on past joys and

lessons learned rather than on facts we cannot and need not change (*Return: Four Phases of Our Mortal Journey Home, Ch. 32*).

104. Can the righteous prolong their lives?

Yes, unless appointed unto death (*see D&C 42:48*). There are at least five ways:

(a) ***Honor parents***: "CHILDREN, obey your parents in the Lord: for this is right. Honour thy father and mother; (which is the first commandment with promise;) That it may be well with thee, and thou mayest live long on the earth" (*Ephesians 6:1-3*).

(b) ***Observe the sacrament covenant***: "For he that eateth and drinketh unworthily, eateth and drinketh damnation to himself, not discerning the Lord's body. For this cause many are weak and sickly among you, and many sleep (*1 Corinthians 11:29-30*). Joseph Fielding Smith interpreted this scripture:

> Evidently Paul meant that many had passed away because of their violation of this commandment. There can be little question raised contrary to the fact that men shorten their lives by violation of the commandments of the Lord. The use of narcotics, liquors, and other drugs and stimulants inevitably weakens and impairs the functions of the body, thus shortening the span of life (*AGQ 3:47*).

"Be not ...wicked, neither be thou foolish: why shouldest thou die before thy time?" (*Ecclesiastes 7:17*).

(c) ***Obtain a priesthood blessing of healing in faith***: "And again, it shall come to pass that he that hath faith in me to be healed, and is not appointed unto death, shall be healed" (*D&C 42:48*). Spencer W. Kimball outlined the three conditions for a faith healing:

> We are assured by the Lord that the sick will be healed if the ordinance is performed, if there is sufficient faith, and if the ill one is "not appointed unto death." All of these three factors should be satisfied. Many do not comply with the ordinances, and great numbers are unwilling or incapable of exercising sufficient faith. But the third

factor also looms important: if they are not appointed unto death (*TD, 9*).

(d) ***Be faithful***. The Lord promised: "whoso is faithful unto the obtaining these two priesthoods of which I have spoken, and the magnifying their calling, are sanctified by the Spirit unto the renewing of their bodies" (*D&C 84:33*). Russell M. Nelson testified of this scripture: "I know of no better choice in preparing for a full and useful life. I have seen this promise realized time and time again" (*The Gateway We Call Death, 68*).

(e) ***Petition the Lord for an extension of life beyond the appointed time***. **Spencer W. Kimball** taught: "I believe we may die prematurely but seldom exceed our time very much. One exception was Hezekiah . . . the Lord yielded unto his prayers, 'I will add unto thy days fifteen years'" (*2 Kings 20:6*). Another was David Patten Kimball, uncle of Spencer W. Kimball (*TD, 10*). David Patten Kimball's experience in the spirit world is told in *Appendix A6* at the end of this book.

105. Can the spirit die?

No. The spirit body is immortal. The First Presidency declared: "A spirit born of God is an immortal being" (*GD, 14*). The spirit body does not deteriorate, decay, or die like the mortal body does (*see GD, 29 and #110*). When the physical body dies, the spirit continues to live on. Eventually, everyone will be resurrected with an immortal physical body (*see 1 Corinthians 15:21-22*).

106. Is the spirit reunited with the body forever in the resurrection?

Yes. "In the resurrection, the immortal spirit is reunited with the same body of flesh and bone it possessed as a mortal, with two major differences: The union will be permanent, and the body will not be subject to aging and death" (*BD, 776*).

107. Can one's death be a positive spiritual experience for the living?

Yes. Like birth, death is a monumental event in the plan of salvation that occurs only as permitted by God. On occasion others close in proximity or in relationship to the deceased may experience supernal out of body or other spiritual experiences similar to an NDE. The Lord sometimes uses another's passing to communicate to loved ones and others. Such events may be a gift or a sign from God that is evidenced by feelings of peace and assurance.

Studies show that so-called *shared death experiences* are very common. Dr. Raymond Moody quoted one psychologist who wrote:

> The deathbed scene is not fully in this world. And although I am not religious, hospice work has awakened me to a spiritual dimension of life. In my opinion, everyone who works with the dying long enough must have some awareness of these experiences. I believe the spiritual experiences of dying people somehow leak out and pervade the area around them. If you step into that area with the right temperament, you will receive, I feel, a sense of the sacred in the presence of the dying (*Glimpses of Eternity, 102*).

CHAPTER TEN

CROSSING INTO THE SPIRIT WORLD

Sunset and evening star And one clear call for me!
And may there be no moaning of the bar, When I put out to sea . . .
For though from out our bourne of Time and Place
The flood may bear me far,
I hope to see my Pilot face to face When I have crossed the bar.
—Alfred Lord Tennyson, Crossing the Bar

108. Do we arrive naked in the spirit world?

Yes. President John Taylor said: "When we go to the spirit world, we go naked, as we came into the world, or if we get any clothing it is as much by our dependence upon others as when we were born into this world" (*Wilford Woodruff, History of His Life and Labors, 541*). The *Bible* teaches: "Naked came I out of my mother's womb, and naked shall I return thither: the Lord gave, and the Lord hath taken away; blessed be the name of the Lord" (*Job 1:21*).

109. Are spirits clothed?

Yes. NDEs and spirit world visions communicate that spirits are clothed. Apparently, as reported in some NDEs, spirits receive clothing upon entering the spirit world. Heber Q. Hale observed groups of women on the other side of the veil preparing "wearing apparel" for spirits about to die (*HQH, 4*). The NDE researcher, Dr. Carol Zaleski, finds that many but not all beings in the spirit world are dressed in white. She summarizes: "the white robes . . . are standard issue for spirits; some, moreover, appear in familiar street clothes, as if to assure the newcomer that normal social life continues on the other side" (*cited in Glimpses, 46-47; see also #148*).

In 1891, nineteen year-old Ella Jensen died and went to the spirit world for three hours. She was called back in a blessing from Lorenzo Snow, who was then President of the Quorum of Twelve Apostles. She observed: "The people were all dressed in white or cream, excepting Uncle Hans Jensen, who had on his dark clothes and long rubber boots, the things he wore when he was drowned in the Snake River." Rudger Clawson, who assisted President Snow in giving Ella the blessing to "come back and live" said that Hans Jensen's body was never found in the Snake river. They didn't know for certain he had drowned until Ella "met him in the spirit world . . . [and] the mystery was solved" (Leroi C. Snow, *IE, October 1929*).

110. Does the spirit change upon death?

Yes and no. Our spirit bodies may change but our disposition and proclivities will not. Daniel H. Ludlow said the "*state* or *condition* of our spirit bodies in the postmortal existence will be essentially the same as when our spirits were in the presence of our Heavenly Father before our birth on earth" (*SW, 400*). Spirits of deceased children revert to their adult form before birth. Spirits of those with decrepit physical bodies revert to their complete and immortal spirit form. Joseph F. Smith described the immortal spirit as "perfection of their spirits . . . the perfection that God designed from the beginning . . . the perfection of her youth" (*GD, 29*). The immortal spirit appearance is reported to be similar to one's age in the prime of young adulthood. For example, Parley P. Pratt saw the "wife of his youth" (*see Appendix B9*). Ludlow continued: "At the time of temporal physical death, the spirit body will be separated from the physical mortal body and will be free of all physical ailments, pains, and sufferings" (*SW, 400*).

An individual's identity and personality is in the spirit which lives on after death. Bruce R. McConkie taught:

> The spirit that enters the body before birth, leaves it at death, and immediately finds itself in the spirit world . . . Men have the same talents and intelligence there which they had in this life . . . They possess the same attitudes, inclinations, and feelings there which they had in this life. They believe the same things, as far as eternal truths are concerned; they continue, in effect, to walk in the same path they were following in this life.
>
> Thus if a man has the spirit of charity and love of the truth in his heart in this life, that same spirit will possess him in the spirit world. If he has the spirit of unbelief and hate in his heart here, so will it be with him when he passes through the door into the spirit world (*MD, 762*).

Amulek anciently said: "That same spirit which doth possess your bodies at the time that ye go out of this life, that same spirit will have power to possess your body in that eternal world" (*Alma 34:34*). Amulek then inferred that one's "same spirit" or level of light, spirit, or intelligence follows him to the spirit world: If "ye have become subjected to the spirit of the devil . . . he doth seal you his" (*Alma 34:35*).

President George Q. Cannon elaborated on this concept:

> We shall enter into the other sphere of existence with the same spirit that we have here. If we were animated by the spirit of the Telestial Kingdom we shall have that, if by the spirit of the Terrestrial Kingdom we shall have that, if by the spirit of the Celestial Kingdom we shall have that. We shall go from this condition of existence into the other sphere with the same feelings, to some extent at least, as we have here. If we have had knowledge, we shall have it there (*Gospel Truth, 60*).

111. Will crossing into the spirit world be a pleasant transition?

Yes. Joseph Smith said: "When men are prepared, they are better off to go hence" (*HC 6:52*). At the funeral of Thomas Williams, Brigham Young taught: "He has now entered upon a higher state of being, that is, his spirit has, than when in this body" *(JD 17:141*). Brigham Young described the pleasant crossing into this higher state:

> [W]e shall turn around and look upon it (the valley of death) and think, when we have crossed it, why this is the greatest advantage of my whole existence, for I have passed from a state of sorrow, grief, mourning, woe, misery, pain, anguish and disappointment into a state of existence where I can enjoy life to the fullest extent as far as that can be done without a body. My spirit is set free, I thirst no more, I want to sleep no more, I hunger no more, I tire no more, I run, I walk, I labor, I go, I come, I do this, I do that, whatever is required of me, nothing like pain or weariness, I am full of life, full of vigor . . . (*JD 17:142*).

Most who experience an NDE report immediate feelings of love, relief, and well-being upon death. They feel enveloped in a comforting light. It is a pleasant and indescribable feeling for them. They generally do not want to return to mortality, until they understand a purpose or obligation to go back, sometimes feeling a responsibility for loved ones left behind. Some cross to the spirit world with feelings of deep regret and disappointment for their lives thus far. They generally come back with a commitment to be better.

112. What do NDEs most frequently convey about crossing into the spirit world?

Jeffrey Long, MD, has studied thousands of NDEs. His large survey, summarized below, revealed that most NDEs have the following elements:

(a) ***Out of body experience***. 75% experienced a "separation of consciousness from the body."

(b) ***Heightened senses***. 74% had "more consciousness and alertness than normal."

(c) ***Intense positive emotions and feelings***. 76% had "incredible peace or pleasantness." 53% experienced "incredible joy."

(d) ***Encountering a brilliant light***. 65% saw a light.

(e) ***Encountering others***. 57% met and saw other beings. Most were deceased relatives.

(f) ***Sense of alteration of time or space***. 61% sensed an "altered space or time." 34% indicated that "everything seemed to be happening all at once."

(g) ***Encountering unworldly realms***. 52% encountered an unearthly realm.

(h) ***Encountering special knowledge***. 56% had a "sense of knowing special knowledge, universal order, and/or purpose."

Some report passing through a tunnel or enclosure (34%); and some experience a life review (22%) (*Evidence, 4-19*).

113. Jehovah said: "In the sweat of thy face shalt thou eat bread, until thou return unto the ground" (*Moses 4:25*). Do we earn our keep in the spirit world?

Apparently not. The above scripture implies we work to sustain ourselves only until we die ("return unto the ground"). Neal A. Maxwell commented, "So many of the cares and demands of the world which press upon us here and now, including doing the chores of this world, will not dominate us there" (*The Promise of Discipleship, 106*).

Victor L. Ludlow noted: "since the physical demands of our bodies will have vanished, the necessity of working for daily bread and of sleeping to rejuvenate our bodies will disappear, and other limitations of the flesh will be left behind (*Principles and Practices of the Restored Gospel, 221*).

This doesn't mean we won't be anxiously engaged, learning, helping others, and taking care of other matters (*#126*).

114. Will illnesses and ailments that plague the physical body continue in the spirit world?

No. Spirit world inhabitants have no physical body pain or hunger. Fatigue is not an issue, so sleep is unnecessary (*see #111*). While bodily ills go away, the wicked will suffer mentally, and those in paradise will "rest from all their troubles and from all care, and sorrow" (*Alma 40:12*).

Neal A. Maxwell said "the spirit body will not suffer certain of the ills and constraints which now beset the mortal body. The result will be added zestfulness there" (*The Promise of Discipleship, 106*).

Brigham Young explained:

Here, we are continually troubled with ills and ailments of various kinds, and our ears are saluted with the expressions: "My head aches," "My shoulders ache," "My back aches," "I am hungry, dry [thirsty], or tired;" but in the spirit world we are free from all this and enjoy life, glory and intelligence (*JD 14:231*).

115. Is there a judgment at death?

Yes. Death results in a separation according to one's righteousness in mortality. This separation constitutes a partial judgment. There is another judgment before the second coming and when one is resurrected (*see #207*); and a final judgment after the millennium and the resurrection of the unjust (*see MM, 516-517, 520*).

Joseph F. Smith taught how this partial judgment at death can be a powerful motivator for us:

> This knowledge is one of the greatest incentives that we have to live right in this life, to pass through mortality, doing and feeling and accomplishing good. The spirits of all men, as soon as they depart from this mortal body, whether they are good or evil, we are told in the Book of Mormon, are taken home to that God who gave them life, where there is a separation, a partial judgment, and the spirits of those who are righteous are received into a state of happiness which is called paradise

> . . . The wicked, on the contrary, have no part nor portion in the Spirit of the Lord, and they are cast into outer darkness, being led captive, because of their own iniquity, by the evil one (*GD, 564-565*).

In a way, we may be our own judge at death if we are given to remember the details of our mortal lives. George Q. Cannon said:

> Memory will be quickened to a wonderful extent. Every deed that we have done will be brought to our recollection. Every acquaintance made will be remembered. There will be no scenes or incidents in our lives that will be forgotten by us in the world to come. You have heard of men who have been drowning or have fallen from a great height describe that in about a second or two every event of their lives passed before them like a panorama with the rapidity of lightning. This shows what power there is latent in the human mind . . . (*Gospel Truth, 60*).

Victor L. Ludlow wrote:

> Although we shed our physical body at death, the memories of the flesh remain with us. The influences of a physical body also remain with us to the extent that we have allowed them power over our spirit. If we have successfully conquered the attractions and appetites of the flesh, our disciplined spirits are freed from the temptations and pains of earth life and enter into a spirit bliss, a tranquil heaven. On the other hand, if our bodies have sinfully ruled our souls in mortality, our spirits remain in bondage to the cravings of the flesh, which cannot be satisfied in a spirit world—thus, we are consigned to a spirit torment, a terrible hell . . . Spirit beings are influenced by the yearnings of the physical world even though they are no longer a part of it. No longer able to manipulate or control a physical body, their relative tranquility or torment depends upon how independent their spirit was of the flesh before death separated the body and spirit (*Principles and Practices of the Restored Gospel, 219*).

Dr. Raymond Moody described how near-death experiencers perceive those in the spirit world who are tied to their mortal desires. They are "unable to surrender their attachments to the physical world." They cannot progress in the spirit world because they are bound to some object, habit or other worldly idol in mortality. These beings are "dulled spirits" until they solve the difficulty that is "keeping them in that perplexed state" (*Reflections on Life after Life, 18*).

It would be well for us to cite our minds forward to the inevitable crossing to the spirit world. Have we overcome the natural man and temptations of the flesh? Imagine a future panoramic life review, which many near-death beholders witness. For example, Alma's life passed before him (*Alma 36:13*). What will our book of life say? Some shudder at the prospects of a life review. Those who have repented need not worry, since that day will be joyous for them. Although we remember our sins, so as not to repeat them, the Lord said "I will remember their sin no more" (*Jeremiah 31:34*). We are to focus on positive actions we can take in the future, not past sins which we have repented of. The challenge is to learn from the past, not dwell on it. President Boyd K. Packer warned that the lesson for the repentant from the experience of Lot's wife is, "Don't look back" (*CR, October 2010*). (*See also #227, #228 and #229.*)

116. On what basis will we be judged upon death?

The Lord told us that we are judged on both our deeds and our desires: "For I, the Lord, will judge all men according to their works, according to the desire of their hearts (*D&C 137:9; see also Mosiah 4:6; 1 Nephi 15:32-33; Alma 41:3*). In passing judgment upon death, the Lord also considers individual circumstances and various degrees of light, knowledge and accountability that individuals possess in mortality.

For example, the scriptures describe those in a state of blindness or ignorance. They never heard the gospel in mortality. The Lord will mercifully bring the gospel to them (*see 1 Nephi13:32-42; Alma 9:16-17*). They "died without the law" (*D&C 76:72*); and "where there is no law given there is no punishment" and no condemnation; therefore they don't go to "hell" (the place of "torment") upon death; and "the mercies of the Holy One of Israel have claim upon them" (*see 2 Nephi 9:25-27; Moroni 8:22*).

An angel taught King Benjamin that the blood of Jesus Christ atones for the sins of those "who have died not knowing the will of God concerning them, or who have ignorantly sinned" (*Mosiah 3:11*). James E. Talmage said "the sinners of this class do not stand condemned, but shall be given opportunity yet to learn and to accept or reject the principles of the Gospel" (*Articles of Faith, 58*).

Individual levels of accountability vary, as does responsibility and condemnation, as taught in a student religion manual published by the Church:

> It should be remembered that all who reach the age of accountability [age 8] are given the light of Christ (*see Moroni 7:15-18*). This allows a man to have at least a foundation of knowing what is good and what is evil. Therefore, all who have reached the age of accountability are not without responsibility, even though the accountability is obviously not the same as one who has been taught the principles of the gospel. "For of him unto whom much is given much is required; and he who sins against the greater light shall receive the greater condemnation" (*D&C 82:3*) (*Book of Mormon Student Manual, 76*).

(*See Chapter 13 for a description of those in spirit prison and see #174 for how spirits are separated in the spirit world.*)

117. Does agency continue in the spirit world?

Yes. Our spirits there can continue to choose and act for ourselves (*2 Nephi 2:27; 10:23*), including decisions to obey or disobey God. John A. Widstoe said "All who die . . . [retain] their free agency" (*Program of the Church of Jesus Christ of Latter-day Saints, 226; see also #178*). Agency is an eternal gift from God which enables us to progress (*see 2 Nephi 2*). In the premortal existence our choice to follow Jesus and Heavenly Father qualified us for mortality. In mortality, correct choices qualify us for more desirable conditions in the spirit world. In the spirit world, correct choices enhance our standing before God and our future destiny.

It is not uncommon in NDEs for an individual to be given the choice of staying in the spirit world or returning to mortality. Of course, we normally only hear about the ones that decided to come back.

118. Do our mortal callings influence our callings in the spirit world?

Yes, at least to some degree. Our callings there will be impacted by the callings we have had here. Joseph F. Smith described his spirit world vision:

> I beheld that the faithful elders of this dispensation, when they depart from mortal life, continue their labors in the preaching of the gospel of repentance and redemption, through the sacrifice of the Only Begotten Son of God, among those who are in darkness and under the bondage of sin in the great world of the spirits of the dead (*D&C 138:57*).

Two other prophets commented on our spirit world callings. In 1949 Elder Harold B. Lee called a man to the position of stake president, but the man died six weeks later. Speaking at the funeral Elder Lee indicated that callings and positions held by men in this life often have a connection with what they will be assigned to do in the next life. President Joseph Fielding Smith, who was on the stand, afterwards spoke to Elder Lee and acknowledged: "If you have called a man to a position in this Church and he dies the next day, that position will have a bearing on what he will be called to do when he leaves this earth" (L. Brent Goates, *Harold B. Lee: Prophet and Seer, 224-25*).

Apparently there are an abundance of callings and activities in the spirit world (*see #126*).

119. In what sense do our works follow us in the spirit world?

There are two ways:

(a) ***The righteous continue their good works in the spirit world*** (*see #118*). John wrote: "Blessed are the dead which die in the Lord . . . that they may rest from their labours; and their works do follow them" (*Revelation 14:13*). In a revelation given to Joseph Smith, the Lord interpreted John's words: "if they die let them die unto me; for they shall rest from all their labors here, and shall continue their works (*D&C 124:86*).

(b) ***We are rewarded according to our works***. **Paul** said the Lord will reward man "according to his works" (*2 Timothy 4:14*). This is the universal law of the harvest that Jesus Christ explained: "Fear not to do good, my sons, for whatsoever ye sow, that shall ye also reap; therefore, if ye sow good ye shall also reap good for your reward" (*D&C 6:33*); "But learn that he who doeth the works of righteousness shall receive his reward, even peace in this world, and eternal life in the world to come" (*D&C 59:23*).

CHAPTER ELEVEN

LIFE IN THE SPIRIT WORLD

And those that were good shall be happy They'll sit in a golden chair
They'll splash at a ten league canvas With brushes of comet's hair
—Rudyard Kipling, When Earth's Last Picture is Painted

120. What is daily life like in the spirit world?

Subsequent chapters summarize the conditions in paradise, spirit prison, and hell. As for everyday living circumstances, our comprehension is, at best, extremely limited because it is a distinct and largely unknown realm. We can only fully understand the truths of daily life in the spirit world when we go there and experience it. The Lord said: "All truth is independent in that sphere in which God has placed it" (*D&C 93:30*).

Regarding relationships, which are what matter most, the spirit world is similar to mortality. Joseph Smith said disembodied spirits "now exist in a place where they converse together the same as we do on the earth" (*TPJS 353*). Other prophets have also taught that relationships will continue in the spirit world and after the resurrection in the kingdoms of glory: "that same sociality which exists among us here will exist among us there" (*D&C 130:2*). In the spirit world, we will not become somebody or something else. The individual spirit is eternal. We will think, act, and intermingle as we do now.

Brigham Young explained:

> [W]hen you are in the spirit world, everything there will appear as natural as things now do. Spirits will be familiar with spirits in the spirit

> world—will converse, behold, and exercise every variety of communication with one another as familiarly and naturally as while here in tabernacles. There, as here, all things will be natural, and you will understand them as you now understand natural things. You will see that those spirits we are speaking of are active; they sleep not (*JD 7:239*).
>
> We have more friends behind the veil than on this side, and they will hail us more joyfully than you were ever welcomed by your parents and friends in this world; and you will rejoice more when you meet them than you ever rejoiced to see a friend in this life (*JD 6:349*).

Joseph Smith reflected on the future reunion with his loved ones in the spirit world:

> I have a father, brothers, children, and friends who have gone to a world of spirits. They are only absent for a moment. They are in the spirit, and we shall soon meet again . . . When we depart we shall hail our mothers, fathers, friends, and all whom we love, who have fallen asleep in Jesus . . . it will be an eternity of felicity" (*HC 6:316*).

Lucy Walker Kimball said Joseph "believed that as soon as the spirit left the body we were shaking hands with and greeting our friends" (*Woman's Exponent, 39:34, 1910*).

121. What does the spirit world look like?

It is in the likeness of the earth we live on, only more beautiful. Jedediah M.Grant, counselor to Brigham Young, described that realm: "I have seen good gardens on this earth, but I never saw any to compare with those that were there. I saw flowers of numerous kinds, and some with from fifty to a hundred different colored flowers growing upon one stalk." Heber C. Kimball added: "He also spoke of the buildings he saw there . . . that the temple erected by Solomon was much inferior to the most ordinary buildings he saw in the spirit world" (*JD 4:136*).

One spirit world beholder who had an NDE described the landscape as follows:

> The new world looked sort of like the world I had left behind, but it was also very different. Everything glowed from the inside with its own light. The colors were beyond anything on earth—they were more vibrant, brilliant, and intense. And there were colors I had never seen before—don't ask me what they were. There were shrubs, trees and flowers, some of which I had seen on earth, like evergreens, and others which I hadn't seen before, and I haven't seen since. They were beautiful, beautiful (Gibson, *Glimpses of Eternity, 238-239*).

Heber Q. Hale, a Stake President from Boise, Idaho, had a heavenly manifestation that the Presidency of the Church asked him to relate at the Genealogical Conference in October 1920. He gave an oft-quoted description of the spirit world:

> The vegetation and landscape were beautiful beyond description; not all green as here, but gold with varying shades of pink, orange, and lavender as the rainbow. A sweet calmness pervaded everything . . . spacious stretches of flowers, grasses, and shrubbery, all of a golden hue, marking the approach to a beautiful building (*HQH, 1-2*).

Brent and Wendy Top summarized the depictions we read in NDE accounts:

> While the descriptions and perceptions may vary, the exhilarating theme of unsurpassable beauty in rarified color and glorious light resounds again and again from near-death accounts. Accounts of NDErs of other faiths are equally as compelling . . . Just about every variety of scenery is mentioned in near-death accounts—mountains, hills, valleys, meadows, woodlands, lakes, rivers, streams, waterfalls—all described as "beautiful," "peaceful," and in glorious hues. Flowers there seem to be active rather than passive parts of the landscape. Cattle, horses, sheep and lions are mentioned as well. Again, the differences in the accounts may be due to the experiences in divergent areas of the spirit world

and/or to individual perceptions and descriptive limitations. Over and over again, we see evidence that the Lord allows his children to perceive things in the way which is most understandable and comforting to them (*Glimpses, 120-22*).

122. How do spirits communicate in the spirit world?

From what little we know, the methods of communicating in the spirit world vary as much or more than they do here. At times, mortals speak in advanced languages. For example, Adam and his posterity down to the Jaredites (approximately 4000 BC to 2200 BC, *see BD, 635*) spoke the pure and undefiled Adamic language, which will apparently be spoken in the millennium (*see MD, 19*). Perhaps these deceased Adamic language speakers use the Adamic language in the spirit world? Some of them have already been resurrected (*see #198*). Could others also learn the Adamic language in the spirit world? Consider that mortals at times speak through the Spirit of inspiration, such as the "tongue of angels" (*2 Nephi 32:2*), which in "some instances" may be the "pure Adamic tongue" (*MD, 19*). The Lord speaks to many mortals through the Spirit. At times kindred spirits on earth experience spirit-to-spirit communication when spoken words are unnecessary. In the spirit world, apparently some spirits will be given power to communicate in these and other advanced ways.

Joseph Smith and Orson Pratt gave us some clues about spirit world communication. Joseph Smith said that deceased spirits of the just may be given to "know and understand our thoughts, [and] feelings" (*TPJS, 326*). Supposedly such just spirits could also communicate among themselves using this mental telepathy. Orson Pratt spoke about how both mortals and spirits can communicate this way if the power is given us.

> For instance, how does God perceive the thoughts of our hearts? Is there not here a language by which He can discover and discern the thoughts and intents of the heart? Suppose we had some of that power resting

> upon us, would not that be a different kind of a language from sound, or from a written language? It would (*JD 3:102*).

Orson Pratt elaborated on other capabilities of the spirit world language.

> There is a language in the spirit world that can communicate more to the mind in one minute than could be learned here in a hundred years of intense study and reasoning. There is an eternity of knowledge . . . worlds, as it were, without number . . . and they all have their way of communication one with another; therefore, when the Apostle [Paul] says, that tongues shall cease, he had reference to the imperfect tongues upon the earth . . . We shall be able by the power of the Holy Ghost to obtain a language by which the angels speak, and by which a higher order of beings speak, and by these means attain to a greater degree of knowledge, that will produce a greater amount of happiness (*JD 3:103-04*).

NDE stories commonly mention the clarity and ease of communication. It seems the messages must be unmistakably clear to avoid miscommunication in the brevity of the moment. Brent and Wendy Top commented on spirit world telepathy:

> Almost all those who encounter spirit beings during their near-death episodes speak of communicating with them instantly—primarily through thought transferral or some form of telepathy rather than through the spoken word. They report that not only thoughts were transmitted but also every feeling, desire, and nuance associated with those thoughts. This suggests a lack of misunderstandings or "communication gaps" in at least some part or parts of the spirit world. It suggests too that genuine loving expressions can be fuller, richer, and more meaningful there than on earth. This being said, we must point out that there have been times when a NDEr was not allowed to completely perceive or remember everything he or she saw and experienced, this presumably being according to the Lord's purposes. In addition we must not construe this to mean that all thought can be read at all times by all spirits (*Glimpses 57-58*).

Robert L. Millet and Joseph Fielding McConkie believe there is a place for our own native languages in the spirit world:

> The heavens have decreed that "every man shall hear the fulness of the gospel in his own tongue, and in his own language, through those who are ordained unto this power" (*D&C 90:11*). We have every reason to suppose that such decrees transcend the veil of death. Those in that world will also be taught by those of their same nation and tongue (*The Life Beyond, 55*). (*See also Appendix C3.*)

In summary, it seems from the limited information we have that there are various methods of communication in the spirit world using thought, feeling, and word in one's native mortal language or advanced languages. According to the will of God, surely many will communicate in glorious ways in the spirit world. We will not fully comprehend these ways until we live in that realm.

123. Will travel be easier in the spirit world?

Yes. Brigham Young said spirits "move with ease like lightning" (*JD 14:231*). Dr. Raymond Moody said: "Travel, once one gets the hang of it, is apparently exceptionally easy in this state. Physical objects present no barrier, and movement from one place to another can be extremely rapid, almost instantaneous" (*Life After Life, 36*). However, such power of movement may be restricted for some. Heber Q. Hale said many "enjoyed unrestricted vision, and unimpeded action, while many others were visibly restricted as to both vision and action" (*HQH, 1; see also #138*). Spirits appear to have the ability to float above the ground, like resurrected beings. Numerous NDEs report this attribute of floating or flying. The resurrected Angel Moroni appeared to Joseph Smith at his bedside, "standing in the air" (*JS-History 1:30*). Joseph Smith saw the Father and the Son, "standing above me in the air" (*JS-History 1:17*).

Orson Pratt suggested that because "whatsoever is light is spirit" (*D&C 84:45*), spirits should be able to travel at the speed of light (*JD 3:104*). Will speeds vary depending on an individual's light or glory? We certainly cannot put a limit on God's power. Are our boundaries restricted depending on our eternal progress? It would seem so.

Brent and Wendy Top gave their view:

> Assuming that the Lord is in agreement, we will apparently be able to arrive at a destination almost instantaneously just by thinking about it or wishing ourselves there. While such a notion may boggle the mortal mind, it is unquestionably the consensus of those who have had near-death experiences . . . Experiencers seem to be able to effect slower travel or movement as well. Some speak of walking or strolling, others of gliding or floating. It usually seems to be a function of the desires of the individual spirit (*Glimpses, 69-70*).

124. Will learning be easier in the spirit world?

Yes. The spirit won't be held back by our temporal infirmities, and our faculties will be expanded. As usual, Brigham Young had something to say on this topic as well:

> I shall not cease learning while I live, nor when I arrive in the spirit world; but shall there with greater facility; and when I again receive my body, I shall learn a thousand times more in a thousand times less time; and then I do not mean to cease learning, but shall continue my researches (*JD 8:10*).

Orson Pratt believed that the entire body will become like the eye, capable of seeing and absorbing light and knowledge. He alluded to other possible senses as well:

> We shall learn many more things there; we need not suppose our five senses connect us with all the things of heaven. Suppose he gave us a sixth sense, a seventh, an eighth, a ninth, or a fiftieth. All these different senses would convey to us new ideas . . . When the Lord imparts . . . we shall find our capacity for obtaining and retaining knowledge to be greatly enlarged (*JD 2:247*).

Spirit world beholders seem to suggest this enhanced learning capability. They report feeling more vibrant, alert, and informed than in mortality. One man said his awareness "stretched out in all three hundred sixty degrees." Another said "it was if my whole body had eyes and ears. I was just so aware of everything" (*Glimpses, 72*).

We can look to the scriptures for examples of man's potential for learning when our minds are touched by the power of God. Consider Enoch (*Moses 7*), the brother of Jared (*Ether 12*), Moses (*Moses 1*), and Abraham (*Abraham 3*), who were quickened by the Spirit and allowed to see and comprehend the particles and souls of the Lord's creations.

125. Does time exist in the spirit world?

Yes. Time appears to exist there as the scriptures seem to suggest. Although "all is as one day with God," time is "measured unto men" (*Alma 40:8*); and there is a "space of time" between the "time of death and the resurrection" (*Alma 40:9*).The deceased remain in the spirit world until "the time of their resurrection"(*Alma 40:14*). Spirit world conditions also seem to indicate that time exists there. Many spirits are very busy preparing for the second coming (*see #137 and Appendix B*). Others are anxiously waiting to have their temple work done (*see Appendix B*). Some will dread having to wait to the end of the millennium to be resurrected (*#161*).

Although time apparently exists in the spirit world, it may be different there. The scriptures indicate that time reckoning is relative: "In answer to the question—Is not the reckoning of God's time, angel's time, prophet's time, and man's time, according to the planet on which they reside? I answer, Yes" (*D&C 130:4-5*). *Abraham Facsimile No. 2 Figure 1* suggests that space and time are related: "one day to a cubit" in "celestial time." Is the spirit world "space of time" (*Alma 40:9*) after death modified from the planet earth to which it belongs? We can imagine ways time could vary because of some dissimilar living conditions there (*see Chapters 11, 12 and 13*).

NDEs commonly convey that time is somehow altered there (*see #112*). Although events happen in sequence, experiencers often report they had no concept of any kind of time span. That can happen to us here too, when we are enjoying ourselves and lose track of time. We don't have particulars from the Lord regarding time in the spirit world. In due time, when it is our time to die, perhaps we'll understand time in the spirit world.

126. What do spirits do in the spirit world?

They are occupied and busy. Heber Q. Hale said:

> The people I met there, I did not think of as spirits but as men and women, self-thinking and self-acting individuals, going about important business in a most orderly manner. There was perfect order there, everybody had something to do and seemed to be about their business (*HQH, 1*).

Various near-death experiencers describe the spirit world as follows:

> A place of intense activity, more like a bustling city than a lonely country scene, nothing like floating on clouds or harps or anything of that sort.
>
> Performing useful tasks is the delight of everyone's life. Joy is obtained through service and lives of usefulness in God's spiritual kingdom. There are so many areas of service . . . and tasks as well, that they cannot be listed for their abundance. There are few in the world by comparison (*Glimpses, 133-137*).
>
> Mormon NDErs also reported seeing people writing family records, painting, cooking, building large houses, participating in meetings, playing music, singing in choirs, considering petitions, preaching, and presiding over various subgroupings (*JNDS, Summer 1993, 236*).

For good people, the spirit world will be a "higher state of being" (*see #111*). We trust the Lord when he said the circumstances will be glorious with plenty to do (*see #119, #120, #132, #152, #157*). Evidently He deems it best for us to not know all the specifics about our activities there. Anticipation and imagination can be an alluring motivation. Rudyard Kipling gave us some thoughts to ponder in his classic poem:

When Earth's Last Picture is Painted

When Earth's last picture is painted And the tubes are twisted and dried
When the oldest colors have faded And the youngest critic has died
We shall rest, and faith, we shall need it Lie down for an aeon or two
'Till the Master of all good workmen Shall put us to work anew
And those that were good shall be happy They'll sit in a golden chair
They'll splash at a ten league canvas With brushes of comet's hair
They'll find real saints to draw from Magdalene, Peter, and Paul
They'll work for an age at a sitting And never be tired at all.
And only the Master shall praise us. And only the Master shall blame.
And no one will work for the money. No one will work for the fame.
But each for the joy of the working, And each, in his separate star,
Will draw the thing as he sees it. For the God of things as they are!

127. Is love encountered in the spirit world?

Yes, most definitely. Love, or charity, is the foremost gift, emotion and feeling, the "greatest of all" (*Moroni 7:46*). It is closely related to spirit world light, because "the fruit of the Spirit [light] is love" (*Galations 5:22*). In its fulness, love constitutes the pinnacle, the most desirable state of man in this life and the next. Nephi defined the meaning of the tree of life as "the love of God, which sheddeth itself abroad in the hearts of the children of men; wherefore, it is most desirable above all things. And he spake unto me, saying: Yea, and the most joyous to the soul" (*1 Nephi 11:21-23*). Love endures in the spirit world. The prophet Gordon B. Hinckley said:

> Love is the very essence of life. It is the pot of gold at the end of the rainbow. Yet it is not found only at the end of the rainbow. Love is at the

> beginning also, and from it springs the beauty that arches across the sky on a stormy day. Love is the security for which children weep, the yearning of youth, the adhesive that binds marriage, and the lubricant that prevents devastating friction in the home; it is the peace of old age, the sunlight of hope shining through death. How rich are those who enjoy it in their associations with family, friends, and neighbors! Love, like faith, is a gift from God. It is also the most enduring and most powerful virtue (*Standing for Something, 3*).

The foremost impression and most prominent message about the afterlife from NDE survivors is the power and importance of love. Many witness beings of light who radiate love in their faces, speech, and mannerisms. They experience potent feelings of love and belonging. Experiencers come back with the realization that how they interact with others matters greatly. They return with greater compassion and charity. According to Dr. Pim von Lommel, based on follow-up studies of near-death experiencers: "People are more forgiving, more tolerant, and less critical of others . . . Appreciation of relationships increases; people spend more time with family, friends, and relatives, and they are more willing and able to share emotions with others. They are more compassionate and caring . . ." (*Consciousness Beyond Life, 53*).

Drawing from his own NDE studies, Dr. Raymond Moody wrote:

> "Have you learned to love?" is a question faced in the course of the episode by almost all NDEers. Upon their return, almost all of them say that love is the most important thing in life. Many say it is why we are here. One NDEr told me: "I used to walk down the street in my own little world, with my mind on a dozen different little problems. Now I walk down the street and I feel I am in an ocean of humanity. Each person I see, I want to get to know, and I am certain that if I really knew them I would love them (*The Light Beyond, 41*).

128. Is there humor in the spirit world?

Yes. "Men are that they might have joy" (*2 Nephi 2:25*). Good humor brings joy so it most assuredly will continue in the hereafter. Brent and Wendy Top observed:

> An interesting and delightful side note to the joy and enjoyment of the next realm is the frequent mention by NDErs of the persistence of humor. It is comforting to know that we will still be able to let go and laugh in the life after death. Immortal life will not be all solemnity and seriousness. That delightful element of joy—humor—is also a part of the light and love of God which pervade that heavenly existence.
>
> It is not hard to imagine that laughter and humor would persist in the afterlife. We can attest to its uplifting power here on earth. Life is so much richer when we can laugh. Almost every prophet in this dispensation has delighted and endeared the Latter-day Saints to himself through his quick refreshing wit and edifying sense of humor. Knowing that these men are representatives and role models of the Savior, we can pretty well rest assured that they and we will be rejoicing in the irreplaceable quality of humor in the world beyond. Such good-natured, loving, edifying heavenly humor is another interesting evidence of the divine love that prevails on the "other side of the veil"—where all is intended to uplift, encourage, and strengthen man's love for God and for his fellow men (*Glimpses, 113-114*).

129. Is there music in the spirit world?

Of course. The Lord said, "my soul delighteth in the song of the heart; yea, the song of the righteous is a prayer unto me" (*D&C 25:12*). Undoubtedly the righteous are "filled with songs of everlasting joy" (*D&C 133:33*) in the spirit world. Angels sang at the birth of Jesus (*Luke 2:13-14*). We read of harps and song in the future celestial world (*Revelation 14:2-3*). King Benjamin, about to die, prayed that "my immortal spirit may join the choirs above in singing the praises of a just God" (*Mosiah 2:28*).

Music is often mentioned in NDEs as a melodious ecstasy, indescribably beautiful, and emoting feelings of love and warmth. Near-death experiencers say they have never heard music quite like it, yet they long to hear it again (*e.g. see Evidence, 15*). The music may come from a variety of instrumental or choral sounds, although the source may not be identifiable. The impression is engrossing and exhilarating.

In a vision, Bruce R. McConkie "saw his brother James leading a great choir in what he understood to be a conference of the Church in the world of spirits" (Joseph Fielding McConkie, *The Bruce R. McConkie Story, 171*).

Brigham Young said, "There is no music in hell" (*JD 9:244*). "However," Neal A. Maxwell explains, "some loud sounds are currently masquerading as music—which would seem to help qualify hell as hell" (*Moving in His Majesty & Power, 74-75*). Brent and Wendy Top elaborated, "Since Brigham Young's day we have seen the emergence of the kind of evil, discordant music that may actually reflect the true spirit of hell. These and other equally negative and unpleasant conditions are, in fact, the very types of things that are being reported to NDE researchers" (*Glimpses, 173*).

CHAPTER TWELVE

PARADISE

And should we die before our journey's through,
Happy day! All is well!
We then are free from toil and sorrow, too;
With the just we shall dwell!
—William Clayton, Come, Come, Ye Saints, Hymns, 30

130. Who goes to paradise upon death?

Two groups go to paradise: (1) faithful saints, and (2) unaccountable children and mentally deficient.

"Paradise is the abode of faithful saints who endured to the end and of innocent children who died before the age of eight, as well as all those who were innocent and not accountable in mortality because of mental deficiency" (Donald W. Parry and Jay A. Parry, *Understanding Death and the Resurrection, Part 1.4*).

"The righteous, those who have received the ordinances of salvation and proven faithful to the attendant covenants, go into paradise at the time of their physical death" (Robert L. Millet and Joseph Fielding McConkie, *DCBofM, 3:299-300*).

Joseph Fielding Smith explained "as I understand it, *the righteous—meaning those who have been baptized and have been faithful*—are gathered in one part and all the others in another part of the spirit world" (*DS 2:230*).

In President Joseph F. Smith's vision of paradise the righteous were "gathered together in one place" when Christ appeared to them after the crucifixion. They were described as (a) the "just, who had been faithful in the testimony of Jesus while they lived in mortality;" (b) who "had offered sacrifice in the similitude of the great sacrifice of the Son of God;" and (c) who "departed the mortal life, firm in the hope of a glorious resurrection, through the grace of God the Father and his Only Begotten Son, Jesus Christ" (*D&C 138:12-14*). To offer a sacrifice (or take the sacrament today) requires baptism. Faithful in testimony implies being true to the Gift of the Holy Ghost given upon confirmation.[viii]

Others who accept the gospel in the spirit prison can also qualify for paradise (*see #178*).

131. What about the crucified Christ's words to the thief: "Today shalt thou be with me in Paradise" (*Luke 23:43*)?

Joseph Smith taught that *paradise* is used here in the broad sense, meaning the *world of spirits*[ix] (*see #21*).

132. What is the condition of the righteous in paradise?

Alma may have said it best: "the spirits of those who are righteous are received into a state of happiness, which is called paradise, a state of rest, a state of peace, where they shall rest from all their troubles and from all care, and sorrow" (*Alma 40:12*).

Joseph F. Smith saw a vision of the righteous who were in paradise prior to Christ's coming to the spirit world following His crucifixion and he witnessed their anticipation of Christ's resurrection: "I beheld that they were filled with joy and gladness, and were rejoicing together because the day of their deliverance was at hand" (*D&C 138:15*). We can imagine that today, those in paradise likewise rejoice in anticipation of Christ's second coming and their own resurrection.

133. What did Christ do when he visited paradise after the crucifixion?

Joseph F. Smith's vision continued with these magnificent words:

> But behold, from among the righteous, he organized his forces and appointed messengers, clothed with power and authority, and commissioned them to go forth and carry the light of the gospel to them that were in darkness, even to all the spirits of men; and thus was the gospel preached to the dead (*D&C 138:30*).

> Thus it was made known that our Redeemer spent his time during his sojourn in the world of spirits, instructing and preparing the faithful spirits of the prophets who had testified of him in the flesh; That they might carry the message of redemption unto all the dead, unto whom he could not go personally, because of their rebellion and transgression, that they through the ministration of his servants might also hear his words (*D&C 138:36-37*).

134. Did Joseph Smith describe spirits in paradise?

Yes. The Prophet Joseph Smith taught the following at the funeral of Patriarch James Adams in Nauvoo:

> [Judge Adams] has had revelations concerning his departure, and has gone to a more important work. When men are prepared, they are better off to go hence. Brother Adams has gone to open up a more effectual door for the dead. The spirits of the just are exalted to a greater and more glorious work; hence they are blessed in their departure to the world of spirits. Enveloped in flaming fire, they are not far from us, and know and understand our thoughts, feelings and emotions, and are often pained therewith (*TPJS, 326*).

135. How are the spirits organized in paradise?

Latter-day prophets tell us spirits are organized as families. President Ezra Taft Benson taught: "They are organized according to priesthood order in family organizations as we are here; only there they exist in a more perfect order. This was revealed to the Prophet Joseph" (*The Teachings of Ezra Taft Benson, 35-36*).

At Jedediah M.Grant's funeral (who was Second Counselor to President Brigham Young), Heber C. Kimball (who was First Counselor to President Brigham Young), gave the following testimony:

> [A dying Brother Grant] said to me, Brother Heber, I have been into the spirit world two nights in succession, and, of all the dreads that ever came across me, the worst was to have to again return to my body, though I had to do it. But O, says he, the order and government that were there! When in the spirit world, I saw the order of righteous men and woman; beheld them organized in their several grades, and there appeared to be no obstruction to my vision; I could see every man and woman in their grade and order. I looked to see whether there was any disorder there, but there was none, neither could I see any death nor any darkness, disorder or confusion. He said that the people he there saw were organized in family capacities; and when he looked at them he saw grade after grade, and all were organized and in perfect harmony. He would mention one item after another and say, "Why it is just as brother Brigham says it is; it is just as he has told us many a time." This is a testimony as to the truth of what brother Brigham teaches us, from what little light I have. He saw the righteous gathered together in the spirit world, and there were no wicked spirits among them. He saw his wife Caroline. She came to him. He saw many that he knew, but did not have conversation with any except his wife Caroline. She came to him, and he said that she looked beautiful and had their little child, that died on the Plains, in her arms, and said, "Mr. Grant, here is little Margaret; you know that the wolves ate her up, but it did not hurt her; here she is all right [*see also #62 and #63*]. "To my astonishment," he said, "when I looked at families there was a deficiency in some, there was a lack, for I saw families that would not be permitted to come and dwell together, because they had not honored their calling here" (*JD 4:135-36*).

136. Does the Priesthood operate in the spirit world?

Yes. Brigham Young said: "When the faithful Elders, holding this Priesthood, go into the spirit world they carry with them the same power and Priesthood that they had while in the mortal tabernacle" (*DBY, 132; see also D&C 124:130*).

There are Latter-day Saint accounts of temples in the spirit world. For example, Heber Q. Hale reported seeing "a wonderful beautiful temple, capped with golden domes" and the Savior emerging from it (*HQH, 3*). Apparently temples in the spirit world are literally a House of the Lord like temples here; although we don't have detailed information on the uses and purposes of spirit world temples.

137. Are spirits in paradise anxiously engaged and busy?

Yes. Peter E. Johnson, an Elder, who visited and returned from the spirit world reported:

> While I was in the spirit world I observed that the people there were busy, and that they were perfectly organized for the work they were doing. It seemed to me a continuation of the work we are doing here—something like going from one stake to another. There was nothing there that seemed particularly strange to me, everything being natural (*Relief Society Magazine, August 1920*).

Ella Jensen had a similar spirit world visit: "A guide was there to meet her and by him she was conducted into a very large building where there were many people, all of whom appeared to be extremely busy, no evidence of idleness whatever" (Leroi C. Snow, *IE, October 1929*).

Wilford Woodruff saw in a vision the Prophet Joseph Smith several years after the Prophet's death. Joseph was hurrying about with scarcely the time to talk to Wilford. Joseph explained to him that there was so much work to do and so little time to do it to be ready for the Savior's second coming. President Woodruff, seeing a glimpse of the activity in the spirit world, said it was a new concept to him to be so busy there (*see The Discourses of Wilford Woodruff, 288-289)*.

Brigham Young said we would be free to "enjoy life, glory, and intelligence; and we have the Father to speak to us, Jesus to speak to us, and angels to speak to us, and we shall enjoy the society of the just and the pure who are in the spirit world until the resurrection" (*JD 14:231*).

138. What travel powers exist in paradise?

Apparently spirits in paradise will be able to travel distances effortlessly (*see #41 and #123*). Depending on God's will, they perhaps will even be able to engage in a type of geographic time travel. Reflect on Brigham Young's amazing discourse at the funeral of Aurelia Spencer:

> I can say with regard to parting with our friends, and going ourselves, that I have been near enough to understand eternity so that I have had to exercise a great deal more faith to desire to live than I ever exercised in my whole life to live.The brightness and glory of the next apartment is inexpressible. It is not encumbered with this clog of dirt we are carrying around here so that when we advance in years we have to be stubbing along and to be careful lest we fall down. But yonder, how different! They [spirits] move with ease and like lightning. If we want to visit Jerusalem, or this, that, or the other place—and I presume we will be permitted if we desire—there we are, looking at its streets. If we want to behold Jerusalem as it was in the days of the Savior; or if we want to see the Garden of Eden as it was when created, there we are, and we see it as it existed spiritually, for it was created first spiritually and then temporally, and spiritually it still remains. And when there we may behold the earth as at the dawn of creation, or we may visit any city we please that exists upon its surface. If we wish to understand how they are living here on these western islands, or in China, we are there; in fact we are like the light of morning . . .
>
> When we pass into the spirit world we shall possess a measure of this power; not to the degree that we will when resurrected and brought forth in the fulness of glory to inherit the kingdoms prepared for us. The power the faithful will possess then will far exceed that of the spirit world; but that enjoyed in the spirit world is so far beyond this life as to be inconceivable without the spirit of revelation. (*JD 14:231*).

Imagine some day, perhaps after the resurrection, traveling instantly to distant places as William W. Phelps wrote:

If you could hie to Kolob
In the twinkling of an eye,
And then continue onward
With that same speed to fly
(If You Could Hie to Kolob, Hymns No. 284)

139. Does Satan have power over the faithful in paradise?

No. Several prophets have said no. George Q. Cannon was one:

> If we listen to the Lord, if we strive to keep His commandments, if we seek to be governed by His Spirit, when death comes Satan's power ceases. He can no more afflict, or torment, or tempt, or annoy those who are thus faithful. His power over them ceases forever (*Juvenile Instructor, 1885, 264*).

140. Are the righteous in paradise subject to temptation?

No. Brigham Young elaborated in two conference addresses below:

> When the faithful Elders, holding this Priesthood, go into the spirit world they carry with them the same power and Priesthood that they had while in the mortal tabernacle. They have got the victory over the power of the enemy here, consequently when they leave this world they have perfect control over those evil spirits, and they cannot be buffeted by Satan. But as long as they live in the flesh no being on this earth, of the posterity of Adam, can be free from the power of the devil (*JD 3:371*).

> If we are faithful to our religion, when we go into the spirit world, the fallen spirits—Lucifer and third part of the heavenly hosts that came with him, and the spirits of wicked men who have dwelt upon this earth, the whole of them combined will have no influence over our spirits. Is

> not that an advantage? Yes. All the rest of the children of men are more or less subject to them, and they are subject to them as they were while here in the flesh. If we conquer here and overcome in the Gospel, in the spirit world our spirits will be above the power of evil spirits (*JD 7:240; see also 14:229*).

There are still weaknesses to overcome beyond the grave (*see Alma 34:34*) and many improvements to be made to our character in the spirit world (s*ee #146*).

141. Will we have to work to learn and grow in paradise?

Yes. George Q. Cannon declared:

> We will have to work there to grow and to make progress just as we have here, though the facilities will be better there than they are here. If we can only pass into the paradise of God without Satan having any power over us, our condition will be a very happy one. But we shall find that knowledge and power will not come to us there as the rain that falls upon us—without any effort of ours to acquire them. We shall have to exercise ourselves and exert our powers there just as we have to here. We shall be rewarded according to our diligence and faithfulness in the exercise of our agency (*Deseret Weekly, Dec. 14, 1895, 51:803*).

142. How many will go to paradise upon death?

Billions. President Joseph F. Smith saw "an innumerable company of spirits" (*D&C 138:12*) who "had departed the mortal life, firm in the hope of a glorious resurrection" (*D&C 138:14*). His vision was of those who lived from Adam to Christ; so obviously the multitudes of people qualified for entrance to paradise have dramatically increased since then. Consider that billions of children and mentally deficient who have died without accountability go to paradise.

In a general priesthood meeting, President Spencer W. Kimball said:

> Brethren, 225,000 of you are here tonight. I suppose 225,000 of you may become gods. There seems to be plenty of space out there in the universe. And the Lord has proved that he knows how to do it. I think he could make, or probably have us help make, worlds for all of us, for every one of us 225,000 (*Ensign, November 1975; see also Alma 13:10-12*).

143. Why do children who die qualify for paradise?

Because "little children are holy, being sanctified through the atonement of Jesus Christ" (*D&C 74:7*). "God, having redeemed man from the fall, men became again, in their infant state, innocent before God" (*D&C 93:38*). These are pure and righteous souls who satisfied their pre-mortal probationary test and did not need the mortal probationary test. Such children will be exalted in the highest degree of the celestial kingdom. Paradise is the appropriate waystation along the way. Joseph Smith taught: "the moment that children leave this world, they are taken to the bosom of Abraham [paradise]" (*HC 4:554*).[x] Children are without sin and under no condemnation until they begin to become accountable at age eight (*Moroni 8:22; D&C 68:27*).

Abinidi wrote: "little children also have eternal life" (*Mosiah 25:25*).

President Joseph Fielding Smith said: "*The Lord will grant unto these children the privilege of all the sealing blessings which pertain to the exaltation*" (*DS 2:54).*

Joseph Smith explained this marvelous truth which is quoted by many Apostles today:

> The Lord takes many away even in infancy, that they may escape the envy of man, and the sorrows and evils of this present world; they were too pure, too lovely, to live on earth; therefore, if rightly considered, instead of mourning we have reason to rejoice as they are delivered from evil, and we shall soon have them again (*TPJS, 196-197*).

Bruce R. McConkie reflected on the Prophet's remarks:

> There are certain spirits who come into this life only to receive bodies; for reasons that we do not know, but which are known in the infinite wisdom of the Eternal Father, they do not need the testing, probationary experiences of mortality. We come here for two great reasons—the first to get a body; the second, to be tried, examined, schooled, and tested under mortal circumstances, to take a different type of probationary test than we underwent in the pre-mortal life. There are some of the children of our Father, however, who come to earth to get a body—for that reason solely. They do not need the testings of this mortality. (*From an address at the funeral of Rebecca Adams, Oct. 28, 1967, cited in The Life Beyond, 114*).

Bruce R. McConkie also quoted a more recent prophet's views on this topic:

> President Joseph Fielding Smith once told me that we must assume that the Lord knows and arranges beforehand who shall die in infancy and who shall remain on earth to undergo whatever tests are needed in their cases . . . It is implicit in the whole plan of things that those of us who have arrived at the years of accountability need the tests and trials to which we are subject . . . [O]ur problem is to overcome the world and attain that spotless and pure state which little children already possess (*Ensign, April 1977*).

144. Will children who die be tested?

No. They were tested in their premortal life, and their exaltation is assured so there will be no more testing for them.

Bruce R. McConkie had a strong opinion on this question:

> Absolutely not! Any idea that they will be tested in paradise or during the millennium or after the millennium is pure fantasy . . . Would the Lord test someone who cannot fail the test and whose exaltation is guaranteed? For that matter, all those billions of people who will be born during the millennium, when Satan is bound, "shall grow up

without sin unto salvation" (*D&C 45:58*) and therefore will not be tested. *"Satan cannot tempt little children in this life, nor in the spirit world, nor after their resurrection. Little children who die before reaching the years of accountability will not be tempted"* (*DS 2:56-57*). Such is the emphatic language of President Joseph Fielding Smith (*Ensign, April 1977*).

145. Why do the mentally deficient qualify for paradise?

They, like children, are pure and innocent and will be exalted. The Lord said: "And he that hath no understanding, it remaineth in me to do according as it is written [for little children]" (*D&C 29:50*). Bruce R. McConkie explained:

> It is with them as it is with little children. They never arrive at the years of accountability and are considered as though they were little children. If because of some physical deficiency, or for some other reason unknown to us, they never mature in the spiritual or moral sense, then they never become accountable for sins. They need no baptism; they are alive in Christ; and they will receive, inherit, and possess in eternity on the same basis as do all children (*Ensign, April 1977*).

146. Does probation end at death for those who go to paradise?

Yes. This is what several prophets have taught us. A careful reading of the scriptures as it pertains to members of the Church who receive Christ in mortality also seems to lead us to this conclusion:

> For strait is the gate, and narrow the way that leadeth unto the exaltation and continuation of the lives, and few there be that find it [in this life], because ye receive me not in the world, neither do ye know me. But *if ye receive me in the world*, then ye shall know me, and shall *receive your exaltation*; that where I am ye shall be also (*D&C 132:22-23 italicized for emphasis*).

> Whatever principle of intelligence [glory, light (*see D&C 93:36*)] we attain unto in this life, it will rise with us in the resurrection (*D&C*

> *130:18*). Ye who are quickened by a portion of the celestial glory shall receive of the same, even a fulness (*D&C 88:29*).

Joseph Fielding McConkie elucidated this concept very well:

> No one apostatizes from paradise. Abraham taught the principle thus: "And they who keep their first estate [premortal life, *see #186*] shall be added upon; and they who keep not their first estate shall not have glory in the same kingdom with those who keep their first estate; and they who keep their second estate [mortal life, *see #186*] shall have glory added upon their heads for ever and ever" (*Abraham 3:26*). The Book of Mormon prophets speak of this life as a time of probation. When the time comes to depart this life and go to paradise, we are no longer on probation. Thus Alma counseled us to "keep your garments spotless, that ye may at last be brought to sit down with Abraham, Isaac, and Jacob, and the holy prophets who have been ever since the world began, having your garments spotless even as their garments are spotless, in the kingdom of heaven *to go no more out"* (*Alma 7:25*; *emphasis added*). The phrase "just men made perfect" is used to describe individuals who have obtained this status. That is, they are men and women whose lives were such that they are justified to expect that in the resurrection they will be made perfect (*see D&C 76:66-69; 129; Hebrews 12:22-23*)" (*Answers, 109-110*).

Bruce R. McConkie expressed the following sentiments at the funeral of Elder S. Dilworth Young:

> If we die in the faith, that is the same thing as saying that our calling and election has been made sure and that we will go on to eternal reward hereafter. As far as faithful members of the Church are concerned, they have charted a course leading to eternal life. This life is the time that is appointed as a probationary estate for men to prepare to meet God, and as far as faithful people are concerned, if they are in the line of their duty, if they are doing what they ought to do, although they may not have been perfect in this sphere, their probation is ended. Now there will be some probation for some other people hereafter. But for the

> faithful saints of God, now is the time and the day, and their probation is ended with their death, and they will not thereafter depart from the path. It is true as the Prophet Joseph Smith said, that there are many things that have to be done "even beyond the grave" (*TPJS, 348*) to work out our salvation, but we'll stay in the course and we will not alter from it, if we have been true and faithful in this life (*cited in* Robert L. Millet and Joseph Fielding McConkie, *The Life Beyond, 141*).

147. Can a person know before he dies that he will go to paradise?

Yes. Bruce R. McConkie explained:

> [A]ll the faithful Saints, all of those who have endured to the end, depart this life with the absolute guarantee of eternal life. There is no equivocation, no doubt, no uncertainty in our minds. Those who have been true and faithful in this life will not fall by the wayside in the life to come. If they keep their covenants here and now and depart this life firm and true in the testimony of our blessed Lord, they shall come forth with an inheritance of eternal life. We do not mean to say that those who die in the Lord, and who are true and faithful in this life, must be perfect in all things when they go into the next sphere of existence. There was only one perfect man—the Lord Jesus whose Father was God. There have been many righteous souls who have attained relative degrees of perfection, and there have been great hosts of faithful people who have kept the faith, and lived the law, and departed this life with the full assurance of an eventual inheritance of eternal life. There are many things they will do and must do, even beyond the grave, to merit the fulness of the Father's kingdom in that final glorious day when the great King shall say unto them "Come, ye blessed of my Father, inherit the kingdom prepared for you from the foundation of the world" (*Matthew 25:34*). But what we are saying is that when the Saints of God chart a course of righteousness, when they gain sure testimonies of the truth and divinity of the Lord's work, when they keep the commandments, when they overcome the world, when they put first in their lives the things of God's kingdom: when they do all these things, and then depart this life—though they have not yet become perfect—they shall nonethe-

less gain eternal life in our Father's kingdom; and eventually they shall be perfect as God their Father and Christ His Son are perfect (*Ensign, November 1976*).

148. What kind of clothing is worn in paradise?

We don't have a definitive scriptural answer to this question. NDE accounts report that spirits of light mostly wear white robes although they dress in other colors.

The notion of white robes in paradise is consistent with John the Revelator's teaching that celestialized beings will be arrayed in white: "they shall walk with me in white: for they are worthy. He that overcometh, the same shall be clothed in white raiment" (*Revelation 3:4-5*). "What are these which are arrayed in white robes? And whence came they? . . . And he said to me, These are they which came out of great tribulation, and have washed their robes, and made them white in the blood of the Lamb" (*Revelation 7:13-14*).

Jesus Christ spoke of one "clothed with light for a covering" (*D&C 85:7*). Is the clothing of the righteous in paradise made of light? Is this the spirit element? These beings reportedly radiate light all over, not just in their faces. Does spirit clothing require some effort to make, like our clothing here? (*see #109*). These are interesting questions, but the detailed answers must not be vital to us now.

149. Is there marriage in paradise?

Yes, for those who qualify. Celestial marriages performed in earthly temples for time and eternity continue in paradise for covenant-keeping couples. Celestial marriages may also be performed in proxy for the dead in temples. The dead who accept the gospel and qualify for the eternal marriage covenant in the spirit world will be married in paradise. Lawful marriages between a husband and wife performed outside the temple are valid only until death when they part. The Lord explained the principle:

> [T]heir covenant and marriage are not of force when they are dead . . . Therefore, when they are out of the world they neither marry nor are given in marriage (*D&C 132:15,16*); All covenants, contracts, bonds, obligations, oaths, vows, performances, connections, associations, or expectations, that are not sealed by the Holy Spirit of promise, of him who is anointed, both as well for time and for all eternity . . . have an end when men are dead (*D&C 132:7*).

Joseph Fielding Smith said that marriage is an eternal principle that was "instituted on this earth" (*Way to Perfection, 251*). Marriage is an earthly ordinance, with a primary purpose of bringing forth children. Evidently, because spirits cannot have children (*see #65*), marriages are not performed in the premortal and postmortal spirit worlds. Douglas E. Brinley explained:

> In the premortal life, each of us was a single adult . . . the only family relationships we experienced were those of sons or daughters of God and brothers or sisters to each other. There we were never intimately involved with one of the opposite sex in a marriage relationship, possessing the ability to create children . . . The Doctrine and Covenants explicitly states that only those who attain to the highest degree of glory remain married and possess the power of increase or 'eternal lives' [ie., have children in the hereafter] (*D&C 131:1-4*). (*Heavens Are Open: The 1992 Sperry Symposium, 85-86, 88*).

Everyone will have the opportunity in this life or the hereafter to choose the path of eternal marriage. President Spencer W. Kimball said: "no soul will be deprived of rich and high and eternal blessings for anything which that person could not help" (*Ensign, October 1979*). Joseph Fielding McConkie and Craig J. Ostler explain:

> Those who accept the gospel of Jesus Christ—in this life or the next—will be given the opportunity to go the house of the Lord with the companion of their choice and be married for time and eternity. Those who reject that opportunity are destined to "remain separately and singly" [D&C 132:17] throughout the endless eternities.

These, we are told, will be "ministering servants" to those who have been married for time and eternity. These will not be exalted; they "cannot have an increase" (D&C 131:4); they will not enjoy the "continuation of lives" (D&C 131:22), that is they will not enjoy the privileges of the family unit nor will they be able to have posterity. As Malachi said, they will be left with neither "root nor branch" (Malachi 4:1) (Revelations of the Restoration, 1062).

CHAPTER THIRTEEN

SPIRIT PRISON

Know this, that every soul is free
To choose his life and what he'll be
For this eternal truth is giv'n
That God will force no man to heav'n
—Anon., ca., 1805, Know This, That Every Soul Is Free, Hymns, 240

150. Who goes to spirit prison upon death?

Everybody who doesn't go to Paradise. Spirit prison in this use of the term comprises the entire spirit world outside of paradise. LDS scholars explain:

> It would appear that all others [who don't go to paradise], including the good and noble men and women of the earth who died without a knowledge of the gospel, enter into hell, outer darkness, or what is sometimes called (in a narrower sense) spirit prison (Robert Millet and Joseph Fielding McConkie, *DCBofM 3:300*).

151. Are there different varieties and grades of spirits in the spirit world?

Yes. Just like here, there seem to be various degrees of good people and wicked people in the spirit world. Speaking of the spirit world spirits, Parley P. Pratt said: "These are of two kinds, viz—Good and evil. These two kinds also include many grades of good and evil" (*KST, 117-118*). Note the following positions that elaborate on this view:

Some people suppose that there are only two kinds of spirits in the spirit world—the righteous in paradise and the wicked in the spirit prison. It is true that there is a basic division between the righteous and the wicked in the spirit world. But there are also as many kinds and grades of spirits there as we have here on earth (Donald W. Parry and Jay A. Parry, *Understanding Death and the Resurrection, Part 1:4*)

There will be just as much distinction between spirits there as you find between spirits here. Those who have made good use of their opportunities here will have the benefit of their diligence and faithfulness there. Those who have been careless and indifferent and have not acquired knowledge and power through the exercise of faith will find themselves lacking there (George Q. Cannon, *Gospel Truth, 60*).

The spirit world will contain the same cross-section of diversity of race and creed that exist upon the earth. The spirit will awaken there with the same religious concept, or the lack of it. There will be Catholics and Protestants of every sect, Jews, Mohammedans, Hindus, Buddhists and others as well as the infidels. All must be taught; must come to a knowledge of the plan of salvation and of the mission of Jesus Christ (Alvin R. Dyer, *Who Am I, 490-491*).

152. Why do honest and noble souls who never knew of the Church go to spirit prison?

Spirit prison is not all bad. It just sounds bad. Even paradise is spirit prison in the scriptural, broad view. The spirit prison is largely a mission field of quality people ready for harvest. Jesus does not condemn "the guiltless" (*Matthew 12:7*) or punish the innocent. The Lord said: "inasmuch as men do good they shall in nowise lose their reward" (*D&C 58:28*); and "all men shall reap a reward of their works" (*Alma 9:28*). Because most people are good, the spirit prison will be a reward to them, a place of peace, rest, learning, and waiting, and not a place of suffering.

Brigham Young referred to noble persons such as John Wesley in the spirit prison. Wesley (d.1791) was a reformer, "Anglican clergyman" and "founder of the Methodist movement" (*EB*):

> Where is John Wesley's abode in the other world? He is not where the Father and the Son live, but he is gone into what is called hades, or paradise, or the spirit-world [speaking in the broad view]. He did not receive the gospel as preached by Jesus Christ and His Apostles; it was not then upon the earth. The power of the Holy Priesthood was not then among men; but I suppose that Mr. Wesley lived according to the best light he had, and tried to improve upon it all the days of his life. Where is the departed spirit of that celebrated reformer? It occupies a better place than ever entered his heart to conceive of when he was in the flesh (*JD 11:126*). (*Note*: *Subsequently John Wesley was baptized in proxy by Wilford Woodruff. If he accepted the gospel Wesley would presumably then qualify for paradise, see Appendix B10 and #12.*)

Parley P. Pratt also acknowledged the noble class of spirits in the spirit world:

> Take another class of spirits—pious, well-disposed men; for instance, the honest Quaker, Presbyterian, or other sectarian, who, although honest, and well disposed, had not, while in the flesh, the privilege of the Priesthood and Gospel. They believed in Jesus Christ, but died in ignorance of his ordinances, and had not clear conceptions of his doctrine, and of the resurrection (*JD 1:12*).

However noble they are, they still need the Gospel. Monte S. Nyman stated: "These various groups are in some degree of darkness until the light of the gospel is carried to them. When vicarious baptism has been performed for them and they have repented and accepted the gospel, they can enter paradise to await the resurrection" (*The Book of Mormon: Alma, the Testimony of the Word, 190-191*). (*See also #178.*)

153. Do these honest, well-disposed souls have to repent?

Yes, if they want to expand on the good they already have, and maximize their progression, they must follow the prescribed path, just as converts do in mortality. That path is faith, repentance, and baptism; and there is only: "One Lord, one faith, one baptism" (*Ephesians 4:5*). However, they won't be forced to repent as the power of choice continues in the spirit world (*see #117*). We all sin and can choose to repent or suffer the judgment of God. (*See D&C 138:33-35; Gospel Principles, 244; #227, #228, #229.*)

154. What did the Prophet Joseph Smith teach about the fate of those in the spirit world who never knew of the Church?

Joseph Smith had great love and hope for his fellowmen, in spite of intense persecution and threats on his life from the time he was fourteen years old. Here are some of his words that show his tremendous compassion and reflects the mercy of our Maker:

> [T]he Great Parent of the universe looks upon the whole of the human family with a fatherly care and paternal regard . . . He is a wise Lawgiver, and will judge all men . . . "according to the deeds done in the body whether they be good or evil," He will judge them, "not according to what they have not, but according to what they have"; those who lived without law, will be judged without law, and those who have a law, will be judged by that law. We need not doubt the wisdom and intelligence of the Great Jehovah.
>
> God judges men according to the use they make of the light which He gives them.
>
> To say that the heathens would be damned because they did not believe the Gospel would be preposterous, and to say that the Jews would all be damned that do not believe in Jesus would be equally absurd; for "how can they believe on him of whom they have not heard, and how can they hear without a preacher, and how can he preach except he be sent" [*see*

Romans 10:14-15]; consequently neither Jew nor heathen can be culpable for rejecting the conflicting opinions of sectarianism, nor for rejecting any testimony but that which is sent of God, for as the preacher cannot preach except he be sent, so the hearer cannot believe [except] he hear a "sent" preacher, and cannot be condemned for what he has not heard, and being without law, will have to be judged without law (*HC 4:595-98; 5:401, cited in Teachings of Presidents of the Church-Joseph Smith, 404-08*) (*see #116*).

155. Did Joseph Smith differentiate between hell and spirit prison?

Yes. Using the common definition of hell, Joseph suggested: "I do not believe the Methodist doctrine of sending honest men and noble-minded men to hell, along with the murderer and the adulterer . . . But I have an order of things to . . . get them saved; for I will send men to preach to them in prison and save them if I can" (*HC 6:365*).

156. What are some of the grades of spirits in the spirit prison?

Such spirits can be classified just like mortals here, living celestial, terrestrial or telestial laws (*see D&C 76)* and they are "judged according to men in the flesh" (*1 Peter 4:6*). Here are some of the grades of spirits in spirit prison:

(a) "***Heirs of the celestial kingdom***:" Those who die "without a knowledge of this Gospel . . . who would have received it with all their hearts" (*D&C 137:7-9*). These will be taught, and receive the gospel with all their hearts in the spirit world. When their temple work is done, they go on to paradise (*see #178*). Bruce R. McConkie elaborated:

> For those who do not have an opportunity to believe and obey the holy word in this life, the first chance to gain salvation will come in the spirit world. If those who hear the word for the first time in the realms ahead are the kind of people who would have accepted the

gospel here, had the opportunity been afforded them, they will accept it there (*BYU Speeches, June 1, 1980*).

(b) ***Heirs of the terrestrial kingdom***: These are "honorable men of the earth, who were blinded by the craftiness of men" (*D&C 76:75*). We can break these down to three types:

Type 1: "These are they who died without law" (*D&C 76:72)* who would not have whole-heartedly received the gospel had they been permitted to tarry (*see D&C 137:7-8*). These evidently receive the gospel in spirit prison but not whole-heartedly (*see D&C 76:101*).

Type 2: These "received not the testimony of Jesus in the flesh, but afterwards received it . . . *when they heard it in prison again*" (*D&C 76:74, italics are Joseph's poetic version, Times and Seasons 4:84*). Thankfully, the Lord Jesus Christ judges what constitutes acceptance and rejection. Theodore M. Burton noted: "God is a God of justice and love and mercy. Every man is entitled to a just chance to know and accept Jesus Christ or to reject him" (*CR, April 1964*).[xi]

Type 3: Those who accept the gospel on earth or the spirit world, but "who are not valiant in the testimony of Jesus; wherefore, they obtain not the crown over the kingdom of our God" (*D&C 76:79*). Being valiant is receiving the gospel "with all their hearts" (*D&C 137:8*).[xii] Again, thankfully, judging valiance, and measuring the heart is for the Lord.

(c) ***Heirs of the telestial kingdom***: These are they who "received not the gospel, neither the testimony of Jesus, neither the prophets, neither the everlasting covenant . . . These are they who are liars, and sorcerers, and adulterers, and whoremongers, and whosoever loves and makes a lie. These are they who suffer the wrath of God on earth" (*D&C 76:101, 103-104*). "These are they who deny not the Holy Spirit. These are they who are thrust down to hell. These are they who shall not be redeemed from the devil until the last resurrection, until the Lord, even Christ the Lamb, shall have finished his work (*D&C 76:83-85*). According to Joseph Smith, they "shall welter for ages in torment, even until they shall have paid the uttermost farthing" (*HC 6:315*).

(d) ***Sons of perdition***. These are "unembodied spirits who supported Lucifer in the war in heaven and were cast out (*Moses 4:1-4*) and mortals who commit the unpardonable sin against the Holy Ghost" (*EM, 1391*). Few mortals have been "identified as sons of perdition" because they must sin "against the greater light and knowledge of God. They willfully and utterly pervert principles of righteousness and truth with which they were once endowed . . ." (*EM, 1391-1392*). (*See also #163 for fate of the sons of perdition.*)

Donald A. and Jay W. Parry indicate: "every soul in the celestial and terrestrial kingdoms will have accepted the gospel of Jesus Christ, either here on earth or in the spirit world. Those who go to the telestial kingdom never do accept the gospel of Jesus Christ—or if they accept it, they subsequently violate their covenants . . . Even though those assigned to the telestial glory do not accept the gospel or testimony of Christ, eventually even they will acknowledge the Kingship of the Lord and serve him" (*see D&C 76:109-112*) (*Understanding Death and the Resurrection, Part 1:4*).

157. What is the condition of the spirit world masses who are neither in hell nor paradise?

They reap a "reward of their works" (*Alma 9:28*) which is the universal law of compensation and restoration. Their condition will be similar to their condition as mortals before they died. Those who are happy will be happy still. Those who are kind and unselfish will be selfless still. The Savior taught, "For with what judgment ye judge, ye shall be judged: and with what measure ye mete, it shall be measured to you again" (*Matthew. 7:2*). Those who died "without the law" (*D&C 76:72*) are under no condemnation and do not live in torment (*see 2 Nephi 9:25-26 and #116*).

Joseph Fielding McConkie described the disparate spirit prison conditions in a manner that rings true:

> [I]t seems unjust to consign to a place of torment those of a terrestrial spirit or, more particularly, those who are of a celestial nature but who have not yet had the opportunity to hear and accept the gospel. Should such be consigned to a place of suffering? To so suppose obviously does not accord with the justice of God. The concern is resolved in a more complete understanding of the nature of the spirit world. It is not eternal burnings. Such language is simply figurative. Certainly some will be in a state of eternal torment, but not everyone will be. Hell [in the broad view] is simply the nation of departed spirits. Its cities have their ghettoes but also their pleasant suburbs. Kindred spirits by nature gather together. Where honorable men and women have gathered, honor prevails. Where people of peace, virtue, and goodness choose to assemble, there such attributes will also be found. Others unlike them would be unwelcome and would seek society among those of like spirit. The scriptures assure us that our works will follow us after death. Men and women of goodness here will be of the same nature there and enjoy the fruits of their labors even as they await the day when they will be taught the gospel (*Answers, 108-09*).

Lorenzo Dow Young (brother of Brigham Young) had an out of body experience and found himself in the spirit world with a guide. He observed spirits in various cities living in conditions of misery or happiness. Some who had apparently died recently were "in a state of expectation" waiting to go to their spirit world abode (*Faith-Promoting Series 6:28*) (*see also #116*).

CHAPTER FOURTEEN

HELL

A man can't be taken to hell, or sent to hell:
You can only get there on your own steam.
—C.S. Lewis, The Quotable Lewis, 292

158. Who goes to hell?

This question refers to the common speech definition of hell, or the place of torment in the spirit prison. Bruce R. McConkie gave us a concise answer:

> This query is abundantly answered in the scriptures. Since those going to a telestial kingdom travel to their destination through the depths of hell and as a result of obedience to telestial law, it follows that all those who live a telestial law will go to hell (*MD, 350*).

Those who live a telestial law and go to hell are the unrepentant wicked who reject the Savior and "who are liars, and sorcerers, and adulterers, and whoremongers" (*see D&C 76:101, 103*). They would not be comfortable in paradise: "ye would be more miserable to dwell with a holy and just God, under a consciousness of your filthiness before him, than ye would to dwell with the damned souls in hell" (*Mormon 9:4*). *(See #12, #21, #24, and #26 for other discussions of hell.)*

159. What is the state or condition of the wicked in hell?

Alma gave us a definitive response:

> [T]he spirits of the wicked, yea, who are evil—for behold, they have no part nor portion of the Spirit of the Lord; for behold, they chose evil works rather than good; therefore the spirit of the devil did enter into them, and take possession of their house—and these shall be cast out into outer darkness [hell]; there shall be weeping, and wailing, and gnashing of teeth, and this because of their own iniquity, being led captive by the will of the devil. Now this is the state of the souls of the wicked, yea, in darkness, and a state of awful, fearful looking for the fiery indignation of the wrath of God upon them, thus they remain in this state, as well as the righteous in paradise, until the time of their resurrection (*Alma 40:13-14*).

Lorenzo Dow Young saw their condition with his spirit world guide:

> As we went on from this place, my guide said, "I will show you the condition of the damned." Pointing with his hand, he said, "Look!" I looked down a distance which appeared incomprehensible to me. I gazed on a vast region filled with multitudes of beings. I could see everything with the most minute distinctness. The multitude of people I saw were miserable in the extreme. "These," said my guide, "are they who have rejected the means of salvation, that were placed within their reach, and have brought upon themselves the condemnation you behold." The expression of the countenances of these sufferers was clear and distinct. They indicated extreme remorse, sorrow and dejection. They appeared conscious that none but themselves were to blame for their forlorn condition. This scene affected me much, and I could not refrain from weeping (*Faith-Promoting Series 6:28*).

160. What constitutes the torment and suffering for the wicked in hell?

There are at least seven elements that contribute to this agony:

(a) ***Remorse of conscience***. Harold B. Lee said: "The greatest hell that one can suffer is the burning of one's conscience" (*The Teachings of Harold B. Lee, 67*). King Benjamin described this condition: "And if they be evil they are consigned to an awful view of their own guilt and abominations, which doth cause them to shrink from the presence of the Lord into a state of misery" (*Mosiah 3:25*). Amulek said "we shall be brought to stand before God . . . and have a bright recollection of all our guilt" (*Alma 11:43*). Alma said that "in this awful state we shall not dare to look up to our God; and we would fain be glad if we could command the rocks and the mountains to fall upon us to hide us from his presence" (*Alma 12:14*). Parley P. Pratt described the feeling: "But, Oh! the pain! the dark despair! the torments of a guilty conscience! the blackness of darkness, in the lower hell, which the guilty wretches will experience before that happy day of deliverance!" (*KST, 80*).

(b) ***Fear of God's presence.*** Joseph Smith elaborated on this anxiety: "There is no pain so awful as that of suspense. This is the punishment of the wicked; their doubt, anxiety and suspense cause weeping, wailing and gnashing of teeth" (*HC 5:340*). Alma exclaimed from personal experience: "the very thought of coming into the presence of my God did rack my soul with inexpressible horror" (*Alma 36:14*). "Now this is the state of the souls of the wicked, yea, in darkness and a state of awful, fearful looking for the fiery indignation of the wrath of God upon them" (*Alma 40:14*).

(c) ***Knowledge of failed potential.*** Hell is not literally fire and brimstone; rather, it is "as a lake of fire and brimstone" (*see 2 Nephi 9:16 and Alma 12:17*). The word *as* indicates the figurative nature of the expression (*see DCBofM, 245*). Joseph Smith described the symbolic essence of this type of anguish:

> A man is his own tormentor and his own condemner. Hence the saying, They shall go into the lake that burns with fire and brimstone. The torment of disappointment in the mind of man is as exquisite as a lake burning with fire and brimstone, I say, so is the torment of man" (*HC 6:314*). "The great misery of departed spirits in the world of spirits, where they go after death, is to know that they come short of the glory that others enjoy, and that they might have enjoyed themselves, and they are their own accusers (*HC 5:425*).

Some portion of this type of disappointment could apply to not only the wicked but to any who come short of exaltation. Harold B. Lee said: "Now, when we fail of that highest degree of glory and realize what we've lost, there will be a burning of the conscience that will be worse than any physical kind of fire that I assume one could suffer" (The Teachings of Harold B. Lee, 67). Consider Amulek's warning that "this life is the time for men to prepare to meet God" (Alma 34:32). Indeed "after this day of life, which is given us to prepare for eternity, behold, if we do not improve our time while in this life, then cometh the night of darkness wherein there can be no labor performed" (Alma 34:33).

John Greenleaf Whittier wrote: "For all sad words of tongue and pen, the saddest are these, 'it might have been.'"

(d) ***Disagreeable society.*** Orson Pratt penned this well-written description:

> There is something that is calculated to render their society disagreeable to themselves, which increases as the degradation of the society is increased. Then a wicked man entering into the company of such beings has not only a hell within himself—a conscience gnawing like a worm, but he sees misery and wretchedness; and they cleave one to another in their wickedness, and in their conversation, and acts, and doings, and intercourse with each other; all these things are calculated in their nature to produce misery and wretchedness, as well as their own consciences. It should then be our constant study to escape this order of things (*JD 2:241*).

(e) ***Evil desires continue.*** Our evil desires plague us. Melvin J. Ballard indicates how the annoyance continues: "Do not let any of us imagine that we can go down to the grave not having overcome the corruptions of the flesh and then lose in the grave all our sins and evil tendencies. They will be with us. They will be with the spirit when separated from the body" (*cited in The Vision, 46; see also #115*).

Brent and Wendy Top found from NDE accounts how spirit world inhabitants are slaves to the evil passions, cravings, and desires they fostered in mortality. For instance, some strove endlessly to obtain alcohol and cigarettes that had mastered them in the flesh (*Glimpses, 179*). We can see why it is important to overcome sin in the flesh (*see #115*).

(f) ***Misery of wickedness.*** **Alma** wrote the great truth: "wickedness never was happiness" (*Alma 41:10*). The carnal state of bitterness without the godly attributes of faith, kindness, mercy, and other virtues contributes to this misery (*see Alma 41:11*).

(g) ***Destitute of love.*** Orson Pratt eloquently explains:

> If we should inquire what constitutes the misery of the fallen angels, the answer would be, they are destitute of love; they have ceased to love God; they have ceased to have pure love one towards another; they have ceased to love that which is good. Hatred, malice, revenge, and every evil passion have usurped the place of love; and unhappiness, wretchedness, and misery are the results. Where there is no love, there will be no desire to promote the welfare of others. Instead of desiring that others may be happy, each desires to make all others miserable like himself; each seeks to gratify that hellish disposition against the Almighty which arises from his extreme hatred of that which is good. For the want of love the torment of each is complete. All the wicked who are entirely overcome by these malicious spirits will have the heavenly principle of love wholly eradicated from their minds, and they will become angels to these infernal fiends, being captivated by them, and compelled to act as they act. They cannot extricate themselves from their power, nor ward off the fiery darts of their malicious tormentors. Such will be the condition of all beings who entirely withdraw themselves from the love of God (*The Seer 1:10, 156*).

161. How long does torment in hell last?

Torment in the spirit world is temporary. George Q. Cannon said those who have "committed abominable crimes—will have this gospel preached unto them, and they will be kept in torment until they repent of their sins" (*Gospel Truth, 63*). Joseph Smith said they welter "in torment, even until they shall have paid the uttermost farthing" (*HC 6:315*). For some, that won't be until the resurrection. Alma revealed that those in hell remain "in darkness, and a state of awful, fearful looking for the fiery indignation of the wrath of God upon them . . . until the time of their resurrection" (*Alma 40:14*). The Lord declared: "These are they who shall not be redeemed from the devil until the last resurrection, until the lord, even Christ the Lamb, shall have finished his work" (*D&C 76:85*).

Harold B. Lee said: "There will be nothing so terrifying to the human soul as to be told on resurrection morning that they will have to wait a thousand years before they shall come forth from the grave in resurrection" (*The Teachings of Harold B. Lee, 67*).

Brigham Young further explained:

> Jesus will bring forth, by his own redemption, every son and daughter of Adam, except the sons of perdition, who will be cast into hell [a permanent hell differentiated from the temporary hell in the spirit world]. Others will suffer the wrath of God—will suffer all the Lord can demand at their hands, or justice can require of them; and when they have suffered the wrath of God till the utmost farthing is paid, they will be brought out of prison. Is this dangerous doctrine to preach? Some consider it dangerous; but it is true that every person who does not sin away the day of grace, and become an angel to the Devil will be brought forth to inherit a kingdom of glory (*JD 8:154*).

162. If hell is temporary, why do the scriptures talk about "endless torment"?

Endless is a name for God. Endless punishment means God's punishment, not punishment without end. The Lord explained:

> Nevertheless, it is not written that there shall be no end to this torment, but it is written *endless torment*. Again, it is written *eternal damnation*...

> For, behold, I am endless, and the punishment which is given from my hand is endless punishment, for Endless is my name. Wherefore—Eternal punishment is God's punishment. Endless punishment is God's punishment (*D&C 19:6-12*).

163. What happens to the sons of perdition?

The sons of perdition are the "only ones who shall not be redeemed in the due time of the Lord, after the sufferings of his wrath" (*D&C 76:38*). They go to perdition (outer darkness) which is a permanent state of hell (*see D&C 76:25-39*). Spencer W. Kimball wrote: "In the realms of perdition or the kingdom of darkness, where there is no light, Satan and the unembodied spirits of the preexistence shall dwell together with those of mortality who retrogress to the level of perdition. These have lost the power of regeneration. They have sunk so low as to have lost the inclinations and ability to repent . . ." (*Miracle of Forgiveness, 125*). "Those who have become sons of perdition while in mortality will be resurrected with unglorified physical bodies . . . Cain, thus resurrected, will then rule over the unembodied Lucifer (*Moses 5:23; MD, 109*)" (*EM, 1391*). Robert L. Millet explained their fate: "The sons of perdition are the only ones who shall be subject to the second spiritual death, the final expulsion from the presence of God. They, after being resurrected and standing before God to be judged (*2 Nephi 9:15*) shall be consigned to a kingdom of no glory" (*Life After Death, 28*).

CHAPTER FIFTEEN

SATAN AND EVIL SPIRITS

I am no devil, for there is none
—Satan, 2 Nephi 28:22

164. What is Satan's purpose?

He has three main purposes. According to President Harold B. Lee the plan of Satan is well-documented:

> *First,* he plans "to destroy the agency of man" (*Moses 4:3*) . . . we may see him in power wherever we see an individual so overwhelmed by his own habits as a result of his sinning and where he seems powerless to control his habits and evil tendencies . . . Likewise in that nation where representative government has given way to the will of dictatorships, there you may see the power of Satan, or the 'prince of this world,' reigning in great demonstration. Satan's *second* purpose is to possess the bodies of Adam and his posterity. The *third* purpose of Satan, which is described carefully and accurately in the scriptures, [is] to make captive the souls of men (*see Alma 34:35; 2 Nephi 26:22*) (*The Teachings of Harold B. Lee, 37-38*).

165. Can Satan and evil spirits from the spirit world influence us?

Yes. Satan and a third part of the spirits in the premortal spirit world were cast out to the earth where they "encompasseth [us] round about" *D&C 76:29*). They live in the spirit world but have power to tempt mortals. Evil spirits may encroach on our world or even possess a human body (*see #168*).

El Ray L. Christiansen described the three ways Satan and his minions tempt us: "Satan knows all the tricks. He knows where we are susceptible to temptations and how to entice us to do evil. He and his messengers [a] suggest evil, [b] minimize the seriousness of sin, and [c] make evil inviting" (*New Era, July 1975*).

Apparently Satan uses every means allowed to influence each person, including print and electronic media, TV, the internet, other individuals, and subtle, direct enticements. Bruce R. McConkie wrote: "Revelations come to men just as easily from devils as they do from holy sources. By rebellion and wickedness men may commune with evil spirits, whereas by obedience and righteousness they might have seen angels and had the communion of the Holy Spirit" (*MD, 246*).

The evil influences may come from wicked disembodied spirits who once lived in mortality. Heber C. Kimball warned: "The spirits of the wicked, who have died thousands of years past, are at war with the Saints of God upon the earth" (*JD 3:229*). Brigham Young said the spirits of the "wicked who have slain the wicked" are "watching us continually for an opportunity to influence us to do evil" (*JD 12:128*). George Q. Cannon testified of Joseph Smith's teachings on the matter:

> I have no doubt that many of my brethren and sisters have sensibly felt in various places and at various times evil influences around them. Brother Joseph Smith gave an explanation of this. There are places in the Mississippi Valley where the influence or the presence of invisible spirits are very perceptibly felt. He said that numbers had been slain there in war, and that there were evil influences or spirits which affect the spirits of those who have tabernacles [physical bodies] on the earth. I, myself, have felt those influences in other places besides the continent of America; I have felt them on the old battle grounds on the Sandwich Islands. I have come to the conclusion that if our eyes were open to see the spirit world around us, we should feel differently on this subject than we do; we would not be so unguarded and careless, and so indifferent whether we had the spirit and power of God with us or not; but we would be continually watchful and prayerful to our heavenly Father

> for His Holy Spirit and His holy angels to be around about us to strengthen us to overcome every evil influence (*JD 11:30*).

Heber Q. Hale, in his vision of the spirit world, observed:

> The wicked and unrepentant have still, like the rest, their free agency, and applying themselves to no useful or wholesome undertaking, seek pleasure about their old haunts and exalt in the sin and wickedness of degenerated humanity. To this extent they are still the tools of Satan. It is these idle, mischievous and deceptive spirits who appear as miserable counterfeits at spiritualist séances, table dancing and Ouija board operation. The noble and great ones do not respond to the call of the mediums and to every curious group of meddlesome inquirers. They would not do it in the world of mortality, certainly they would not do it in their increased state of knowledge in the world of immortality (*HQH, 3*).

166. When is communicating with the dead good and when is it bad?

It is good when it is authorized by God, i.e. when it is inspired and comes with light or Spirit. Because we don't pray to the deceased or seek to communicate with specific deceased individuals, approved communication is generally unexpected. Mediums have become practiced in communing with evil spirits. Isaiah taught:

> And when they shall say unto you: Seek unto them that have familiar spirits, and unto wizards that peep, and mutter; should not a people seek unto their God? for the living to hear from the dead? To the law and to the testimony; and if they speak not according to this word, it is because there is no light in them (*Isaiah 8:19-20 JST*).

Bruce R. McConkie gave this commentary on Isaiah's words:

> Thus, no matter how sincerely mediums may be deceived into thinking they are following a divinely approved pattern, they are in fact turning to an evil source "for the living to hear from the dead." Those who are truly spiritually inclined know this by personal revelation from the true

> Spirit; further, the information revealed from spirits through mediums is not according to "the law and to the testimony." Accordingly, though some true facts may be found in it, yet its acceptance and use has the effect of leading souls into the clutches of those evil powers which give the data (*MD, 760*).

Elder McConkie warned about the evils of mediums (witches), sorcery, divination, fortune telling, hypnotism, necromancy, soothsaying, etc. (*MD, 759*). "Ouija boards, séances, spiritualism, or Satan worship . . . are tools of Satan" that we have been counseled to completely avoid (*Aaronic Priesthood Manual 2:37*).

We should also avoid frequent discussions of evil spirits. President Harold B. Lee told about a "wave of incidents in which evil spirits were inflicting missionaries and Saints" in Brazil. At every conference, missionaries were relating these experiences. The mission president told the missionaries to stop talking about it, and there was an "almost immediate cessation of the power of evil spirits when the people confined their testimonies to the works of the Lord rather than of Satan." President Lee admonished: "stop talking about the works of the devil, but confine [our] conversation to the works of God and bear testimony to His goodness and blessings, and stop giving discourses on the subjects that the devil would like us continue to talk about—his works" (*The Teachings of Harold B. Lee, 41*).

Along these lines, we would be wise to avoid movies and books that embellish the dark side, are devoid of the spirit, and leave evil fingerprints of mystical and psychic activity.

167. How can one be delivered from the power of Satan or evil spirits?

First, pray. Moses' experience is a pattern for us to follow. Moses prayed and then commanded Satan to depart in the name of the Jesus Christ: "Moses began to fear exceedingly . . . Nevertheless, calling upon God, he received strength . . . saying: In the name of the Only Begotten, depart hence, Satan" (*Moses 1:18-22*). Spencer W. Kimball commented on this event:

> When he is challenged, Satan is angry, as he was with Moses. He cried with a loud voice, trembled, and shook, and he departed from Moses who was resolute . . . There was nothing else for him to do. He has to leave when you say, "Depart from me, Satan." Every soul who has mortality is stronger than Satan, if that soul is determined (*Ensign, March 1976*).

Wilford Woodruff prayed when attacked by hordes of evil spirits (*Appendix B8*).

Heber C. Kimball saw an evil spirit standing at the foot of his wife Vilate's bed where she lay sick. "Kneeling down he prayed, and then rebuked the apparition in the name of Jesus" (Orson F. Whitney, *Life of Heber C. Kimball, 472*).

168. The Savior cast out evil spirits. Have evil spirits been cast out of mortals in our day?

Yes. And as in Biblical times, it may require priesthood power. Joseph Smith "rebuked the devil, and commanded him in the name of Jesus Christ to depart" when casting an evil spirit from Newel Knight, in what Joseph said was the first miracle experience in the restored Church (*see HC 1:82-84*).

Elder F. Enzio Busche fervently prayed when faced with the problem of helping a missionary who was possessed with an evil spirit. Apprehensive and uncomfortable, the scripture "perfect love casteth out fear," came to Elder Busche's mind (*1 John 4:18; and Moroni 8:16*). Then his mind was drawn to *Moroni 7:48*: "Wherefore . . . pray unto the Father with all the energy of heart, that ye may be filled with this love." He prayed with all the energy of his heart: "Father, fill my soul with love." Suddenly he was filled with the spirit, driving out all fear. The Spirit directed him what to do. He knelt in front of the young man who was sitting and shaking uncontrollably. Then he put his arms around him, pulling him gently to his chest, and told him, with all the strength of his soul, "I love you, my brother." In the very moment he did that, the evil spirit left. The missionary came to his senses, looked at him and said, "I love you, too" (*Yearning for the Living God, 268-71*).

In speaking about the practice of exorcism, Bruce R. McConkie wrote: "In imitation of the true order whereby devils are cast out of people, false ministers (having no actual priesthood power) . . . attempt to expel evil spirits from persons or drive them away from particular locations by incantations, conjuration, or adjuration. Commonly some holy name is used in these false rituals" (*MD, 259*). Anciently seven exorcists attempted to cast out an evil spirit by imitating Paul using

> the name of the Lord Jesus, saying, We adjure you by Jesus whom Paul preacheth . . . And the evil spirit answered and said, Jesus I know, and Paul I know; but who are ye? And the man in whom the evil spirit was leaped on them, and overcame them, and prevailed against them, so that they fled out of that house naked and wounded" (*Acts 19:13,15-16*).

169. Do some of the wicked fight against righteousness in the spirit world?

Yes. Brigham Young described the battle going on there:

> Take those that were wicked designedly, who knowingly lived without the Gospel when it was within their reach, they are given up to the devil, they become tools to the devil and spirits of devils. Go to the time when the Gospel came to the earth in the days of Joseph, take the wicked that have opposed this people and persecuted them to the death, and they are sent to hell. Where are they? They are in the spirit world, and are just as busy as they possibly can be to do everything they can against the Prophet and the Apostles, against Jesus and His Kingdom. They are just as wicked and malicious in their actions against the cause of truth, as they were while on the earth in their fleshly tabernacles. Joseph, also, goes there, but has the devil power over him? No, because he held the keys and power of the eternal Priestood here, and got the victory while here in the flesh (*JD 3:370*). (*See also #44.*)

CHAPTER SIXTEEN

SPIRIT WORLD LIGHT

Teach me to know of the things that are right;
Teach me, teach me to walk in the light.
—Clara W. McMaster, Teach Me to Walk in the Light, Hymns, 304

170. Is the light of Christ in the spirit world?

Yes. Here are three ways the light of Christ is in the spirit world:

(a) ***Light fills the immensity of space, earth, and the spirit world***. The light of Christ, which is in the sun, moon, stars, and earth, and which constitutes the power thereof by which they were made "proceedeth forth from the presence of God to fill the immensity of space" (*D&C 88:12; see 88:6-13*). Most NDE beholders encounter this light in the spirit world (*#112*). They find it difficult to define, but the feelings are consistent with the light of Christ: comfort, joy, love, warmth and belonging, reassurance, peacefulness, and understanding (*see* Migliore, *Measure of Heaven, 56; #43*).

(b) ***All individual spirits have "light . . . which giveth life,"*** (*D&C 88:13*) the "light *of* truth" which can "act for itself" (*D&C 93:29-30, italics for emphasis*). This is the source of life and individuality and is contained in the spirit body that continues after death in the spirit world (*see #45*).

(c) ***Each person is born with the light of Christ***, the glory of God, intelligence, "or, in other words, light *and* truth" (*D&C 93:36, italics for emphasis*) which can be acted upon (*see #43*). This is the Spirit that "giveth light to every man that cometh into the world; and the Spirit enlighteneth every man through the world, that hearkeneth to the voice of the Spirit" (*D&C 84:46*). Individual light development continues after death for those who seek it according to this marvelous promise: "he that receiveth light, and continueth in God, receiveth more light; and that light groweth brighter and brighter until the perfect day" (*D&C 50:24*). "He that keepeth his [God's] commandments receiveth truth and light, until he is glorified in truth and knoweth all things" (*D&C 93:28*). Spirit world visitors report that this type of light (Spirit) is much more visible and detectable in spirits than in coarser mortals (*see also #43 and #171*).

171. What are the phases or milestones of individual light development?

We progress in godliness on our individual merits and God's grace in the premortal, mortal, and postmortal worlds. The measuring stick for one's advancement is light. President Marion G. Romney spoke in general conference on the three phases of the light of Christ. Summarizing, they are: (a) the light of Christ we are born with; (b) the gift of the Holy Ghost; and (c) the more sure word of prophecy, which is obtained by making one's calling and election sure, thereby receiving the other Comforter. "This Comforter is the promise which I give unto you of eternal life, even the glory of the celestial kingdom (*D&C 88:3-4*)" (*Ensign, May 1977*). Joseph Smith said that when one obtains this second Comforter "he will have the personage of Jesus Christ to attend him" (*TPJS, 151*). President Romney called this third phase the "full light of Christ" (*Ensign, May 1977*). For some, that glorious day may be in Paradise.

Joseph F. Smith saw the righteous saints in paradise: "Their countenances shone, and the radiance from the presence of the Lord rested upon them, and they sang praises unto his holy name" (*D&C 138:24*). Joseph Smith taught that the faithful go to paradise where they become spirits of the just, "revealed in flaming fire and glory." Later they are resurrected and become "angels [that] have advanced further [than the spirits of the just], their light and glory being tabernacled; and hence they appear in bodily shape" (*TPJS, 325*).

The Lord gave us the formula for receiving this light. We are to set our hearts on "treasures in heaven" and not "treasures upon earth." "For where your treasure is, there will your heart be also" (*3 Nephi 13: 19-21*). The Lord then gave this incredible promise to those who keep their heart and mind's eye focused on the things of God:

> The light of the body is the eye; if, therefore, thine eye be single, thy whole body shall be full of light (*3Nephi 13:22*). And if your eye be single to my glory, your whole bodies shall be filled with light, and there shall be no darkness in you; and that body which is filled with light comprehendeth all things. Therefore sanctify yourselves that your minds become single to God, and the days will come that you shall see him; for he will unveil his face unto you, and it shall be in his own time, and in his own way, and according to his own will (*D&C 88:67-68*).

Light is an important concept we should ponder and seek, even if it is not always readily apparent in mortality. Truman G. Madsen, in his fine essay, *Man Illumined,* described the radiance of soul as "like a search light turned on within" to the godly who witness it. Apostles especially have this gift of discernment:

> At the everyday level there are the light-variations in the human face, almost infinitely intimate and animated. "You will always discover in the first glance of a man, in the outlines of his features, something of his mind," said the Prophet Joseph (*TPJS, 299*). Particularly around the eyes ("the light of the body is the eye" [*Matthew 6:22*]), the forehead, and the lips one sees recorded a person's past and present encounters with light. It has nothing to do with fairness of complexion, with age, with cosmetic skill, with habitual patterns of facial set or mood, or even with the features we are accustomed to identify as "attractive." (*The Radiant Life, 27*).

Most near-death experiencers, upon entering the spirit world, readily identify this spiritual light and the effects of its accompanying peace and fruits of the spirit (*see #112*). The light is often described as visible, all-pervading, bright, and beautiful, but not blinding. The light is accompanied by powerful feelings of love and belonging. Some encounter beings of light and glory, perhaps ministers who God maketh "a flaming fire" (*Psalm 104:4; Hebrews 1:7*). These may be spirits of the just or possibly others advancing on the path of light.

Significantly, the only thing we can take with us to the spirit world is our spirit bodies and its accompanying light or Spirit. Our light constitutes what we have become and the eternal truths we know. The fulness of light or Spirit is the heavenly treasure (*see D&C 19:38; Helaman 5:8*).

172. What is the source of spirit world light?

It comes from the same source from which we get it here (*see #43*). Brigham Young explained how the principle is the same in the spirit world:

> God is the source, the fountain of all intelligence, no matter who possesses it, whether man upon the earth, the spirits in the spirit world, the angels that dwell in the eternities of the Gods, or the most inferior intelligence among the devils in hell. All have derived what intelligence, light, power, and existence they have from God—from the same source from which we have received ours (*JD 8:205*).

173. Do spirits in the spirit world differ in light or glory?

Yes. Spirits differ in the level of light, glory, intelligence, or spirit quickening they attain. Intelligence is light in this definition. "The glory of God is intelligence, or, in other words, light and truth" (*D&C 93:36*). Individuals have a celestial, terrestrial, or telestial spirit or glory in mortality and in the spirit world depending on the celestial, terrestrial or telestial laws being lived. We are then resurrected with a portion of that same light or spirit, eventually receiving a fulness of the respective glory (*see D&C 88:21-31*). "Whatever principle of intelligence [light] we attain unto in this life [which must include the spirit world for those who didn't have the opportunity in mortality], it will rise with us in the resurrection" (*D&C 130:18*). The Lord wants his disembodied spirit children to be blessed with the Spirit through obedience to his laws: "Because of this, is the gospel preached to them who are dead, that they might be judged according to men in the flesh, but live in the spirit according to the will of God" (*JST 1 Peter 4:6*).

174. Are classes of spirits in the spirit world separated?

Yes. Joseph F. Smith saw the righteous dead "gathered together in one place" in paradise (*D&C 138:12*). Heber C. Kimball referred to Jedediah M. Grant's deathbed NDE: "He saw the righteous gathered together in the spirit world, and there were no wicked spirits among them" (*JD 4:136*). Monte Nyman, referring to Brigham Young's description of classes of spirits in spirit prison (*see # 15 and JD 3:368*), observed that spirits are "apparently separated by the state or condition of their spirit" (*see also #156*). These "classes of people described above do not seem to be separated by a physical barrier, such as a wall or fence. However there are other restrictions imposed" (*BofMC 3:525*).

Heber Q. Hale, President of the Boise Stake, had a vision in 1920 of the spirit world "as real to me as any experience of my life." He reported:

> [T]he wicked and unrepentant are confined to a certain district by themselves, the confines of which are as definitely determined and impassable as the line marking the division of the physical from the spiritual world. A mere film but impassable until the person himself has changed . . . There was much activity within the different spheres, and the appointed ministers of salvation were seen coming from the higher to the lower spheres in pursuit of their missionary appointments (*HQH, 1*).

Joseph Smith said: "It would seem also, that wicked spirits have their bounds, limits, and laws by which they are governed and controlled" (*TPJS, 208*). In Nephi's vision of the spirit world, he saw that the "justice of God did also divide the wicked from the righteous; and the brightness thereof was like unto the brightness of a flaming fire" (*1 Nephi 15:30*).

The spirits of the just are "enveloped in flaming fire" (Joseph Smith (*TPJS, 326*).

Monte Nyman provided this thought-provoking commentary and opinion:

> The brightness of the justice of God, likened to a flaming fire, is probably the Spirit of the Lord that envelops the spirits of the just as the Prophet Joseph said. Either the flaming fire of the Spirit of the Lord would prevent wicked spirits from passing through it, or perhaps restrictions were placed upon them. If there were restrictions, they would be imposed by the priesthood.
>
> The priesthood is an eternal power, and is held by some people in the spirit world (*see Alma 13:7-9*). Those not meeting the prerequisites, such as worthiness or receiving priesthood ordinances, would not be allowed to enter certain areas where the righteous were assembled. It would be similar today when a person cannot enter the temple without a recommend from their bishop and endorsed by a member of the stake presidency (*BofMC 3:526*).

175. Do temptations continue in the spirit world for those not in paradise?

Yes. Temptations continue (except for those in paradise, *see #139*) so they can be judged according to men in the flesh. There is much to be done in the hereafter by both those in paradise and the spirit world to merit any of the degrees of glory (*see #11 and #146*). Heber C. Kimball made an interesting observation, apparently pertaining to those who did not abide their gospel opportunities in mortality: "If men and women do not qualify themselves and become [sufficiently] sanctified and purified in this life, they will go into a world of spirits where they will have a greater contest with the devils than ever you had with them here" (*JD 3:230*).

176. What is the great gulf Jesus described, that separated Lazarus in paradise and the certain rich man in hell? (*see Luke 16:19-31*)

Bruce R. McConkie articulated the answer succinctly:

> Until the death of Christ these two spirit abodes [paradise and spirit prison] were separated by a great gulf, with the intermingling of their respective inhabitants strictly forbidden (*Luke 16:19-31*). After our Lord bridged the gulf between the two (*see 1 Peter 3:18-21; Moses 7:37-39*) . . . righteous spirits began teaching the gospel to wicked ones (*MD, 762*).

In the parable, the rich man found himself in hell and the beggar Lazarus was in Abraham's bosom (paradise). The rich man called out for Abraham to send Lazarus to comfort him. Abraham answered there was no passage between hell and paradise. Lazarus then asked Abraham to send Lazarus to his five mortal brothers to warn them about the torments in hell. Abraham said they would not be persuaded by a spirit "from the dead" if "they hear not Moses and the prophets" (*see Luke 16:30,31*).

Although the great gulf has now been bridged by Christ, the wicked are still separated from paradise (*see #174*). The parable also suggests these principles which may apply in the spirit world today:

(a) One's spirit world condition of comfort or torment depends upon one's righteousness and service on earth.

(b) Friends and acquaintances will know of each other in the spirit world. They will be aware of their former lives of good or evil and will be their own judge.

(c) We should follow the prophets and repent to prepare for the spirit world. Those who will not hear the prophets will not be persuaded to repent "though one rose from the dead" (*Luke 16:31*). Signs from the dead alone do not convert the soul (*see #6*).

Following Jesus' visit after the crucifixion, spirits in paradise do missionary work in spirit prison, and repentant spirits in spirit prison can join the righteous in paradise when baptisms and confirmations are done on their behalf (*see #178*).

177. Is there light in hell?

There is the kind of "light . . . which giveth life" (*D&C 88:13*) because the spirits are alive. However, in Hell there is no Spirit, or light of Christ. Alma said they "have no part nor portion of the Spirit of the Lord" (*Alma 40:13*). The "glory of God . . . or in other words . . . light and truth forsake that evil one" (*D&C 93:36-37*). Those thrust down to hell "have become subjected to the spirit of the devil, and he doth seal you his; therefore, the Spirit of the Lord hath withdrawn from you, and hath no place in you, and the devil hath all power over you" (*Alma 34:35*). Without the Spirit, they are in "outer darkness" (*D&C 101:91*). "They love darkness rather than light, because their deeds are evil" (*D&C 10:21*). Darkness in this definition refers to the condition of an evil existence and the absence of the Spirit. Apparently there is some form of physical light with which to see in hell. In Jesus' parable the rich man in hell could "lift up his eyes" and "seeth Abraham afar off, and Lazarus" (*Luke 16:*23). NDE visitors to hell report being able to see things there (*e.g., see George G. Ritchie, Return from Tomorrow, 74-79*).

CHAPTER SEVENTEEN

GREAT SPIRIT WORLD WORK

Far and wide we tell the Father's story,
Far and wide his love proclaim.
—Grace Gordon, Called to Serve, Hymns, 249

178. What happens to those who died without baptism or knowledge of the gospel?

This was one of Clement's questions for Peter (*see Introduction*). Here is Hugh Nibley's summary of the interview:

> One of the first things Clement asks Peter upon being introduced to him, in the *Clementine Recognitions,* is, "Shall those be wholly deprived of the kingdom of heaven who died before Christ's coming?" for he was thinking probably of his own forebears . . . his dead father and mother. He then assures Clement that his parents are not in hell, although they never were baptized, and that ample provisions have been made for their salvation . . . When their bodies died [they] went in the spirit to be retained in good and happy places, that at the resurrection of the dead each might be empowered to receive an eternal heritage for the good he had done (*CWHN 3:168 and 17:341*).

The *Gospel Principles* manual states the following regarding spirits in spirit prison who have not yet heard the gospel of Jesus Christ: "These spirits have agency and may be enticed by both good and evil. If they accept the gospel and the ordinances performed for them in the temples, they may leave the spirit prison and dwell in paradise" (*Gospel Principles, 244*).

179. What is the great work in the spirit world?

Bruce R. McConkie declared: "The great work . . . is the preaching of the gospel to those who are imprisoned by sin and false traditions" (*MD, 762*).

Joseph Smith said: "All those who have not had an opportunity of hearing the Gospel . . . must have it hereafter, before they can be finally judged" (*HC 3:29*).

Since the number of converts has been a relatively small percentage of the world's population thus far, it is easy to see why missionary work to the ignorant billions in the spirit world is such a massive and great work.

Neal A. Maxwell expounded further:

> The vastness of the work in the spirit world of preaching the gospel is confirmed in the 1918 vision of President Joseph F. Smith, which was accepted by the Church in 1976 as a revelation. That work is proceeding, "even to all the spirits of men" (*D&C 138:30*). Billions and billions of them! . . . Therefore an interesting constituency awaits us, such as those "who had died in their sins, without a knowledge of the truth" (*D&C 138:32*). This group is obviously very large! None is to be left out, however, even those in the spirit prison who once "rejected the prophets" or who are there "because of their rebellion and transgression, that they through the ministration of his servants might also hear his words" (*D&C 138:32,37*) (*The Promise of Discipleship, 108-109).*

180. What will be preached in the spirit world?

The principles of the gospel. Joseph F. Smith saw spirits investigating the gospel in vision:

> These were taught faith in God, repentance from sin, vicarious baptism for the remission of sins, the gift of the Holy Ghost by the laying on of hands, And all other principles of the gospel that were necessary for them to know in order to qualify themselves that they might be judged according to men in the flesh, but live according to God in the spirit. And so it was made known among the dead, both small and great, the un-

> righteous as well as the faithful, that redemption had been wrought through the sacrifice of the Son of God upon the cross (*D&C 138: 33-35*).

181. What happens to those who repent?

Joseph F. Smith's vision continued with this answer:

> The dead who repent will be redeemed, through obedience to the ordinances of the house of God, And after they have paid the penalty of their transgressions, and are washed clean, shall receive a reward according to their works, for they are heirs of salvation (*D&C 138:58-59*).

Those in spirit prison and hell may repent (*see #185*). Heirs of the celestial and terrestrial kingdoms will repent and receive the gospel in mortality or the spirit world (*see #156, #173, #178*). For those who do not repent, "the residue of the wicked have I kept in chains of darkness until the judgment of the great day, which shall come at the end of the earth" (*D&C 38:5*) (*see #156, #161*).

Repentance is necessary to be released from a condition of sin and ignorance to enjoy a condition of righteousness, peace, and comfort. Bruce R. McConkie wrote:

> Repentance opens the prison doors to the spirits in hell; it enables those bound with the chains of hell to free themselves from darkness, unbelief, ignorance, and sin. As rapidly as they can overcome these obstacles—gain light, believe truth, acquire intelligence, cast off sin, and break the chains of hell—they can leave the hell that imprisons them and dwell with the righteous in the peace of paradise (*MD, 755*).

Although the worthy dead who have repented enjoy some conditions of paradise, including "some intermingling" (MD, 762) with the saints from paradise and a just "reward according to their works" (D&C 138:59), apparently they still require vicarious baptism and confirmation "ordinances of the house of God" (D&C 138:58) to enter the place of paradise (see #130, #178, #185, #189). The Encyclopedia of Mormonism explains:

> As teaching and missionary work proceed in the spirit prison and ordinances for the dead are performed in temples on the earth, the once uninformed and the disobedient but now repentant and purified spirits may enter into paradise and enjoy association with the righteous and the blessings of the gospel (*EM, 1063*).

182. How successful will missionary work be in the spirit world?

Several prophets have suggested the gospel will be largely accepted there. President Wilford Woodruff stated: "There will be few, if any, [in the spirit world] who will not accept the gospel." (Stuy, *Collected Discourses 4:74*). President Lorenzo Snow declared: "When the Gospel is preached to the spirits in prison, the success attending that preaching will be far greater than that attending the preaching of our Elders in this life. I believe there will be very few indeed of those spirits who will not gladly receive the Gospel when it is carried to them. The circumstances there will be a thousand times more favorable" (Stuy, *Collected Discourses 3:363*).

A Patriarch, Charles R. Woodbury, reported this temple experience which supports the prophets' statements above:

> As I witnessed baptisms one day in the Manti Temple, when the first name was called out for baptism, a voice said to me, "This person has had the gospel taught to him, has accepted it, and desires baptism." As the second name was read, the voice said: "This person has not heard the gospel yet." Another name was called, and I was told, "This person has heard the gospel and was not converted." I witnessed 300 baptisms, each time being advised by the voice as to those who accepted of their baptism, and those who did not. Twenty-five of the 300 whose baptism had been done for them were not ready for it; they had as yet not been converted to the gospel. The remaining 275 were prepared, and rejoiced that their work was being done. This is my testimony to the world that the departed spirits know and most of them appreciate and rejoice when their work is done in the temples

of the Lord. It is our great responsibility to do the temple work for our departed kindred dead, so that they, like us, can enjoy the blessings of the gospel" (Jensen, When Faith Writes the Story, 224-225).

183. Will all the spirits in spirit prison be given a chance to hear the gospel?

Yes. Neal A. Maxwell points out: "Only in the spirit world, it appears, will 'all the spirits of men' receive either a first, full, or last chance to hear the gospel (*D&C 138:30*)" (*Whom the Lord Loveth, 149-150*).

184. Do those who had a full opportunity to accept the gospel in mortality but did not receive it with all their heart get another chance in the spirit world?

Yes and no. Bruce R. McConkie explains the seeming contradiction:

> *There is no such thing as a second chance to gain salvation by accepting the gospel in the spirit world after spurning, declining, or refusing to accept it in this life.* It is true that there may be a second chance to hear and accept the gospel, but those who have thus procrastinated their acceptance of the saving truths will not gain salvation in the celestial kingdom of God. Salvation for the dead is the system by means of which those who *"die without a knowledge of the gospel"* (D&C 128:5) may gain such knowledge in the spirit world and then, following the vicarious performance of the necessary ordinances, become heirs of salvation on the same basis as though the gospel truths had been obeyed in mortality. *Salvation for the dead is limited expressly to those who do not have opportunity in this life to accept the gospel but who would have taken the opportunity had it come to them (MD, 685-686).*

The Lord described heirs of terrestrial glory as those who "received not the testimony of Jesus in the flesh, but afterwards received it [in the spirit world] *when they heard it again*" (*D&C 76:74, italics are from Joseph's poetic version*). Moroni taught: "let us labor diligently; for if we should cease to labor, we should be brought under condemnation; for we have a labor to perform whilst in this tabernacle of clay, that we may conquer the enemy of all righteousness, and rest our souls in the kingdom of God" (*Moroni 9:6*).

Marion G. Romney's opinion on the subject is well-stated:

> In light of these teachings, it would seem to be most unwise to rely upon the doctrine of the so-called second chance and wait until after death to perform our good works. I am acquainted with the doctrine that those who have had no opportunity to hear and receive the gospel in this life will have that opportunity in the world to come, and I rejoice in it . . . I have never found anything in the scriptures nor in the teachings of the prophets which encourages me to believe that those who have the gospel taught to them here will be able to make up their loss if they choose to wait for the next life to obey it. I would not advise anyone to take that chance. As I understand the scriptures, taking such a hazard would be fatal (*CR, April 1954*).

Finally, note the concurring view of Robert L. Millet and Joseph Fielding McConkie:

> When Amulek spoke of death as the "night of darkness wherein there can be no labor performed" (*Alma 34:33*), he had reference to those who had full opportunity to accept the gospel in the flesh and did not do so. It is a serious doctrinal error to suppose that those who reject that opportunity in this life because they have no desire to conform to gospel standards may correct the matter in the spirit world. The willfully disobedient will not be cleansed from their sins simply because they have the good fortune to have someone labor in their behalf after they are dead. The book of life from which each man will be judged will be the book he has written on his own soul (*The Life Beyond, 41-42*).

185. Is there a time when a spirit can't seek or look to God?

No. Not according to the compassionate Joseph Smith:

> There is never a time when the spirit is too old to approach God. All are within the reach of pardoning mercy, who have not committed the unpardonable sin, which hath no forgiveness, neither in this world, nor in the world to come. There is a way to release the spirits of the dead; that is by the power and authority of the Priesthood—by binding and loosing on earth. This doctrine appears glorious, inasmuch as it exhibits the greatness of divine compassion and benevolence in the extent of the plan of human salvation (*HC 4:425*).

Whether in this life or the spirit world, obedience enhances our standing before God. There are countless individual circumstances and levels of devotion to the Lord; and there are multiple levels within kingdoms to reward His children. He will judge righteously in mercy and wisdom. We should make every effort to be obedient, repent, and do good in this life, in spite of past mistakes, knowing that all righteous desires, and good works count in the eyes of our Maker.

186. Is the spirit world part of our second estate?

Yes. We sometimes say that our second estate ends upon death. "Premortal life is often called the *first estate*, and mortality is called the *second estate*" (*Relief Society Personal Study Guide 3, 32*). Apparently that is true in the narrow usage of the term. However, Neal A. Maxwell gives us an expanded definition that is insightful:

> Sometimes in the Church we speak imprecisely at funerals and otherwise as if individuals who die go immediately to the celestial kingdom and are at once in the full presence of God. We tend to overlook the reality that the spirit world and paradise are part, really, of the second estate. The work of the Lord, so far as the second estate is concerned, is completed before the Judgment and the Resurrection (*The Promise of Discipleship, 110-111*).

Victor L. Ludlow echoed this extended definition of the second estate:

> The postmortal spirit world is a natural continuation of earth life. It comprises the other vital portion of our second estate. The second estate began with our birth as our spirit and physical body were joined together, and it continues until they are reunited again in a resurrected state . . . Both phases of the second estate are probationary periods where we learn, develop, and test our spiritual commitments. Our priorities must be developed and refined before we can exit from the postmortal spirit world (*Principles and Practices, 225-226*).

187. Do we continue to walk by faith in the spirit world?

Yes. Neal A. Maxwell addressed this in two different books:

> Since those who go to the celestial kingdom include, as revealed, those who "overcome by faith" (*D&C 76:53*), the same efforts and triumph would need to occur in the spirit world before they receive resurrection and the entitlement to enter the celestial kingdom (*The Promise of Discipleship, 111*).

> We do not know precisely how God handles things in the spirit world so that life there is an extension of walking by faith. Death does not suddenly bestow upon the disbeliever full awareness of all reality, thereby obviating the need for any faith. Instead, what follows death is a continuum of the basic structure in mortality—until the Judgment Day, when every knee shall bow and every tongue confess that Jesus is the Christ (*see Romans 14:11; Philippians 2:10; D&C 76:110*). Until then, we "walk by faith, not by sight" (*2 Corinthians 5:7*) (*That Ye May Believe, 93-94*).

188. How will God ensure this condition of faith in the spirit world?

Neal A. Maxwell continues:

> We do not know. Yet He has certainly so handled the second estate in relation to the first estate hasn't He? The memories of the first estate are not accessible in the second estate. The spirit world will be so arranged

> that there will be no legitimate complaints later over the justice and mercy of God (*see Mosiah 27:31; Alma 12:15*) (*That Ye May Believe, 94*).

189. "If God blocks out the memory of our first estate while we are here in the second estate, to make choosing fair and a matter of faith, does He also block off the memory of the second estate when we go to the spirit world?" (Neal A. Maxwell)

In his answer to his own question above, Neal A. Maxwell acknowledges our lack of spirit world knowledge, but he certainly gives us thoughts to ponder:

> Perhaps the memories of the mortal second estate are had by all in the spirit world, thus giving those who are disbelievers here some advantage there. Perhaps the memories of the second estate are accessed only by those in paradise. In any case, those in the spirit world must accept and have faith in the gospel and receive the Holy Ghost, if they are to move from the spirit prison to paradise. If not, why send the missionaries to the spirit world? Spirit prison is a term that may seem too harsh, too graphic, and too simplistic. Yet it describes unmistakably a restraining barrier that actually exists. Only further revelation will supply details (*Moving in His Majesty and Power, 90*).

190. "Do people who have been wicked and agnostic, when they pass through the veil of death, suddenly and fully realize that there is, in spite of their earlier skepticism, life beyond the grave? Do they thus have an advantage over those who have had to develop faith in mortality concerning that prospect?" (Neal A. Maxwell)

Elder Maxwell again uses his questions as a teaching tool in responding:

> If, for instance, the same attitudes with which we die persist, then there will be no automatic or immediate flip-flop into a totally different way of thinking. Such can occur there, just as it does here, upon our accepting the gospel and responding with both faith and repentance (*Alma 34:34*).

> Again, our existence in the spirit world is part of the mortal sector of our Father's plan which culminates with the Judgment and the Resurrection (*The Promise of Discipleship, 111*).

191. Will the veil of forgetfulness of our first estate be removed immediately upon physical death?

No. Some in the Church, in the past especially, have assumed the first estate veil of our premortal life would be automatically removed upon death. Nowadays, we're taught otherwise. Here is the view of Neal A. Maxwell:

> The veil of forgetfulness of the first estate apparently will not be suddenly, automatically, and totally removed at the time of our temporal death. This veil, a condition of our entire second estate, is associated with and is part of our time of mortal trial, testing, proving, and overcoming by faith—and thus will continue in some key respects into the spirit world (*The Promise of Discipleship, 111*).

Joseph Fielding McConkie gave his opinion on the subject:

> The idea that at death our memory of the premortal existence is restored to us disrupts any notion that the blessings of the gospel are dispensed there as they are here or, as Peter said it, "according to men in the flesh" (*1 Peter 4:6*) . . . If the sacred truths of heaven are dispensed in this life according to the preparation we have made, we can have every assurance that the same will be the case in the spirit world. The memory of our premortal experience will be revealed to us only as we are worthy to receive it. This means that some will never have that knowledge restored to them (*Answers, 107*).

Alma teaches that God reveals his mysteries to mankind according to the "heed and diligence which they give unto him . . . and he that will not harden his heart, to him is given the greater portion of the word . . . until he knows them in full. And they that will harden their hearts, to them is given the lesser portion of the word until they know nothing concerning his mysteries" (*Alma 12: 9-11*). This scripture seems to imply that one can lose his sacred knowledge. Perhaps God will mercifully withhold or remove the pre-earth heavenly memory of living with Heavenly Parents from the followers of Satan who remain hardened in their hearts and are not redeemed (*see #163*).

We don't have revealed details from the Lord on memory restoration. Some scholars expect that after the resurrection and final judgment there is no reason to withhold our former memory. Daniel H. Ludlow suggested that the timing of the veil removal depends on individual righteousness, but only until the resurrection: "In the post-earthly spirit world, the spirit continues to be tested and proven until the 'veil of forgetfulness' is removed through righteousness or until the spirit and the physical body are reunited through the resurrection" (*SW, 388*).

192. "By what means is the veil of forgetfulness removed?" (Daniel H. Ludlow)

"By the power of the individual's spirit, working in conjunction with the Spirit of our Heavenly Father," responded Daniel H. Ludlow. "Jesus Christ and perhaps some other righteous persons have been so faithful and diligent in this life that the veil of forgetfulness has been removed from them while they were still living on earth" (Daniel H. Ludlow, *SW, 290; see also D&C 8:1-4)*.

CHAPTER EIGHTEEN

RESURRECTION

He is risen! He is risen!
Tell it out with joyful voice.
He has burst his three days' prison;
Let the whole wide earth rejoice.
Death is conquered; man is free.
Christ has won the victory.
—Cecil Frances Alexander, He Is Risen, Hymns, 199

193. What is the resurrection?

Hyrum M. Smith gave a classic definition: "Death is the dissolution of the body, and the resurrection is the reanimation of the body; yea the actual and literal reuniting of the spirit with the body" (*CR, April 1917*). The ancient prophet Alma wrote: "The soul shall be restored to the body, and the body to the soul; yea, and every limb and joint shall be restored to its body; yea, even a hair of the head shall not be lost; but all things shall be restored to their proper and perfect frame" (*Alma 40:23*).

194. Will everyone be resurrected?

Yes, all earthlings will be resurrected. Daniel H. Ludlow specified: "The resurrection applies to every person who has ever lived or will ever live on this earth, without exception. Even those who becomes sons of perdition in the flesh will be resurrected (*see 1 Corinthians 15:22; Alma 11:44*)" (*SW, 264*).

Satan and the third part who rebelled in the premortal spirit world will not be resurrected because they never receive a body with which to be resurrected (*see EM, 381*).

195. Will all living things be resurrected, such as animals, insects, and plants?

Daniel H. Ludlow answered this question:

> Yes. The resurrection even applies to the earth itself (*see D&C 88:17-18, 25-26*) and to everything that has ever lived on this earth (*D&C 29:24-25*). Some leaders of the Church have suggested that the resurrection of Jesus Christ also applies to everything that has ever lived on any of the earths created by Jesus Christ (*SW, 265*).

The *Bible Dictionary* states: "Animals are resurrected from the dead, and there are animals in heaven, redeemed by the blood of Christ (*Revelation 5:11-14; D&C 77:3, HC 5:343*)" (*BD, 763*).

C.S. Lewis humorously commented about insects in the hereafter:

> Nor am I greatly moved by jocular inquires such as, "Where will you put all the mosquitoes?"—a question to be answered on its own level by pointing out that, if the worst came to worst, a heaven for mosquitoes and a hell for men could very conveniently be combined" (*The Problem of Pain, 140-141*).

196. By what power is the resurrection accomplished?

By the power of God and Jesus Christ. "God hath both raised up the Lord, and will also raise us up by his own power" (*1 Corinthians 6:14*). "For as in Adam all die, even so in Christ shall all be made alive" (*1 Corinthians 15:22*). The resurrection is like our mortal birth when God takes "man's spirit and put it into him" (*Abraham 5:7*): "Thus saith the Lord GOD unto these bones: Behold, I will cause breath to enter into you, and ye shall live" (*Ezekial 37:5*).

Brigham Young suggested the involvement of another person with priesthood keys: "Some person holding the keys of the resurrection, having previously passed through that ordeal, will be delegated to resurrect our bodies, and our spirits will be there and prepared to enter into their bodies" (*JD 9:139*).

Joseph F. Smith indicated there is effort on our part as well: "[As] Jesus, the Only Begotten of the Father . . . had power to lay down his life and take it up again . . . we too, in his name and through his redeeming blood, will have power in due time to resurrect these our bodies after they shall have been committed to the earth" (*JD 18:277*).

197. What is the first resurrection and second resurrection?

The first resurrection is for the just, heirs of the celestial and terrestrial kingdoms; and the second resurrection is for the unjust who go to the telestial kingdom or to perdition (*see #201*).

Daniel H. Ludlow clarified:

> The term "first resurrection" refers to the resurrection of the righteous or just. If a person is resurrected at the first opportunity he has to be resurrected after his death, then he comes forth in the morning of his first resurrection. The second resurrection refers to the resurrection of the wicked or unjust" (*SW, 268; see also John 5:28-29; Revelation 20; D&C 76*).

Therefore, the resurrection at the time of Christ is called a first resurrection, and the resurrection at his second coming is also a first resurrection.

198. When did the first general resurrection occur?

At the time Jesus Christ was resurrected. Jesus was "the first that should rise" from the grave (*2 Nephi 2:8*). Then, "the graves were opened; and many bodies of the saints which slept arose, And came out of the graves after his resurrection, and went into the holy city, and appeared unto many" (*Matthew: 27:52-53*). Also, in the Americas, the Book of Mormon records that "many saints did arise [from their graves] and appear unto many and did minister unto them" (*3 Nephi 23:11*). Parley P. Pratt wrote: "The first general resurrection took place in connection with the resurrection of Jesus Christ. This included the Saints and Prophets of both hemispheres, from Adam down to John the Baptist; or, in other words, all those who died in Christ before his resurrection" (*KST, 135*).

199. "Has there been a general resurrection since the resurrection of Jesus Christ?" (Daniel H. Ludlow)

"No. The next general resurrection will be at the time of the second coming of Jesus Christ" (Daniel H. Ludlow, *SW, 268*).

200. "Can a righteous person who has passed through the experience of temporal death be resurrected now if it is in keeping with the plan and purpose of our Heavenly Father for that person?" (Daniel H. Ludlow)

"Yes, if it is necessary for a specific person who died after the resurrection of Jesus Christ to be resurrected in order to perform a mission here on earth requiring a physical body, that person might be resurrected" (Daniel H. Ludlow, *SW, 268*).

Bruce R. McConkie wrote: "We have no knowledge that the resurrection is going on now or that any persons have been resurrected since the day in which Christ came forth excepting Peter, James, and Moroni, all of whom had special labors to perform in this day which necessitated tangible resurrected bodies" (*MD, 639*).

201. What is the order and timing of resurrections within the first and second resurrections which are to come?

Angels will sound trumps: the first two trumps as part of the first resurrection, the resurrection of the just; and the third and fourth trumps as part of the second resurrection, which is the last resurrection, or the resurrection of the unjust.

(a) ***First trump***. The morning of the first resurrection, when Christ comes in glory. "They are Christ's, the first fruits, they who shall descend with him first . . . They who have slept in their graves . . . who are first caught up to meet him." These are Saints qualifying for celestial glory (*see D&C 88:94-102*), and who will be resurrected and meet Him as He descends in glory.

(b) ***Second trump***. "And after this [the first trump] another angel shall sound, which is the second trump; and then cometh the redemption of those who are Christ's at his coming; who have received their part in that prison which is prepared for them, that they might receive the gospel, and be judged according to men in the flesh" (*D&C 88:99*). Bruce R. McConkie explained: "This is the *afternoon* of the first resurrection; it takes place after our Lord has ushered in the millennium. Those coming forth at that time do so with terrestrial bodies and are thus destined to inherit a terrestrial glory in eternity" (*MD, 640; see also D&C 76:71-80*). We don't know the length of the second trump resurrection except that it doesn't extend past the third trump.

(c) ***Third trump***. The second resurrection won't begin until the end of the millennium, which is not "until the thousand years are ended" (*D&C 88:101*). These are the wicked who will inherit a telestial glory (*see D&C 76:81-112*).

(d) ***Fourth trump.*** After the third trump, at the latter end of the second resurrection. This is for the sons of perdition, "who shall remain filthy still" (*D&C 88:102*), and who go to the second hell, or perdition, which is the second death.

202. Will the body be fully restored in the resurrection?

Yes. "The spirit and the body shall be reunited again in its perfect form; both limb and joint shall be restored to its proper frame . . . even there shall not so much as a hair of their heads be lost" (*Alma 11:43-44*); "every part of the body should be restored to itself" (*Alma 41:2*).

Brigham Young spoke specifically about this in general conference in 1875:

> Man's body may be buried in the ocean, it may be eaten by wild beasts, or it may be burned to ashes, they may be scattered to the four winds, yet the particles of which it is composed will not be incorporated into any form of vegetable or animal life, to become a component part of their structure . . . and at the sound of the trumpet of God every particle of our physical structures necessary to make our tabernacles perfect will be assembled, to be rejoined with the spirit, every man in his order. Not one particle will be lost (*Scrapbook of Mormon Literature 2:41*).

John Taylor said:

> It will be just as Ezekial [*Ezekial 37:1-14*] has described it—bone will come to its bone, and flesh and sinew will cover the skeleton, and at the Lord's bidding breath will enter the body, and we shall appear, many of us, a marvel to ourselves (*JD 18:333*).

203. "But some man will say, how are the dead raised up? and with what body do they come?" (*1 Corinthians 15:35*)

We will be resurrected with our own, physical, natural bodies, but they will be spiritual, or immortal. Paul referred to the resurrected body as "a spiritual body" (*1 Corinthians. 15:44*). The Lord likewise called this resurrected body that shall "also rise again, a spiritual body . . . the same body which was a natural body, even ye shall receive your bodies." This natural, but "spiritual body" will be "quickened" by the spirit, and "your glory shall be that glory by which your bodies are quickened" (*D&C 88:27,28*).

204. The scripture above states that in the resurrection we will receive our same, natural bodies. Is that literal?

Yes. The scriptures are consistent with this message: "Their sleeping dust was to be restored unto its perfect frame, bone to his bone, and the sinews and the flesh upon them" (*D&C 138:*17); "every part of the body should be restored to itself" (*Alma 41:2*). *Webster's 1828 Dictionary* defines "restored" as "brought back; retrieved; recovered; and re-established" (*AD*). Just as Jesus Christ was resurrected with the identical body he laid down, our same bodies will be brought back in the resurrection. Heber J. Grant said that in the pattern of Christ's resurrection "every man, woman, and child that ever lived shall come forth from the grave a resurrected being, even as Christ is a resurrected being" (*Millenial Star 99:395-396*). Joseph F. Smith said Christ is "the true type of the resurrection [and all] will rise from the dead . . . precisely as He did" (*Millenial Star 74:803*).

Resurrected bodies are the same physical bodies, except they will be restored to a perfect, immortal frame, with "spirit in their [veins] and not blood" (*WJS, 270; see also TPJS, 200*).

Even though a body may be decomposed, destroyed, or cremated, God can restore the elements. Dissolution is not permanent extinction. The primary elements in one's physical body are resurrected in that individual alone. Joseph Smith explained:

> There is no fundamental principle belonging to a human system that ever goes into another in this world or in the world to come; I care not what the theories of men are. We have the testimony that God will raise us up, and he has the power to do it. If anyone supposes that any part of our bodies, that is, the fundamental parts thereof, ever goes into another body, he is mistaken (*HC 5:339*).

Robert J. Matthews commented:

> It would be helpful if we had a more extensive explanation from the Prophet Joseph on what he meant by "fundamental parts." I have inter-

> preted this to mean that there is something in each cell of a person's body that is uniquely the property of the owner of the body; hence no matter what I eat, nothing else's fundamental parts ever become my fundamental parts, and no matter what becomes of my body, my fundamental parts never become the fundamental parts of any living organism (A *Bible! A Bible! 202).*

> If we do not get our *same* bodies in the resurrection and get other bodies instead, that is a type of reincarnation, which doctrinally we could not subscribe to. Such would also negate the concept of resurrection being a restoration, as in *Alma 11:43-45; 41:2-3* (*Selected Writings of Robert J. Matthews, 520*).

205. What is the condition of the body when it first rises from the dead?

Although there is some disagreement about just how perfected the body will be when if first comes forth from the grave, the predominant thinking today seems to indicate the resurrected body will come forth with its imperfections and some of the effects of age, young or old, when it died, apparently including certain physical defects, injuries, and scars. Over time, perhaps a short time, the imperfections will go away. The resurrected body is a spiritual body, without disease or sickness. Though imperfect when first coming forth from the grave, it is nonetheless glorified and beautiful.

Daniel H. Ludlow commented:

> The physical body will come forth from the grave as it is laid down, except that the blood will be replaced by spirit. Immediately after the resurrection, the physical body of an infant or child begins to grow further and the physical body of all resurrected beings begins to develop toward its perfect condition (*SW, 269*).

Joseph Smith taught that resurrected beings come forth as they died, but with a glorious body blossomed in radiant beauty:

> As concerning the resurrection, I will merely say that all men will come from the grave as they lie down, whether old or young; there will not be "added unto their stature one cubit," neither taken from it . . . having spirit in their bodies, and not blood (*TPJS, 199-200*). They must rise just as they died; we can there hail our lovely infants with the same glory—the same loveliness in the celestial glory, where they all enjoy alike. They differ in stature, in size, the same glorious spirit gives them the likeness of glory and bloom; the old man with his silvery hairs will glory in bloom and beauty. No man can describe it to you—no man can write it (*TPJS, 368*).

Joseph F. Smith was specific:

> What a glorious thought it is . . . that those from whom we have to part here, we will meet again and see as they are. We will meet the same identical being that we associated with here in the flesh—not some other soul, some other being . . . but the same identity and the same form and likeness, the same person we knew and were associated with in our mortal existence, even to the wounds in the flesh. Not that a person will always be marred by scars, wounds, deformities, defects or infirmities, for these will be removed in their course, in the proper time according to the merciful providence of God. Deformity will be removed; defects will be eliminated, and men and women shall attain to that perfection of their spirits, to the perfection that God designed in the beginning (*GD, 28-29*).

Robert J. Matthews elaborated on President Smith's statement:

> We note here that President Smith's statement that the body's scars, wounds, and deformities are still present at the moment of the resurrection is a strong argument in favor of the concept that the dead are raised with the very same bodies they had in mortality. Such wounds and scars would not be present if resurrected bodies were fashioned from new materials (*A Bible! A Bible! 203*).

Finally, Daniel H. Ludlow gave this thought-provoking perspective:

> [I] rejoice when I realize my body will come forth from the grave with its imperfections, for *then* after the resurrection my spirit can help my physical body overcome these defects and deformities. If I lay down a body with scars and imperfections, and yet resurrect a perfect body, who or what has been tampering with my physical body while it has been in the grave and while my spirit has been away from it in the postmortal spirit world? (*SW, 270*)

206. Has anyone seen the resurrection in a vision?

Yes. Joseph Smith had amazing visions and understanding of the resurrection described in the following passages (*see also Joseph Smith quote at #205, TPJS, 368*):

> So plain was the vision, that I actually saw men, before they had ascended from the tomb, as though they were getting up slowly. They took each other by the hand and said to each other, "My father, my son, my mother, my daughter, my brother, my sister." And when the voice calls for the dead to arise, suppose I am laid by the side of my father, what would be the first joy of my heart? To meet my father, my mother, my brother, my sister; and when they are by my side, I embrace them and they me (*HC 5:362*).

> God has revealed His Son from the heavens and the doctrine of the resurrection also; and we have a knowledge that those we bury here God will bring up again, clothed upon and quickened by the Spirit of the great God; and what mattereth it whether we lay them down . . . Let these truths sink down in our hearts, that we may even here begin to enjoy that which shall be in full hereafter (*TPJS, 296*).

> All your losses will be made up to you in the resurrection, provided you continue faithful. By the vision of the Almighty I have seen it (TPJS, 296).

In 1835 Wilford Woodruff had a vision of the resurrection of the dead not knowing whether he was in or out of the body: "In the first resurrection those that came forth from their graves seemed to be all dressed alike, but in the second resurrection they were as diverse in their dress as this congregation . . . (*Discourses of Wilford Woodruff, 284*).

207. Is the resurrection a type of judgment?

Yes. Daniel H. Ludlow summarized why: "at the time of resurrection, each will come forth with a body that is particular to one of the degrees of glory or one without glory. Thus the resurrection might be considered a type of judgment" (*SW, 273*).

Elder Melvin J. Ballard described the differences in resurrected bodies: "Those who come forth in the celestial glory with celestial bodies have a body that is more refined. It is different. The very fibre and texture of the celestial body is more pure and holy than a telestial or terrestrial body, and a celestial body alone can endure celestial glory" (Hinckley, *Sermons and Missionary Services of Melvin Joseph Ballard, 256*).

There may even be a difference among celestial bodies. For example, only souls to be exalted, those in the celestial kingdom's highest degree, will have bodies capable of procreation (*see D&C 132*).

208. Are we approaching the time of the latter-day first resurrection?

Yes. That is what the prophets have told us. In the 1920s, Elder Orson F. Whitney often said we are in the Saturday evening of time:

> According to received chronology—admittedly imperfect, yet approximately correct—four thousand years, or four of the seven great days given to this planet as the period of its "temporal existence," had passed before Christ was crucified; while nearly two thousand years have gone by since. Consequently, Earth's long week is now drawing to a close, and we stand at the present moment in the Saturday Evening of Time, at or near the end of the sixth day of human history. Is it not a time for thought, a season for solemn meditation?" (*Saturday Night Thoughts, 12*).

Other prophets have used this term, including N. Eldon Tanner: "I plead with all of us today, in the Saturday evening of time, to make it a priority to remember who we are" (*Ensign, January 1983*).

Compared to the eons of time we lived before we came to earth, there isn't much time before the second coming and the latter-day first resurrection. While we can't predict the timing, we are warned to be ready and watchful. Consider as merely an illustration and not speculation, that if an evening starts at 6 pm, then Saturday evening to midnight is 214 years when extrapolated from 6000 years. Whether it is 50, 100, or 200 years or more until Christ comes, it doesn't really matter for this discussion. The point is that the comparative briefness is sobering, considering our eternal judgment at stake.

For many if not most of us, our next critical judgment day will be death (*#115*), not the second coming. Death is likely within the next 80 years for those who read these words. That's not really very long. Neal A. Maxwell reminded us: "One's life, therefore, is brevity compared to eternity—like being dropped off by a parent for a day at school. But what a day! (*Ensign, November 1985*).

CHAPTER NINETEEN

MINISTERING BEINGS

Or have angels ceased to appear unto the children of men? . . .
Behold I say unto you, Nay
—Moroni 7:36-37

209. What types of beings visit and minister on the earth?

Gods, resurrected beings, translated beings, premortal spirits (unembodied spirits), and postmortal spirits (disembodied spirits) (*see #88, #210, #211, #216, #218*).

210. What are angels?

"Ordinarily the word angel means those ministering persons who have a body of flesh and bone, being either resurrected from the dead (reembodied), or else translated, as were Enoch, Elijah, etc" (*BD, 608*). Joseph Smith taught that generally angels "are resurrected personages, having bodies of flesh and bones" (*D&C 129:1*). "A person who is a divine messenger is called an angel. Thus Moroni, John the Baptist, Peter, James, John, Moses, Elijah, and Elias all ministered to Joseph Smith as angels" (*BD, 608*). Sometimes the Lord uses unembodied spirits, disembodied spirits or mortals as angels to carry out his purposes. Elder Jeffrey Holland said: "My beloved brothers and sisters, I testify of angels, both the heavenly and the mortal kind . . . may we all try to be a little more angelic ourselves—with a kind word, a strong arm, a declaration of faith . . ." (*CR, October 2008*).

The Lord promised us: "I will go before your face. I will be on your right hand and on your left, and my Spirit shall be in your hearts, and mine angels round about you, to bear you up" (*D&C 84:88*).

211. What is the difference between an angel and a ministering spirit?

Joseph Smith said:

> There are two kinds of beings in heaven, namely: Angels, who are resurrected personages, having bodies of flesh and bones—For instance, Jesus said; *Handle me and see, for a spirit hath not flesh and bones, as ye see me have.* Secondly: the spirits of just men made perfect, they who are not resurrected, but inherit the same glory (*D&C 129:1-3*).

Just men made perfect are disembodied spirits in paradise who are ministering spirits (*see #129*).

Joseph Smith explained that typically angels minister to embodied beings (mortals or resurrected persons) while deceased spirits minister to other deceased spirits. Apparently many of the numerous angels who visited and taught Joseph Smith were resurrected beings.

> The [angel is] a resurrected or translated body . . . ministering to embodied spirits—the other a disembodied spirit, visiting and ministering to disembodied spirits. Jesus Christ became a ministering spirit (while His body was lying in the sepulcher) to the spirits in prison . . . After His resurrection He appeared as an angel to His disciples . . .[i.e.,] Jesus Christ went in body after His resurrection, to minister to resurrected bodies (*HC 4:425*).

Sometimes ministering spirits (deceased, disembodied spirits) also minister to mortals. These ministering spirits are sometimes called angels. For example, the angel Gabriel (the disembodied Noah, *HC 3:386*) ministered to Daniel (*see Daniel 8:16, 9:21*), and then approximately 600 years later to Zacharias and Mary (*see Luke 1:11-19; 26-38*). Gabriel wasn't resurrected until after Christ's resurrection, Christ being first to rise from dead (*see 2 Nephi 2:*8). The angel Michael (Adam) comforted

Daniel (*Daniel 10:13, 21*). Joseph F. Smith said the "ancient prophets who died were those who came to Abraham, to Isaac, and to Jacob" (*GD, 548*). We have numerous reports of communications from ministering spirits to mortals in these latter-days (*see #85*).

212. What do angels look like?

They have bodies of flesh and bones. They are resurrected with a visible celestial glory. Joseph Smith described the angel Moroni: "Not only was his robe exceedingly white, but his whole person was glorious beyond description, and his countenance truly like lightning. The room was exceedingly light, but not so very bright as immediately around his person" (*JS-History 1:32*).

Joseph Smith taught: "An angel of God never has wings" (*TPJS, 162*). However, the Lord uses the symbolism of wings. Joseph Fielding Smith explained that cherubim and seraphim "are terms that are sometimes applied to angels" (*AGQ 2:96*). In reference to the wings of seraphs described in the Revelation of John (*Revelation 5:6*) the Lord said "their wings are a representation of power, to move, to act, etc" (*D&C 77:4*). Isaiah referred to seraphims with wings (*see Isaiah 6:2*). Ezekial had a vision of cherubims with wings (*see Ezekial 10:21*). The images in Solomon's Temple are cherubs with wings (*see 1 Kings 6:21-23*). The Ark of the Covenant was fashioned with cherubims with wings covering the mercy seat (*see Exodus 25:20*).

Joseph Fielding Smith elaborated:

> The cherubim . . . were placed there as symbolic figures, representing guardians, whose wings protected the altar. These, like the figures seen by Ezekiel, were symbolic, not necessarily living beings, and by them the Lord was teaching Ezekiel a lesson in relation to his mission to Israel. The same is true in relation to the several beasts seen by the Revelator John. All of these visions by symbolic representation had something to do with history which the Lord was revealing, the full meaning of which has not been made clear to our understanding (*AGQ 2:97*).

213. Where do resurrected angels live?

After they are resurrected, they leave the spirit world and reside in a world of resurrected beings. "The angels do not reside on a planet like this earth; But they reside in the presence of God" (*D&C 130:6-7; see #78*). Resurrected angels may visit the earth or the spirit world as the Lord requires (see #*78*).

214. What are translated beings?

The *Encyclopedia of Mormonism* defines these individuals as beings who are:

> changed from a mortal state to one in which they are temporarily not subject to death, and in which they experience neither pain nor sorrow except for the sins of the world . . . Resurrection is a step beyond translation, and persons translated prior to the resurrection of Christ [such as Moses, Elijah, Alma, Enoch, and Zion's inhabitants] were resurrected with him (*see D&C 133:54-55*); it is expected that those translated since Christ's resurrection will be resurrected at his second coming (*EM, 1485*).

Translated beings will be "changed in the twinkling of an eye" to a resurrected state (*3 Nephi 28:8*).

215. Where is the habitation of translated beings?

Some translated beings, such as John the Revelator and the Three Nephites have a calling to minister among mortals on earth until the second coming (*see #216*). Others, such as Enoch and the inhabitants of his city of righteousness were taken up by God to an unknown terrestrial habitation until their resurrection.

Joseph Smith elaborated on their location:

> Many have supposed that the doctrine of translation was a doctrine whereby men were taken immediately into the presence of God, and into an eternal fulness, but this is a mistaken idea. Their place of habita-

> tion is that of the terrestrial order, and a place prepared for such characters He held in reserve to be ministering angels unto many planets, and who as yet have not entered into so great a fulness as those who are resurrected from the dead (*TPJS, 170*).

The Lord showed Enoch that "Zion, in process of time, was taken up into heaven" (*Moses 7:21*). These resurrected beings are in the heavens now. Bruce R. McConkie taught: "It will be resurrected, not translated beings, who shall return with the city of Enoch" (*MD, 808*).

216. Which translated beings are not yet resurrected?

These are the translated beings we know of that are still ministering on earth or other planets:

(a) ***John the Revelator*** (Matthew 16:28; John 21:21-23; D&C 7; 3 Nephi 28:6-8).

(b) ***The Three Nephites*** (3 Nephi 28:1-23).

(c) ***Some who were with Jesus*** "There be some standing here which shall not taste of death, till they see the Son of man coming in his kingdom" (*Matthew 16:28*).

(d) ***Possible others*** "which I have reserved unto myself, holy men that ye know not of." (*D&C 49:8*).

217. Do we have communication with premortal spirits?

Yes. Scriptural evidence establishes the precedence. Jehovah, the premortal Jesus Christ who was the God of the Old Testament (*see BD, 710*), visited the earth frequently as a premortal spirit (*see GD, 549*). Also, an "angel of the Lord appeared unto Adam, saying: Why dost thou offer sacrifices unto the Lord?"'(*Moses 5:6*). Perhaps this angel was a premortal spirit because Adam was the first mortal man on earth and there were no other mortals, translated, or resurrected beings associated with this earth that we know of, besides God, at this early time.

Joseph Fielding Smith said the cherubim

> that guarded the way to the tree of life were angels. Evidently faithful personages belonging to this world who had not, at the time, received the privilege of partaking of mortality, for the Lord revealed to the Prophet Joseph Smith that "there are no angels who minister to this earth but those who do belong to it" (*D&C 130:5*) (*AQC, 97*).

We know far more about the postmortal spirit world than the premortal spirit world. Evidently in His wisdom the Lord arranged a stronger veil between the premortal and mortal worlds because communication with premortal spirits is apparently rare.

218. Which postmortal spirits minister to mortals?

Disembodied spirits are sometimes allowed or called to help mortals. Among these are: "the spirits of just men made perfect, they who are not resurrected, but inherit the same glory" (*D&C 129:3*). Apparently these spirits are those who died and entered paradise and will eventually be exalted and "made perfect through Jesus the mediator of the new covenant" (*D&C 76:69*).

Joseph Smith remarked on the demise of James Adams: "Patriarch Adams is now one of the spirits of the just men made perfect . . . [Such] spirits can only be revealed in flaming fire and glory. Angels have advanced further, their light and glory being tabernacled; and hence they appear in bodily shape" (*HC 6:51*). "Brother Adams has gone to open up a more effectual door for the dead. The spirits of the just are exalted to a greater and more glorious work; hence they are blessed in their departure to the world of spirits" (*HC, 52*).

Parley P. Pratt described these spirits who are sometimes granted permission to contact mortals:

> The good spirits, in the superlative sense of the word, are they who, in this life, partook of the Holy Priesthood, and of the fulness of the gospel.

> This class of spirits minister to the heirs of salvation, both in this world and in the world of spirits. They can appear unto men, when permitted; but not having a fleshly tabernacle, they cannot hide their glory. Hence, an unembodied spirit, if it be a holy personage, will be surrounded with a halo of resplendent glory . . . (*KST, 118*). (*See also #38.*)

George Q. Cannon said: "A just man made perfect, who has not received the resurrection, if he appears, will be seen in his glory; for that is the only way he can appear (*Gospel Truth, 56*).

Elder Melvin J. Ballard said:

> I am sure that our departed loved ones are near us, and belong to this sphere; yet they have difficulty in talking to us. We sometimes wish we could meet them, shake their hands, and counsel with them, although they operate in another world—I suppose there is a good reason why we cannot. There must be some law which prevents the law-abiding spirit from talking with man in the flesh . . . but the law-abiding spirits abide the law under which they dwell and do not come unless there is some very good reason, and special permission given; and occasionally that permission is granted" (*Crusader for Righteousness, 271*).

Latter-day Saint annals contain numerous stories of returning spirits to visit loved ones (*e.g., see Appendix* B). Joseph F. Smith, speaking at the funeral of Elizabeth H. Cannon, and referring to Jesus' mission after death said:

> In like manner our fathers and mothers, brothers, sisters and friends who have passed away from this earth, having been faithful, and worthy to enjoy these rights and privileges, may have a mission given them to visit their relatives and friends upon the earth again, bringing from the divine Presence messages of love, of warning, of reproof and instruction, to those whom they had learned to love in the flesh. And so it is with Sister Cannon. She can return and visit her friends, provided it be in accordance with the wisdom of the Almighty. There are laws to which

they who are in the Paradise of God must be subject, as well as laws to which we are subject (*GD, 549*). (*See also #36 and #85.*)

219. For what purpose do postmortal spirits visit mortals?

Jeffrey Holland described the purposes of angels and divine messengers, affirming that the day of miracles has not ceased (*see Moroni 7:29-30; 35-37*). Summarizing Elder Holland's words, they sometimes come to teach, counsel, guide, or warn. But most often they convey love and provide comfort or some form of merciful attention in difficult times. They reassure us of God's care. Usually such beings are not seen. Sometimes they are. But seen or unseen they are always near. Assignments may be grand and have world-wide significance or the messages may be private (*see CR, October 2008*). (*See also #36.*)

We read stories of spirits who attend funerals (such as their own) and other meetings or events. Spirits may come to prepare the dying for death or accompany them to the spirit world. At times, they serve as guardian angels to mortals as Wilford Woodruff said: "these men who have died and gone into the spirit world had this mission left with them, that is, a certain portion of them to watch over the Latter-day Saints" (*JD 21:318*).

Heber Q. Hale, from the vantage point of the spirit world, was "permitted to view the earth and what was going on here." He saw his wife and children at home; and he saw the current President of the Church at the time, Heber J. Grant. He gave his opinion about permission required in the spirit world to view earthly activities:

> There came to me the unmistakable impression that this earth and scenes and persons upon it are open to the vision of the spirits only when special permission is given or when they are assigned to special service here. This is particularly true of the righteous who are busily engaged in two fields of activity at the same time (*HQH, 3*).

President Wilford Woodruff actually put in a request to attend his own funeral in his last will and testament: "If the laws and customs of the spirit world will permit, I should wish to attend my funeral myself, but I shall be governed by the counsel I receive in the spirit world" (*Wilford Woodruff, History of His Life and Letters, 622*).

220. Do postmortal spirits who are not from paradise appear to mortals?

Yes. There are numerous reported instances where unbaptized spirits have appeared to mortals, such as to request that their temple work be done. For example, George Washington and the signers of the Declaration of Independence appeared to Wilford Woodruff for that purpose (*see Appendix B10; see also #85*). The Lord may assign spirits to watch over his children or convey messages according to his purposes. There are many reports of after-death communications from deceased loved-ones among people of all walks of life (*see #36*).

CHAPTER TWENTY

CELESTIAL MUSINGS

Press forward, Saints, with steadfast faith in Christ
With hope's bright flame alight in heart and mind,
With love of God and love of all mankind.
Alleluia! Alleluia! Alleluia!
—Marvin K. Gardner, Press Forward, Saints, Hymns, 81

221. What do we know about the celestial kingdom?

John the Revelator saw in vision the future celestial earth set in a "new heaven" (*Revelation 21:1*). He saw Jesus Christ and the "great white throne" (*20:11*) of God the Father (*3:21*). The dead are judged "according to their works" out of the "book of life" (*20:12*) which can only be opened by Jesus Christ (*5:6*). John saw the exalted saints, "clothed in white raiment" (*3:5*) singing and harping praises (*14:2-3*) and participating in the "marriage supper of the Lamb" (*19:9*). John viewed one hundred million and "thousands of thousands" (*5:11*) of angels praising the Lamb. A celestial city of exquisite beauty is described with walls of precious stones (*21:19*), pearly gates (*21:21*), and streets of pure gold (*21:21*). There is "no need of the sun" because "the glory of God did lighten it, and the Lamb is the light thereof" (*21:23*). This glory is described by Isaiah as "everlasting burnings" (*Isaiah 33:14*).

Joseph Smith received these revelations describing the celestial kingdom:

> I beheld the celestial kingdom of God . . . I saw the transcendent beauty of the gate through which the heirs of that kingdom will enter, which was like unto circling flames of fire; Also the blazing throne of God,

> whereon was seated the Father and the Son. I saw the beautiful streets of that kingdom, which had the appearance of being paved with gold (*D&C 137:1-4*).

> This earth, in its sanctified and immortal state, will be made like unto crystal and will be a Urim and Thummim to the inhabitants who dwell thereon, whereby all things pertaining to an inferior kingdom . . . will be manifest to those who dwell on it; and this earth will be Christ's. Then the white stone mentioned in *Revelation 2:17*, will become a Urim and Thummim to each individual who receives one, whereby things pertaining to a higher order of kingdoms will be made known (*D&C 130: 9-10*).

222. How limited is our knowledge about heaven and the celestial kingdom?

Joseph Smith described just how limited our knowledge is:

> Could we read and comprehend all that has been written from the days of Adam, on the relation of man to God and angels in a future state, we should know very little about it. Reading the experience of others, or the revelation given to *them*, can never give *us* a comprehensive view of our condition and true relation to God. Knowledge of these things can only be obtained by experience through the ordinances of God set forth for that purpose. Could you gaze into heaven five minutes, you would know more than you would by reading all that ever was written on the subject (*HC 6:50*).

In his marvelous discourse on the three degrees of glory, the Apostle, Melvin J. Ballard said:

> Do you comprehend it, you who gain celestial glory, the privilege of dwelling in the presence of God and his Christ forever and ever? What did it mean to have in the world, during his ministry, for three brief years the Lord Jesus Christ—not the Father, just the Son? It was the most wonderful privilege the world has ever had. What would you give tonight for the privilege of standing in the presence of the Son for five

minutes? You would give all your earthly possessions for that privilege. Then can you comprehend the full meaning and significance of the statement that those who gain celestial glory will have the privilege of dwelling in the presence of the Father and the Son forever and ever? That, in itself, will be reward enough for the struggle to obtain the prize. Yea, it is beyond price and earthly possessions. Even the giving of life itself would be a trifle for the privilege to dwell forever and ever in the presence of the Father and the Son (Hinckley, *Sermons and Missionary Services of Melvin Joseph Ballard, 242*).

CHAPTER TWENTY-ONE

SO WHAT NOW?

Come, let us anew our journey pursue
—Charles Wesley, Come Let Us Anew, Hymns, 217

223. How can we prepare for the spirit world?

How did Jesus counsel us to handle mortality? He said, "Wherefore, be not weary in well-doing for ye are laying the foundation of a great work. And out of small things proceedeth that which is great" (*D&C 64:33*). Small acts of service matter to Jesus. Consider the poor widow's two mites (*Mark 12:43*). Jesus said, "Inasmuch as ye have done it unto one of the least of these my brethren, ye have done it unto me" *(Matthew 25:40*). The small positive efforts we make daily will help us become more Christlike and better prepare us for the hereafter. Little actions can carry great impact: "by very small means the Lord doth confound the wise and bringeth about the salvation of many souls" (*Alma 37:6-7*). What small things can we do? We can give compliments, encourage others, express thanks, be more aware and notice things, call someone to see how they are doing, listen more, give to the poor, be more interested in strangers and acquaintances, and follow impulses to serve even in small ways.

One near-death experiencer who had lived selfishly found his life review "nauseating" to watch, but he saw a few positive moments: "I got to see, when my sister had a bad night one night, how I went into her bedroom and put my arms around her. I didn't say anything. I just lay there with my arms around her. As it turned out, that experience was one of the biggest triumphs of my life" (Gibson, *Glimpses of Eternity, 281*).

Surely all of our righteous endeavors, no matter how small spread love and goodwill and count in the eyes of our Maker. With a bit of effort, little acts of service can become second nature, helping us lose our lives in service. Jesus said: "He who seeketh to save his life shall lose it; and he who loseth his life for my sake shall find it" (*Matthew 10:34 JST*). David Dunn wrote a wonderful book about the importance of little warm-hearted impulses. He said they are as important as the big ones—more important in a way, for they help you to form the habit of giving yourself away (*Try Giving Yourself Away, 10*).

224. What motivation can we glean from our kindred dead in the spirit world?

Monte Nyman reminded us about our duty: "May we be diligent both in preaching the gospel here upon the earth and in finding the names of our departed dead and performing the vicarious ordinances for them so they can live in the paradise until the Resurrection" (*The Book of Mormon: Alma, the Testimony of the Word, 193*).

225. What are our greatest responsibilities in mortality?

President Gordon B. Hinckley (in 2003) and Elder L. Tom Perry (in 2006) specified our four responsibilities:

"First, we have a responsibility to our families. It is imperative that you not neglect your families. Nothing you have is more precious."

"Second, we have a responsibility to our employers. Be honest with your employer."

"Third, we have a responsibility to the Lord's work. Budget your time to take care of your Church responsibilities."

"Fourth, we have a responsibility to ourselves. Every Church leader has an obligation to himself. He [she] must get needed rest and exercise. He needs a little recreation. He must have time to study" (*Worldwide Leadership Training Meeting, June 2003 and February 2006*).

Apparently our paramount responsibility to family extends to our kindred dead. Joseph Smith said as much and prophets since have quoted him: "The greatest responsibility in this world that God has laid upon us is to seek after our dead" (*HC 6:313*). "This doctrine was the burden of the scriptures. Those Saints who neglect it in behalf of their deceased relatives, do it at the peril of their own salvation" (*HC 4:426*). Paul said "that they without us should not be made perfect (*Hebrews 11:40*).

President Hinckley said that in mortality: "None of us will accomplish all we might wish to. But let us do the best we can. I am satisfied that the Redeemer will then say, 'Well done, thou good and faithful servant' (*Matthew 25:21*)" (*Worldwide Leadership Training, June 2003*).

226. What is a person's most important time in eternity?

Joseph Fielding Smith declared: "This life is the most vital period in our eternal existence" (*DS 1:69*).

Bruce R. McConkie echoed this counsel:

> In a very real and literal sense the life that we are now living is the final examination for that infinite period of preparation that we had in the premortal life. Now if we do not respond as we ought to respond . . . then in effect we are throwing away all of the preparation that we made in the premortal life . . . Now this life is not only the final examination for the life, the eternity, that went before, but this mortal probation is an entrance examination to determine the sphere, and the place, and the kingdom and the reward that we will have that are in the mansions ahead . . . In a very real and definite sense, that singles out this mortal probation as the most important part of all eternity (*Official Report of the Brisbane Area Conference, February 29 and March 1, 1976, 15*).

227. What is our great test in mortality?

President Ezra Taft Benson said: "The great task of life is to learn the will of the Lord and then do it" (*Ensign, May 1988*). What does He want us to do? Repent! Someone said the most important commandment is the one we're not keeping. After the Lord had driven Adam and Eve from Eden, he commanded: "thou shalt repent and call upon God in the name of the Son forevermore" (*Moses 5:8*). Among the Lord's first words when he appeared to the Nephites were: "This is my doctrine . . . that the Father commandeth all men, everywhere, to repent" (*3 Nephi 11:32*). In Jesus' parable of the rich man and Lazarus, what message did the rich man in hell want to send to his five brothers? To repent! (*Luke 16:19-31*).

Hugh Nibley, speaking on repentance at his friend's funeral, said:

> This is not a popular doctrine. In my thirty-five years at BYU, I have heard only one sermon (given by Stephen L. Richards, incidentally) on repentance. And it was not well received. "Don't tell us to repent. Repentance is for the bad guys."The test for this life is not for knowledge; it is not for intelligence, or for courage, or for anything like that. That would be a huge joke. None of us knows very much, none of us is very brave, none of us is very strong, none of us is very smart. We would flunk those tests terribly. Alma said, we are only to be tested on one thing—the desires of our heart (*Alma 41:3*); that is what we are really after . . . You yourself can see your own life; you can test yourself. Thus we don't need to go on forever suffering the same nonsense in order to see the things we can be tested for, namely the two things and the only two things we are good at: we can forgive and we can repent. These are the two things the angels envy us for, as the church fathers said[xiii]. . . All must repent constantly, each for himself. *Ezekiel 33:18-19* defines a righteous man. Who is righteous? Anyone who is repenting. No matter how bad he has been, if he is repenting he is a righteous man. There is hope for him. And no matter how good he has been all his life, if he is not repenting, he is a wicked man . . . The direction we are facing, that is repentance; and that is what determines whether we are good or bad. (*CWHN 9:300-302*).

President Thomas S. Monson said: "One day, each of us will run out of tomorrows. Let us not put off what is important" (*Ensign, May 2003*).

228. What is the process of constant repentance?

It is the same process after baptism as before baptism. The key is to keep doing it.

Hugh Nibley explained:

> Do what Peter tells us to do: Have faith that there is more than you know; repent of all your present shallowness and silliness; wash off everything of this world in the waters of baptism, and be reborn, not in the self congratulatory one-shot manner of pop religion, but to a course of action requiring perpetual, progressive repentance. Then "ye shall receive the gift of the Holy Ghost" and get all the guidance you need (*Acts 2:38*). [It's] perpetual repentance . . . until you are full of grace and truth, which is nowhere within the foreseeable future. Meanwhile, "an unexamined life is not worth living," as Socrates said (*CWHN 9:283*).

The prophet King Benjamin said one can retain "a remission of your sins from day to day, that ye may walk guiltless before God" (*Mosiah 4:26*). Because none of us is perfect, we need to repent daily. Brigham Young gave the "secret" for living in this constant state of guiltlessness and worthiness: "if you commit an overt act, repent of that immediately, and call upon God to deliver you from evil and give you the light of His Spirit . . . If I commit an overt act, the Lord knows the integrity of my heart, and, through sincere repentance, He forgives me" (*JD 12:103*).

George Q. Cannon said:

> Now, how much better it is for us, while this day of probation lasts and while God gives us life and power and opportunities, to live according to the laws of God, so that every day our sins will be remitted. Let us confess our sins to our Father every day, and if we have sinned against our brethren and sisters, obtain forgiveness of them. Then, when the hour of death approaches, no matter where it may find us, we shall be

found prepared to enter into the presence of our God" (*Gospel Truth, 62*).

229. Is it easier to repent now than in the spirit world?

Yes. Elder Melvin J. Ballard gave us this valuable admonition:

> But this life is the time in which men are to repent. Do not let any of us imagine that we can go down to the grave not having overcome the corruptions of the flesh and then lose in the grave all our sins and evil tendencies. They will be with us. They will be with the spirit when separated from the body.
>
> It is my judgment that any man or woman can do more to conform to the laws of God in one year in this life than they could do in ten years when they are dead . . . It is much easier to overcome and serve the Lord when both flesh and spirit are combined as one. This is the time when men are more pliable and susceptible. When clay is pliable it is much easier to change than when it gets hard and sets.
>
> This life is the time to repent. That is why I presume it will take a thousand years after the first resurrection until the last group will be prepared to come forth. It will take them a thousand years to do what it would have taken, but three score years and ten to accomplish in this life.
>
> Then, every man and woman who is putting off until the next life the task of correcting and overcoming the weakness of the flesh are sentencing themselves to years of bondage, for no man or woman will come forth in the resurrection until he has completed his work, until he has overcome, until he has done as much as he can do (Bryant S. Hinckley, *Sermons and Missionary Services of Melvin J. Ballard, 241-42*).

230. Can we be successful in our quest for exaltation?

Yes! We can if we want to succeed. Elder Dallin H. Oaks said: "We are accustomed to thinking that our actions make us what we are. But since our actions are stimulated by our desires, it is more accurate to say that our desires make us what we are" (*Pure in Heart, 51*). He quoted Bruce C. Hafen: "Not only will the righteous desires of our hearts be granted, but also the unrighteous desires of our hearts. Over the long run, our most deeply held desires will govern our choices, one by one and day by day, until our lives finally add up to what we have really wanted" (*The Believing Heart, 26*).

So how do we shape our desires? "Let this desire work within you" (*Alma 32:27*). Ponder the possibilities. Imagine the light and love in the spirit world. Pray for the desire. Elder Oaks said: "When we have a vision of what we can become, our desire and our power to act increase enormously" (*CR, April 2011*).

God designed the plan so we can achieve exaltation. He declared: "For behold, this is my work and my glory—to bring to pass the immortality and eternal life of man" (*Moses 1:39*). In his book, *Odds Are, You're Going to be Exalted, Evidence that the Plan of Salvation Works,* Alonzo L. Gaskill reminds us of "each individual's potential and ability through the atonement of Christ to achieve *all* that God has in mind for us" (*Book Jacket*). Contemplate the simple, but persuasive words of the inspired hymn by Reid N. Nibley:

I Know My Father Lives

I know my Father lives
And loves me too.
The Spirit whispers this to me
and tells me it is true,
And tells me it true.
He sent me here to earth,
By faith to live his plan.
The Spirit whispers this to me
and tells me that I can,
And tells me that I can.
—Hymns, 302

APPENDIX A

SELECTED VISITATIONS TO THE SPIRIT WORLD

1. Samuel Turnbow's spirit left his body and he embraced his deceased wife in the spirit world. Then a man gave Turnbow the names of over one-hundred relatives and told him that he must return to his body and do the work for them. When he came back, he asked his son to write the names. Later he learned from a cousin that the names and relationships were correct *(Genealogical and Blessing Book of Samuel Turnbow with a Brief Sketch of His Life, 1804-1876, 25).*

2. John Peterson, from Mt. Pleasant, Utah had a near-death experience in 1857 at age 22 while in Gottenberg, Sweden where he had recently joined the Church. He spent approximately five hours in the spirit world before returning. He saw the ancient Apostle, Matthias, who replaced Judas Iscariot, and the martyred Parley P. Pratt in the spirit world preaching to a congregation. Peterson noted there was no hand shaking, just head nodding in the spirit world. Matthias asked him: "Would you as soon go back . . . to redeem your forefathers?" John Peterson had been ill with consumption and replied that his lungs were gone. Matthias replied that he would be healed because "it is easy to grow new lungs in a man." John agreed to return and regained his health shortly thereafter *(Juvenile Instructor, October 15, 1906, 4:20, 609-610).*

3. Michelle Sorenson was a teenager when her heart stopped as a result of a serious infection. Her spirit left her body, and from above she observed the frantic activity of her family. A spirit messenger told her she was dead and asked if she wanted to be dead. She was hesitant to go back because she had been relieved of the pain and enjoyed the light and love she experienced out of her body. The

messenger told her to look at what she would miss. She then had a vision of a tall blond man walking with two children, a boy and a girl. She recognized them as being her future family. "Yes, I want to go back" she said. Then she returned to her body. Michelle later married a tall, blond former basketball player and they had two children, a boy and a girl (Melvin Morse, MD, *Closer to the Light, 122-123).*

4. Mitchell Dalton died at age 11 in 1895. Mitchell's father was the Manassa, Colorado Ward Bishop. His father begged and prayed to God to let his boy live. He came back to life and asked, "Oh, Papa and Mama, why did you call me back. I have been to such a beautiful place." People came from far and near to hear him tell of the marvelous things he had seen. His father held him constantly in his arms because he was so weak. Finally, Mitchell looked up into his father's eyes and said, "Papa, may I go now?" His father replied, "Yes, Mitchell," then he immediately died. Mitchell's experience was a powerful testimony of the life hereafter for many in the community *(Deseret News Church Section, December 5, 1931, 3).*

5. Spencer W. Kimball wrote about his uncle's visit to the spirit world:

   > My uncle, David Patten Kimball, left his home in Arizona on a trip across the Salt River desert. He had fixed up his books and settled accounts and had told his wife of a premonition that he would not return. He was lost on the desert for two days and three nights, suffering untold agonies of thirst and pain. He passed into the spirit world and described later, in a letter of January 8, 1882, to his sister, what happened there. He had seen his parents. "My father . . . told me I could remain there if I chose to do so, but I pleaded with him that I might stay with my family long enough to make them comfortable, to repent of my sins, and more fully prepare myself for the change. Had it not been for this, I never should have returned home, except as a corpse. Father finally told me I could remain two years and to do all the good I could during that time, after which he would come for me . . . He mentioned four others that he would come for also . . . " Two years to the day from that experience on the desert he died easily and apparently without pain. Shortly before he died he

looked up and called, "Father, Father." Within approximately a year of his death the other four men named were also dead *(TD, 10-11).*

6. When an NDE is corroborated by another, it's an extraordinary event. The Apostle Rudger Clawson told the story about the Apostle Marriner W. Merrill (first president of the Logan Temple) who was ill when he was called to administer to a bedridden young woman. They both died, met and conversed with each other and others in the spirit world, and then returned. They both remembered the incidents *(Related by J. Berkeley Larsen to the BYU student body, in "The Reality of Life After Death," BYU Speeches, Oct. 6, 1953).*

7. Hugh Nibley had a near-death experience in 1936 at the age of 26. The story as told in Nibley's biography is summarized here. The desperate times of the depression had left Nibley depressed, which led him to see "certain flaws in the gospel," as he put it; "I was terribly bothered about this afterlife business and that sort of thing. I had no evidence for that whatever." He heard Matthias F. Cowley speak at a sacrament meeting. After the meeting, Hugh's mother took him to the front of the meeting hall to meet Brother Cowley. "As soon as he took my hand, he said, 'come with me,' Hugh says. "He took me into the back room there and he said, 'I want to give you a blessing.'" In the blessing, Cowley said the Lord knew his questions and "would give me an answer immediately."

   Within the week, Hugh contracted appendicitis and taken to the hospital. When the ether was turned on, Hugh "swallowed his tongue and stopped breathing." The resuscitator was nowhere to be found by the hospital staff. Nibley reports:

   > I remembered Socrates, the turning cold of the feet, icy, incredibly cold, and it got higher, higher, and higher, and (pause) I couldn't believe anything could get that cold. Absolute numbness, absolute nothing, but curiosity all the time. Something big's going to happen, and sure enough. Then, pop! Then it happened. Then all of a sudden, down this thing like a tube . . . and you come out . . . Boy, I know everything, everything is there and this is what I wanted to know, three

> cheers and all this sort of thing, and I started solving problems . . . but all I wanted to know was whether there was anything on the other side; and when I came out there, I didn't meet anything or anybody else, but I looked around, and not only was I in all possession of my faculties, but they were tremendous. I was light as a feather and ready to go, you see, and above all I was interested in problems. I had missed out on a lot of math and stuff like that . . . Well, five minutes and I can make up for that.

Hugh was resuscitated and the operation was a success. The experience had a profound effect on Nibley. His doubts about the afterlife were dramatically and instantly resolved. "My land," he exclaimed, "I could no more doubt that than I could doubt that I am here now." In addition, the experience was a "higher" form of education which helped him focus on life as a period when we are "tested for our moral qualities." It was a pivotal experience that enabled him to keep perspective throughout his life (*see* Boyd Jay Petersen, *Hugh Nibley, A Consecrated Life, 114-121).*

8. John Hernandez was part of a crew of firefighters battling a mountain fire. Suddenly the wind shifted, trees exploded, and the fire engulfed the immediate area depriving the firefighters from oxygen. The crew fell to the ground and their spirits left their bodies. "One of John's crew members had a defective foot which he had been born with. As he came out of his body John looked at him and said: 'Look, Jose, your foot is straight.' John saw his deceased great-grandfather who became his guide. He also met other ancestors before he found himself in his body again. All of the crew survived and all had undergone some type of near-death experience, including meeting deceased family members. They were given the choice of remaining in the spirit world or returning. The crew was comprised of a "diverse ethnic and religious group of Hispanics, Caucasians and American Indians." The experience was "so profound that upon escaping from what they had supposed would be sure death, the diverse group of saved people knelt in prayer to thank the Lord for their deliverance." *(Gibson, They Saw Beyond Death, 144-146).*

APPENDIX B

SELECTED VISITATIONS FROM THE SPIRIT WORLD

1. Bishop A.J. Graham was visited three times by his deceased parents from the spirit world who wanted him to perform temple work for the family ancestors. The parents said: "They pray as earnestly for you, that you might have money and the necessities of life, and that your heart will be moved so that you will do this work for them, just as sincerely as you pray for things you need. Why don't you get started? The longer you wait the harder it will be for you. These poor people are waiting" *(Deseret News Church Section, June 25, 1932, 2).*

2. A university professor in California was devastated from the loss of his 4-year-old son who died in an automobile accident. He suffered from terrible depression as he struggled "between a state of denial and the fear of accepting the reality" that his son was gone. He couldn't cope with the idea that his son would no longer be there. Two weeks after his son died, he saw his son come right through the front door without opening it. He looked just as he did before he was killed, except he was dressed in white and "was clothed in light—light seemed to pervade the whole area." The son was "very cheerful and exceedingly happy." He assured his father that he was "all right and everything is fine." From then on the father began to heal. (Bill and Judy Guggenheim, *Hello from Heaven!, 305).*

3. Lerona A. Wilson was visited by her deceased father, mother, sister, daughter in law and two other ancestors she didn't know. Her father spoke of numerous noble spirit world progenitors who had accepted the gospel and were anxious for their baptisms to be done in proxy. She promised to do the work. "The time is short," he said, "our people can not be put off. Their work must be done so they can be

ready for the coming of the Savior." With divine assistance, she obtained the records and with the help of friends did the temple work for several thousand of her dead ancestors" (*Deseret News Church Section, July 16, 1932, 5*).

4. George Farnsworth, a Bishop in Mount Pleasant, Sanpete County had an amazing experience at the time of the Manti temple dedication. While traveling on a country road in 1888 with a team of horses he saw a vast multitude of men. One said: "These are your kindred! And we have been waiting, waiting, waiting! Waiting for your temple to be finished. It is now dedicated and accepted by our Father. You are our representative, and we want you to do for us what we cannot do for ourselves. You have the privilege of hearing the gospel of the Son of God: we had not that great blessing!" He asked how he would find out their names. He was told, "when that will be required it will be made known." The names were soon provided by a temple recorder who had felt impressed to gather the names on a previous trip overseas (*Young Women's Journal, 1:214-15*).

5. Sammie Mitton, a deaf and dumb boy from Wellsville, Utah, died from a diphtheria epidemic, and later appeared to a friend. The friend said, "Why Sammie, you are not deaf and dumb any more." Sammie replied: "That belonged to the body, that didn't belong to the spirit" (*cited in Joseph Heinerman, Spirit World Manifestations, 121*).

6. The Apostle Marriner W. Merrill could not reconcile himself to his son's death, until he received a visit from his deceased son. Bryant S. Hinckley tells the story:

   > On one occasion soon after the death of his son, as he was returning to his home, he sat in his carriage so deeply lost in thought about his son that he was quite oblivious to things about him. He suddenly came into a state of awareness when his horse stopped in the road. As he looked up, his son stood in the road beside him. His son spoke to him and said, "Father, you are mourning my departure unduly! You are over concerned about my family (his son left a large family of small children) and their welfare. I have much work to do and

> your grieving gives me much concern. I am in a position to render effective service to my family. You should take comfort, for you know there is much work to be done here and it was necessary for me to be called. You know that the Lord doeth all things well." So saying, the son departed (Hinckley, *The Faith of Our Pioneer Fathers, 182-83*).

7. William L. Hansen, a missionary serving in the Swiss and German mission was extremely homesick and discouraged. He prayed contritely and fervently in a grove of trees and the Spirit filled his soul. Upon arising from his knees, he saw his mother, who had died when he was six years old. She wore white robe, and her whole countenance radiated. She expressed her joy at being able to visit, as she had been chosen to answer his prayers, explaining that her visit was divinely authorized and appointed. She said the evil one had tried hard to discourage him, but he was to be preserved to complete a worthy and successful mission. They spent at least two more hours together. She said she knew he was struggling with the German language, and asked him to meet her for help in the language, at the same grove the next day at the same time, although he would not see her as he saw her that day. The next day he did not see her or hear her voice, yet there seemed to be just as divine a presence, as thoughts were exchanged rapidly and clearly, and "an unquestionably clear conversation under a much higher law." The following day was the same in every way as the second day, although the time was spent in recalling Sunday school and Gospel teachings. After this experience his German language abilities and overall outlook improved dramatically (*Deseret News Church Section, May 27, 1933, 8*).

8. Wilford Woodruff related an experience he had while on a mission in England in which three divine messengers protected him and his missionary companions when they were attacked by hordes of evil spirits. The three messengers could have been angels or translated beings:

   > When Brother Heber C. Kimball, Brother George A. Smith, and myself went to London, we encountered these evil spirits. They sought

> to destroy us. The first house that was opened to us was filled with devils. They had gathered there for our destruction, so that we could not plant the gospel in that great city. Brother Kimball went to Manchester on some business, and left Brother George A. Smith and myself there. One night we sat up till 11 o'clock, talking Mormonism, and then we went to bed. We had only just laid down when these spirits rested upon us, and we were in a very fair way of losing our lives. It was as if a strong man had me by the throat, trying to choke me to death. In the midst of this a spirit told me to pray. I did so, and while praying, the door opened, the room was filled with light, and three messengers came in. Who they were I know not. They came and laid their hands upon us, and rebuked . . . the whole army of devils that were in that great city, and bound them so they had never troubled any elder from that day to this (*The Deseret Weekly, November 7, 1896, 642*).

9. Elder Parley P. Pratt wrote of his deceased wife's visit while he was held in a Missouri dungeon in 1839. After months of captivity, he prayed to know if he would ever escape:

> After some days of prayer and fasting, and seeking the Lord on the subject, I retired to my bed in my lonely chamber at an early hour, and while the other prisoners and the guard were chatting and beguiling the lonesome hours in the upper apartment of the prison, I lay in silence, seeking and expecting an answer to my prayer, when suddenly I seemed carried away in the spirit, and no longer sensible to outward objects with which I was surrounded. A heaven of peace and calmness pervaded my bosom; a personage from the world of spirits stood before me with a smile of compassion in every look, and pity mingled with the tenderest love and sympathy in every expression of the countenance. A soft hand seemed placed within my own, and a glowing cheek was laid in tenderness and warmth upon mine. A well-know voice saluted me, which I readily recognized as that of the wife of my youth, who had for near two years been sweetly sleeping where the wicked cease from troubling and the wary are at rest. I was made to realize that she was sent to commune with me, and answer my question.

> Knowing this, I said to her in a most earnest and inquiring tone, "Shall I ever be at liberty again in this life and enjoy the society of my family and the Saints, and preach the gospel as I have done?" She answered definitely and unhesitatingly, "YES!" I then recollected that I had agreed to be satisfied with the knowledge of that one fact, but now I wanted more. Said I: "Can you tell me how, or by what means, or when I shall escape?" She replied, "That thing is not made known to me yet." I instantly felt that I had gone beyond my agreement and my faith in asking this last question, and that I must be contented at present with the answer to the first.
>
> Her gently spirit then saluted me and withdrew. I came to myself. The doleful noise of the guards, and the wrangling and angry words of the old apostate again grated on my ears, but heaven and hope were in my soul.
>
> Next morning I related the whole circumstance of my vision to my two fellow prisoners, who rejoiced exceedingly. This may seem to some like an idle dream, or a romance of the imagination, but to me it was and always will be a reality, both as it regards what I then experienced and the fulfillment afterwards (*Autobiography of Parley P. Pratt, 238-239*).

10. President Wilford Woodruff reported the appearance of the signers of the Declaration of Independence in the St. George Temple:

> I am going to bear my testimony to this assembly, if I never do it again in my life, that those men who laid the foundation of this American Government and signed the Declaration of Independence were the best spirits the God of Heaven could find on the face of the earth. They were choice spirits, not wicked men. General Washington and all the men that labored for the purpose were inspired of the Lord. Another thing I am going to say here, because I have a right to say it. Every one of those men that signed the Declaration of Independence, with General Washington, called upon me, as an Apostle of the Lord Jesus Christ, in the Temple at St. George, two consecutive nights, and demanded at my hands that I should go forth and attend to the ordinances of the House of God for them.

> Men are here, I believe, that know of this, Brothers J. D. T. McAllister, David H. Cannon and James C. Bleak. Brother McAllister baptized me for all these men, and I then I told these brethren that it was their duty to go into the Temple and labor until they got endowments for all of them. They did it. Would those spirits have called upon me, as an Elder in Israel, to perform that work if they had not been noble spirits before God? They would not. I bear this testimony, because it is true. The spirit of God bore record to myself and the brethren while we were laboring in that way (*CR, April 10, 1898*).

> I will say here, before closing, that two weeks before I left St. George, the spirits of the dead gathered around me, wanting to know why we did not redeem them. Said they: "You have had the use of the Endowment House for a number of years, and yet nothing has ever been done for us. We laid the foundation of the government you now enjoy, and we never apostatized from it, but we remained true to it and were faithful to God." These were the signers of the Declaration of Independence, and they waited on me for two days and two nights. I thought it very singular, that notwithstanding so much work had been done, and yet nothing had been done for them. The thought never entered my heart, from the fact, I suppose, that heretofore our minds were reaching after our more immediate friends and relatives. I straightway went into the baptismal font and called upon Brother McAllister to baptize me for the signers of the Declaration of Independence, and fifty other eminent men, making one hundred in all, including John Wesley, Columbus, and others; I then baptized him for every President of the United States except three; and when their cause is just, somebody will do the work for them (*JD 19:229-CR, Sept. 16, 1877*).

11. The Reverend Norman Vincent Peale told of the experience he had when he learned his mother died. He was alone, thinking, praying and grieving the loss:

> At that moment, I felt two strong hands, cupped together, as light as a feather, on the back of my head. And I had the distinct impression of her person indicating to me that it was all right, and that she was happy, and to grieve no more . . .

> This leads me to the conclusion that this other world is not way off in the sky someplace, but that it is superimposed upon the world in which we live. That other world is simply on a higher, or, at least, a different frequency than we on earth occupy. And the line of demarcation becomes, under certain circumstances, so thin that there can be vibration, or the sense of a presence, so that we know those whom we have loved and lost are not far from us (*cited in Glimpses, 116-117*).

12. One woman from Oregon struggled with a lingering question after her mother died of cancer unexpectedly. Her mother was a "real strong-minded lady" and the daughter cried a lot as she grew up. The daughter felt that her mother was more loving to her sister. When her mother died she was sorrowful that she couldn't talk to her mother. A month later, she saw her mother standing at the foot of her bed. She looked about thirty years old, "so pretty and so young with an absolutely beautiful face." The mother smiled with "all the love she could give" and then told her "I really loved you, and I wish you had known it more." The daughter said it was a "great reconciliation" (Guggenheim, *Hello from Heaven! 307*).

13. Bill and Judy Guggenheim have collected a number of accounts where deceased persons have appeared to more than one person at the same time. They note: "Reports of shared ADCs [after death communications] provide credible evidence that after-death communications are genuine experiences with deceased loved ones and not products of overactive imaginations." Some of them involve an adult and a child. Here is one example. A middle-aged business executive in Florida was mourning the loss of her father who died from a stroke. He appeared in her hotel room the night before the funeral and told her: "Be strong and take care of your mother. Remember, I love you. Good-bye." He was gone in just a few seconds. Her little boy, who she thought was asleep, got up and said, "My granddaddy! My granddaddy!" She said, "Your granddaddy is gone." And he said, "No! My granddaddy was right here!" So both the daughter and grandson witnessed his appearance. (*Hello from Heaven! 290*).

APPENDIX C

INSIGHTFUL STORIES ABOUT THE SPIRIT WORLD

1. Kent F. Richards of the Seventy related an incident in the April 2011 general conference:

   > Thirteen-year-old Sherrie underwent a 14-hour operation for a tumor on her spinal cord. As she regained consciousness in the intensive care unit, she said: "Daddy, Aunt Cheryl is here . . . and Grandpa Norman . . . and Grandma Brown . . . are here. And Daddy, who is that standing beside you? . . . He looks like you, only taller . . . he says he's your brother, Jimmy." Her uncle Jimmy had died at age 13 of cystic fibrosis. For nearly an hour, Sherrie . . . described her visitors, all deceased family members. Exhausted, she then fell asleep. Later she told her father, "Daddy, all of the children here in the intensive care unit have angels helping them" (*Ensign, May 2011, see Michael R. Morris, Sherrie's Shield of Faith, Ensign, June 1995*).

2. Heber J. Grant related the story of Wilford Woodruff's bitterness over the death of his son, Brigham Woodruff. Finally, Brother Woodruff was told by the Lord that his boy was needed on the other side to carry the Gospel to his relatives for whom Brother Woodruff was to do the vicarious labor in the temples when they were completed. This reconciled Brother Woodruff to the inexplicable, though previously he could not feel satisfied regarding the loss of that boy. Brother Woodruff said: "I had lived in hopes that this boy would some day follow me. He was more brilliant than I am, and I hoped he might some day be one of the Apostles of the Lord Jesus Christ, and it was a terrible shock to me when he died. But I shall never cease to be grateful to the Lord for giving me a special manifestation to the effect that my boy had gone where he was needed more than he was needed here" (IE, February 1931). "The Lord revealed to him that he

was doing such an extensive work in the Temples for the dead, his son Brigham was needed in the spirit world to preach the gospel and labor among those relatives there" (*Latter-day Saint Biographical Encyclopedia 1:24*).

3. Robert J. Matthews tells a true story, occurring in 1949, which he verified with participants, as well as reviewing the written reports and diaries:

> Mark Johnson Vest, a Lamanite of the Maricopa tribe, was an elder and president of the Cocopah Branch in Mesa, Arizona. He was the only one from his family who was a member of the Church. He was an active missionary and had brought some thirty to forty Lamanites into the Church. He was a very large man, 6'5" tall and nearly 300 pounds in weight. On 18 April, 1949 he died unexpectedly of a heart attack in a bus depot. When arrangements were being made for the funeral, his family expressed the wish to have him cremated according to tribal custom, but members of the Church, including the district president, objected to this on the basis that the Church has traditionally disapproved of cremation. It was finally agreed that there should be two funerals, one in the Papago Ward chapel and the other on the Lehi Indian Reservation. The matter of cremation, however, was not resolved.
>
> In those days Arizona was part of the California Mission. President Harold Wright, the district president, called Oscar W. McConkie Sr., president of the California Mission in Los Angeles, and arrangements were made for President McConkie to speak at the LDS funeral, which was to be held on 22 April. President McConkie had met Mark Vest previously. President Wright would conduct the LDS services.
>
> As were the other members of the Church, President McConkie was uneasy about the plans for cremation. Brother McConkie was a very able and good man, well acquainted with the guidance that comes from the Spirit of God. Early on the day of the funeral, while pondering the matter and preparing what he would say, he began to have an unusual experience. He said he did not see with

his natural eyes or hear any voices with his ears, but in his mind he became aware of a happening in the world of spirits with Mark Vest teaching the gospel. I quote from President McConkie's journal, which includes a report he made to the Brethren about the occasion:

> I could almost see Elder Vest towering above the crowd, standing and talking to a great congregation of his own people in the spirit world . . . Some of the people cried out, saying, 'He is not a Lamanite. Give no heed to him. He is a Nephite'. . . Elder Vest replied, 'I am a Lamanite. I observed the traditions of my people, and when I died my body was cremated according to the custom of my people.' Then he gained control of them by his words and preached the gospel with power unto those rebellious spirits and they quieted and listened and heard his words.

President McConkie explained further that Elder Vest's audience in the spirit world seemed to number twenty to thirty thousand. He said that the event was so clear in his mind that he saw one heckler rise and stretch forth his arm toward Elder Vest.

As a result of that spiritual communication, President McConkie assured the district president that in this case the restriction against cremation would be overruled for good. At the LDS funeral both President Wright and President McConkie spoke. President McConkie told about the spirit world and explained the role Mark Vest would have in teaching the gospel to his people in the world of spirits.

After the LDS services, President Wright and President McConkie attended the tribal funeral and the cremation. President Wright told me that the mourners brought food, new clothes, suitcases, shoes, pants, shirts, hats, and blankets and placed them on the heap of wood to be burned. President Wright said he talked to the tribal leader about the waste of so much new clothing and was told that "white men buy flowers . . . we buy good clothes and useful things [and] the spirit carries them to be used in the heavens" (*Selected Writings of Robert J. Matthews, 498-500*).

4. Authors and researchers Bill and Judy Guggenheim wrote: "Many bereaved parents of infants who died before they were baptized fear that their child will not be granted entrance to heaven." They have collected a number of accounts that suggest their concerns are unnecessary. One involved a mother who was devastated when her six-week-old son died of sudden infant death syndrome. She was agonizing over the guilt she felt, compounded by her belief that her son would burn in hell forever because the baby hadn't been baptized. She had a remarkable vision of Christ holding her baby. The message she got was that her baby had a special place with Christ (Guggenheim, *Hello from Heaven! 302*).

APPENDIX D

LIST OF QUOTED PERSONS

Cecil Frances Alexander, d.1895, Irish Hymn writer *(OLDH) 192*

Richard Bach, American Author *101*

Melvin J Ballard, Apostle 1919-1939 *(CA) 160, 207, 222, 229*

William Barclay, Christian Theologian, Professor of Divinity, and Author *12,*

Ezra Taft Benson, Apostle 1943-1985, President 1985-1994 *(CA) 85, 135, 227*

Douglas E. Brinley, LDS Scholar, Brigham Young University *(EM) 149*

F. Enzio Busche, Seventy 1977-2000 *(CA) 168*

Charles A. Callis, Apostle, 1933-1947 *(CA) 85*

George Q. Cannon, Apostle, 1860-1873, 1877-1880, 1887-1889; First Presidency, 1874-1877, 1880-1887, 1889-1901 *(CA) 10, 44, 110, 139, 141, 151*

Kevin Christensen, LDS Writer *(Journal of Book of Mormon Studies)* 35

El Ray L. Christiansen, Assistant to the Twelve, 1951-1975 *(CA) 165*

Rudger Clawson, Apostle, 1898-1943 *(CA) 109*

William Clayton, Secretary to Joseph Smith, LDS pioneer *(OLDH) 129*

David Dunn, American writer *(Try Giving Yourself Away) 223*

Alvin R Dyer, Apostle 1967-1968, First Presidency 1968-1970 *(CA) 151*

Matthew George Easton, d.1894 , Writer of Bible dictionary *12*

John C. Eccles, d.1997, Nobel prize-winning Neurophysiologist *(EB) 47*

Lawrence R. Flake, LDS Scholar, Church Educational System *(EM) 79*

St. Francis of Assisi, d.1226, Roman Catholic Saint *(EB) Chapter 2 Introduction*

Marvin K. Gardner, Assistant Managing Editor-Ensign *(OLDH) Chapter 20 Introduction*

Alonzo L. Gaskill, LDS Scholar, Brigham Young University *(Odds Are, You're Going to be Exalted) 230*

Grace Gordon, Hymn Author *(Hymns) Chapter 17 Introduction*

Jedediah M. Grant, First Presidency 1854-1856 *(CA) 121, 135, 174*

Bruce C. Hafen, Seventy 1996-2010 *(CA) 230*

Heber Q. Hale, Boise Stake President, LDS Church, had a heavenly manifestation in *1920 (HQH) 44, 62, 109, 12, 123, 126, 136, 174, 219*

Robert D. Hales, Apostle 1994- *(CA) 103,*

Robert Hamerton-Kelly, Christian Theologian, United Methodist Pastor, Author *13*

Bryant S. Hinckley, General Board of YMMIA, Author *(LDS Biographical Encyclopedia) B6*

Gordon B. Hinckley, Apostle, 1961-1980; First Presidency, 1981-1995, President, 1995-2008 *(CA) 54, 127, 225*

Jeffrey R. Holland, Apostle 1994- *(CA) 210, 219*

Heidi J. Hornik, Professor of Art History, Theology Author *(www.baylor.edu) 12*

Howard W. Hunter, Apostle 1959-1994, President 1994-1995 *(CA) 28*

John Jaques, Member of Martin Handcart Co., Assistant Church Historian *(OLDH) Chapter Three Introduction*

Ella Jensen, Latter-day Saint from Brigham City, Utah, brought back to life in 1891 after being dead for three hours by her Uncle, the Apostle Lorenzo Snow *(Young Woman's Journal, January 1893) 109, 137*

LIST OF QUOTED PERSONS

Benjamin F. Johnson, Colonizer, Public Servant, LDS Church Leader *(LeBaron) 69*

Peter E. Johnson, Latter-day Saint who had an NDE *(Relief Society Magazine, August 1920) 137*

Heber C. Kimball, Apostle 1935-1847, First Presidency 1847-1868 *(CA) 73, 121, 135, 165, 167, 174, 175. Appendix B8*

Rudyard Kipling, d. 1936, English Writer, Poet, *(EB) 126*

Lucy Walker Kimball, Wife of Apostle Heber C. Kimball *120*

Spencer W. Kimball, Apostle 1943-1973, President 1973-1985 *(CA) 96, 97, 98, 100, 104, 142, 149, 163, 167, A5*

Harold B. Lee, Apostle 1941-1970, First Presidency 1970-1972, President 1972-1973 *(CA) 17, 85, 118, 160, 161, 164, 166,*

C.S. Lewis, d.1963, British Scholar, Author and Christian Apologist *(EB) 59, Chapter 14 Introduction, 195,*

Pim von Lommel, MD, Cardiologist, NDE Expert and Author *(Consciousness Beyond Life) 127*

Jeffrey Long, MD, Radiation Oncologist, NDE Researcher and Author *(Evidence) 29, 34, 35, 92, 112*

Daniel H. Ludlow, LDS Scholar, Brigham Young University *(EM) 50, 96, 110, 191, 192, 194, 195, 197, 199, 200, 205, 207*

Victor L. Ludlow, LDS Scholar, Brigham Young University *(EM) 186*

Martin Luther, d. 1546, German Priest who sparked the Reformation *(EB) 12*

Truman G. Madsen, LDS Scholar and Apologist, Brigham Young University *(EM) 171*

Robert J. Matthews, LDS Scholar, Brigham Young University *(EM) 59, 75, 204, 205, C3*

Neal A. Maxwell, Apostle 1981-2004 *(CA) 9, 10, 11, 77, 80, 84, 95, 99, 113, 114, 129, 156 Note, 179, 183, 186, 187, 188, 189, 190, 191, 208*

Bruce R. McConkie, Apostle 1972-1985 *(CA) 1, 9, 22, 43, 44, 47, 58, 60, 73, 82, 101, 110, 129, 143, 144, 145, 146, 147, 156, 158, 165, 166, 168, 176, 179, 184, 200, 201, 215, 226*

Joseph Fielding McConkie, LDS Scholar, Brigham Young University *(EM) 5, 22, 27, 46, 69, 75, 122, 129, 130, 146, 149, 150, 157, 184, 191,*

Oscar W. McConkie, LDS Scholar, Attorney *(EM) 64*

David O. McKay, Apostle 1906-1934, First Presidency 1934-1950, Apostle 1950-1951, President 1951-1970 *(CA) 91*

Clara W. McMaster, Primary General Board, Tabernacle Choir, *(OLDH) Chapter 16 Introduction*

Marriner W. Merrill, Apostle 1889-1906 *(EM) A6, B6*

Vince Migliore, NDE Researcher and Compiler *(A Measure of Heaven) 36, 170*

Robert L. Millet, LDS Scholar, Brigham Young University *(EM) 21, 27, 46, 75, 89, 101, 122, 130, 146, 150, 163, 184*

Thomas S. Monson, Apostle, 1963-1985, First Presidency, 1985-2008, President, 2008- *(CA) 227*

Raymond Moody, MD, PhD, Psychiatrist, NDE Researcher and Author *(Life after Life) 29, 31, 62, 107, 123, 127*

Melvin Morse, MD, Pediatrician, NDE Researcher and Author *(Closer to the Light) 31*

N. L. Nelson, LDS Scholar, Brigham Young University *33, 80, 82, 83, 86*

Russell M. Nelson, Apostle 1984- *(CA) 21, 33, 90, 104*

Hugh Nibley, LDS Scholar and Apologist, Brigham Young University *(EM) Introduction, 5, 7, 12, 13, 47, 81, 178, 227, 228, A7*

Reid M. Nibley, Concert Pianist, Brigham Young University *(OLDH) 230*

Monte S. Nyman, LDS Scholar, Brigham Young University *(EM) 130, 152, 174, 224*

LIST OF QUOTED PERSONS

Dallin H. Oaks, Apostle 1984- *(CA) Introduction, 90, 101, 230*

Boyd K. Packer, Apostle 1970- *(CA) 82, 115*

Jay A. Parry, LDS Scholar, Senior Editor at Deseret Book *(www.deseretbook.com) 130, 151, 156*

Donald W. Parry, LDS Scholar, Brigham Young University *(EM) 130, 151, 156*

Mikeal C. Parsons, Professor of Religion, Author *(www.baylor.edu) 12*

Charles W. Penrose, Apostle 1904-1911; First Presidency 1911-1925 *(CA) 39, 83*

Fran Peek, Author, Father and Principal Caretaker of Kim Peek, *(The Real Rain Man) 51*

L. Tom Perry, Apostle 1974- *(CA) 225*

William W. Phelps, d.1872, Scribe to Joseph Smith, Hymnal Editor, Pioneer *(OLDH) 58, Chapter 8 Introduction, 88, 138*

Parley P. Pratt, Apostle 1835-1857 *(CA) 14, 19, 38, 39, 40, 41, 42, 43, 44, 46, 52, 57, 64, 78, 110, 151, 152, 160, 198, 218, A2, B9*

Orson Pratt, Apostle 1835-1842, 1843-1881 *(CA) 50, 59 Note, 70, 122, 123, 124, 160*

Kent F. Richards, Seventy 2009- *(CA) C1*

Kenneth Ring, PhD, Professor and Author, Founding Editor of *Journal of Near-Death Studies* and past president of the International Association for Near-Death Studies *(Lessons from the Light) 33, 36, 85*

George G. Ritchie, MD, Psychiatrist, NDE Experiencer, Author *(Return from Tomorrow) 177*

Marion G. Romney, Apostle 1951-1988, First Presidency 1972-1985 *(CA) 171, 184*

Michael Sabom, MD, Cardiologist, NDE Researcher and Author *(www.zondervan.com) 33*

Katharina von Schlegel, b.1697, Protestant Scriptorian *(OLDH) Chapter 5 Introduction*

Mark W. Sheffield, Compiler, Author of *Postmortal Spirit World*

Joseph Smith, Apostle 1829-1832, President 1832-1844 *(CA) Introduction, 2, 5, 7, 8, 9, 10, 13, 15, 16, 17, 18, 23, 24, 28, 31, 37, 38, 44, 53, 55, 59, 60, 61, 65, 66, 69, Chapter 7 Introduction, 71, 72, 74, 76, 78, 79, 81, 82, 87, 94, 98, 111, 119, 120, 122, 123, 131, 134, 137, 143, 146, 154, 155, 156, 160, 167, 168, 171, 174, 179, 185, 204, 205, 206, 210, 211, 212, 215, 218, 221, 222, 225*

Joseph F. Smith, Apostle or First Presidency 1866-1901, President 1901-1918 *(CA) Chapter 1 Introduction, 8, 9, 22, 25, 45, 50, 56, 61, 63, 65, 79, 70, 85, 87, 99, 110, 115, 118, 130, 132, 133, 142, 179, 180, 181, 196, 204, 205, 211, 218*

Joseph Fielding Smith, Apostle 1910-1965, First Presidency 1965-1970, President 1970-1972 *(CA) 9, 42, 45, 48, 66, 98, 99, 101, 104, 118, 130, 143, 144, 149, 212, 217, 226*

Hyrum M. Smith, Apostle 1901-1918 *(CA) 193*

William Smith, d.1893, English Lexicographer (editor and writer of dictionaries) *12*

Eliza R. Snow, Second General President of the Relief Society 1866-1887, Known as Zion's Poetess, Sealed to Joseph Smith, Wife of Brigham Young *(EM) 58*

Leroi C. Snow, General Board of Y.M.M.I.A., Son of Lorenzo Snow *(I.E. 1929) 137*

Lorenzo Snow, Apostle 1849-1873; First Presidency 1873-1889; Apostle 1889-1898; President 1898-1901 *(CA) 7, 182*

James E. Talmage, Apostle 1911-1933 *(CA) 116*

Nathan Eldon Tanner, Apostle 1962-1963, First Presidency 1963-1982 (CA) 208

LIST OF QUOTED PERSONS

John Taylor, Apostle 1938-1980, President 1980-1987 *(CA) 74, 79, 108, 202*

William Taylor, Bodyguard of Joseph Smith *(www.taylorassociation.org) 10*

Alfred Lord Tennyson, d.1892, English Poet *(EB) Chapter 10 Introduction*

Brent L. Top, LDS Scholar, Brigham Young University *(EM) 62, 109, 121, 122, 123, 124, 126, 128, 129, 160*

Wendy C. Top, LDS Scholar, Author *(Glimpses) 62, 109, 121, 122, 123, 124, 126, 128, 129, 160*

Darold Treffert, MD, Psychiatrist, Savant Syndrome Expert *(www.daroldtreffert.com) 51*

Charles Wesley, English Clergyman, Poet, and Hymnwriter, Started the Methodist movement in the Church of England with his brother, John *(EB) Chapter 21 Introduction*

John Wesley, Reformer, Anglican Clergyman *(EB) 152*

Harold A. Widdison, PhD, NDE Scholar and Researcher *(JNDS) 33*

Orson F. Whitney, Apostle 1906-1931 *(CA) 120, 167*

John Greenleaf Whittier, d.1892, American Poet and Abolitionist *(EB) 2, 160*

John A. Widstoe, Apostle 1921-1952 *(CA) 117*

Charles R. Woodbury, d. 1963 Delta, Utah, LDS Patriarch *(www.gailsgenealogy.atspace.com) 182*

Wilford Woodruff, Apostle 1839-1889, President 1889-1898 *(CA) 9, 81, 87, 137, 152, 167, 182, 206, 219, 220, B8, B10, C2*

William Wordsworth, d.1850, English Poet *(EB) Chapter 6 Introduction*

Brigham Young, Apostle 1835-1847, President 1847-1877 *(CA) 7, 9, 14, 15, 16, 17, 19, 21, 38, 39, 44, 57, 74, 77, 79, 84, 87, 111, 114, 120, 121, 123, 124, 129, 135, 136, 137, 138, 140, 152, 161, 169, 172, 174, 196, 202, 228*

APPENDIX D

Lorenzo Dow Young, LDS Pioneer, Brother of Brigham Young *(www.young.parkinsonfamily.org) 157, 159*

Carol Zaleski, PhD, NDE Author and Researcher, *(www.smith.edu) 109*

APPENDIX E

LIST OF QUESTIONS

Chapter 1: Spirit World in General

1. What is the postmortal spirit world?
2. Why should we learn about the spirit world?
3. Why learn about the spirit world from Latter-day Saints (LDS)?
4. Is knowledge of the spirit world consistent among all LDS?
5. What constitutes official doctrine regarding the spirit world?
6. How do we identify misinformation taught about the spirit world?
7. How can we recognize the feeling of the guidance of the Spirit?
8. What are the principle scriptures and revelations from God on the spirit world and the hereafter?
9. Will more be revealed about the spirit world?
10. How familiar was the Prophet Joseph Smith with the spirit world
11. Do mortal beings grasp the scope of the spirit world?
12. Do Christians today, in general, believe in the spirit world?
13. Do Christians today, in general, believe in a premortal existence?

Chapter 2: Spirit World Geography

14. Where is the postmortal spirit world?
15. Explain, so where on earth is the spirit world?

16. Do the righteous and wicked go to the same spirit world?
17. Do spirits from other worlds go to our spirit world?
18. Can mortals go to the spirit world?
19. Are the spirit world and the world of resurrected beings the same place?
20. Are the premortal spirit world and the postmortal spirit world the same place?

Chapter 3: Spirit World Terminology

21. What terms are used for the entire postmortal world of spirits?
22. In the scriptures is the spirit world called the spirit prison?
23. How is the entire spirit world a prison?
24. In what sense is the entire spirit world sometimes called hell?
25. What are the major divisions in the spirit world?
26. What is hell in common speech?
27. What is outer darkness?

Chapter 4: Evidences of Life after Death

28. Can it be proven that there is life after death and a spirit world?
29. What is an NDE (near-death experience)?
30. Do the scriptures contain examples of near-death experiences?
31. Can LDS theology accommodate near-death accounts?
32. Do NDEs contribute to our gospel understanding?
33. What other cautions are in order concerning NDEs?
34. Do NDEs accurately describe the spirit world?
35. Do NDEs provide evidence of life after death?

36. Do other spiritual experiences provide evidence of life after death?

Chapter 5: Nature of a Spirit

37. What is a spirit?
38. Can a mortal see a spirit?
39. Do spirits see and feel spirits?
40. Do spirits have senses that mortals have?
41. Can spirits travel easily?
42. Can a spirit eat?
43. What is the Spirit that is the influence of the Holy Ghost?
44. What is a ghost?
45. What gives life?
46. Where do our intellect and feelings reside?
47. Is the mind or consciousness able to exist outside the brain?
48. Surely the brain must have something to do with the mind?
49. Does the brain then affect the mind?
50. Is a spirit capable of remembering everything?
51. What is the potential of a human mind?
52. Besides omniscience, what potential does the human mind have?
53. Is a spirit able to communicate with God in mortality?

Chapter 6: Our Divine Genealogy

54. Who is Heavenly Father?
55. Do we have a Heavenly Mother?
56. Were we reared to maturity in heaven before we were born?

57. Did we actually live with God and know Him?
58. How many at a time were reared to maturity in the family circle of His heavenly mansions?
59. Was God once a mortal who died and was resurrected?
60. Why is mankind born upon this earth?
61. Are spirits full-grown before birth in the world and after death as a child?
62. Does that mean there are no children in the spirit world?
63. Would one recognize a son or daughter in the spirit world who died in infancy?
64. What is the nature of the spirit in a baby?
65. Can a spirit bear children?
66. Do resurrected beings have blood?
67. Can a resurrected being bear physical children with flesh and bones?
68. What does *in the flesh* mean?
69. If God begat Adam, are we then physically direct descendants of God, the Father?
70. In what sense can we become sons and daughters of Christ?

Chapter 7: Heavens

71. What is heaven?
72. Do we have a description of heaven, the residence of God?
73. Upon death, do the righteous immediately go to heaven?
74. Where was the earth formed?
75. What steps were involved in the creation of the earth and the spirit world?

Chapter 8: The Veil

Chapter 9: Physical Death

94. Why do we shun death?

95. Should we have no anxieties over death?

96. Should we mourn for those who die?

97. Why do innocent tragedies of death happen? Why doesn't the Lord protect such victims? Why is a young mother, a father providing for a family, a child, or a missionary taken?

98. In death is one called home by God?

99. We are commanded to acknowledge or confess "his hand in all things" *(D&C 59:21)*. Does God have a hand in all things, even deaths?

100. What does Ecclesiastes 3:2, "A time to be born, and a time to die" mean?

101. Do the righteous die before their time?

102. Does agency play a role in the timing of one's death?

103. Should survivors feel guilty upon the death of a loved one?

104. Can the righteous prolong their lives?

105. Can the spirit die?

106. Is the spirit reunited with the body forever in the resurrection?

107. Can one's death be a positive spiritual experience for the living?

Chapter 10: Crossing into the Spirit World

108. Do we arrive naked in the spirit world?

109. Are spirits clothed?

110. Does the spirit change upon death?

111. Will crossing into the spirit world be a pleasant transition?

112. What do NDEs most frequently convey about crossing into the spirit world?

113. Jehovah said: "In the sweat of thy face shalt thou eat bread, until thou return unto the ground" (*Moses 4:25*). Do we earn our keep in the spirit world?
114. Will illnesses and ailments that plague the physical body continue in the spirit world?
115. Is there a judgment at death?
116. On what basis will we be judged upon death?
117. Does agency continue in the spirit world?
118. Do our mortal callings influence our callings in the spirit world?
119. In what sense do our works follow us in the spirit world?

Chapter 11: Life in the Spirit World

120. What is daily life like in the spirit world?
121. What does the spirit world look like?
122. How do spirits communicate in the spirit world?
123. Will travel be easier in the spirit world?
124. Will learning be easier in the spirit world?
125. Does time exist in the spirit world?
126. What do spirits do in the spirit world?
127. Is love encountered in the spirit world?
128. Is there humor in the spirit world?
129. Is there music in the spirit world?

Chapter 12: Paradise

130. Who goes to paradise upon death?
131. What about the crucified Christ's words to the thief: "Today shalt thou be with me in Paradise" *(Luke 23:43)*?

132. What is the condition of the righteous in paradise?
133. What did Christ do when he visited paradise after the crucifixion?
134. Did Joseph Smith describe spirits in paradise?
135. How are the spirits organized in the spirit world?
136. Does the Priesthood operate in the spirit world?
137. Are spirits in paradise anxiously engaged and busy?
138. What travel powers exist in paradise?
139. Does Satan have power over the faithful in paradise?
140. Are the righteous in paradise subject to temptation?
141. Will we have to work to learn and grow in paradise?
142. How many will go to paradise upon death?
143. Why do children who die qualify for paradise?
144. Will children who die be tested?
145. Why do the mentally deficient qualify for paradise?
146. Does probation end at death for those who go to paradise?
147. Can a person know before he dies that he will go to paradise?
148. What kind of clothing is worn in paradise?
149. Is there marriage in paradise?

Chapter 13: Spirit Prison

150. Who goes to spirit prison upon death?
151. Are there different varieties and grades of spirits in the spirit world?
152. Why do honest and noble souls who never knew of the Church go to spirit prison?

Chapter 14: Hell

Chapter 15: Satan and Evil Spirits

Chapter 16: Spirit World Light

170. Is the light of Christ in the spirit world?
171. What are the phases or milestones of individual light development?
172. What is the source of spirit world light?
173. Do spirits in the spirit world differ in light or glory?
174. Are classes of spirits in the spirit world separated?
175. Do temptations continue in the spirit world for those not in paradise?
176. What is the great gulf Jesus described that separated Lazarus in paradise and the certain rich man in hell? *(see Luke 16:19-31)*
177. Is there light in hell?

Chapter 17: The Great Spirit World Work

178. What happens to those who died without baptism or knowledge of the gospel?
179. What is the great work in the spirit world?
180. What will be preached in the spirit world?
181. What happens to those who repent?
182. How successful will missionary work be in the spirit world?
183. Will all the spirits in spirit prison be given a chance to hear the gospel?
184. Do those who had a full opportunity to accept the gospel in mortality but did not receive it with all their heart, get another chance in the spirit world?
185. Is there a time when the spirit can't seek or look to God?
186. Is the spirit world part of our second estate?
187. Do we continue to walk by faith in the spirit world?

188. How will God ensure this condition of faith in the spirit world?

189. If God blocks out the memory of our first estate while we are here in the second estate, to make choosing fair and a matter of faith, does He also block off the memory of the second estate when we go to the spirit world?

190. Do people who have been wicked and agnostic, when they pass through the veil of death, suddenly and fully realize that there is, in spite of their earlier skepticism, life beyond the grave? Do they thus have an advantage over those who have had to develop faith in mortality concerning that prospect?

191. Will the veil of forgetfulness of our first estate be removed immediately upon physical death?

192. By what means is the veil of forgetfulness removed?

Chapter 18: Resurrection

193. What is the resurrection?

194. Will everyone be resurrected?

195. Will all livings things be resurrected, such as animals, insects, and plants?

196. By what power is the resurrection accomplished?

197. What is the first resurrection and second resurrection?

198. When did the first general resurrection occur?

199. Has there been a general resurrection since the resurrection of Jesus Christ?

200. Can a righteous person who has passed through the experience of temporal death be resurrected now if it is in keeping with the plan and purpose of our Heavenly Father for that person?

201. What is the order and timing of resurrections within the first and second resurrections which are to come?

202. Will the body be fully restored in the resurrection?
203. But some man will say, how are the dead raised up? and with what body do they come? *(1 Corinthians 15:35)*
204. The scripture above states that in the resurrection we will receive our same, natural bodies. Is that literal?
205. What is the condition of the body when it is first rises from the dead?
206. Has anyone seen the resurrection in a vision?
207. Is the resurrection a type of judgment?
208. Are we approaching the time of the latter-day first resurrection?

Chapter 19: Ministering Beings

209. What types of beings visit and minister on the earth?
210. What are angels?
211. What is the difference between an angel and a ministering spirit?
212. What do angels look like?
213. Where do resurrected angels live?
214. What are translated beings?
215. What is the habitation of translated beings?
216. Which translated beings are not yet resurrected?
217. Do we have communication with premortal spirits?
218. Which postmortal spirits minister to mortals?
219. For what purpose do postmortal spirits visit mortals?
220. Do postmortal spirits who are not from paradise appear to mortals?

Chapter 20: Celestial Musings

221. What do we know about the celestial kingdom?
222. How limited is our knowledge about heaven and the celestial kingdom?

Chapter 21: So What Now?

223. How can we prepare for the spirit world?
224. What motivation can we glean from our kindred dead in the spirit world?
225. What are our greatest responsibilities in mortality?
226. What is a person's most important time in eternity?
227. What is our great test in mortality?
228. What is the process of constant repentance?
229. Is it easier to repent now than in the spirit world?
230. Can we be successful in our quest for exaltation?

NOTES

[i] (#2) There is an exception for some who will skip the spirit world. They are the righteous who survive the second coming of Christ, and live worthy in the millennium until the "age of at tree" (100 years per *Isaiah 65:20*) when they are "changed in the twinkling of an eye," from mortality to immortality and "shall be caught up , and his rest shall be glorious" (*D&C 101:30-31*). They do not suffer death, but are resurrected instantly.

[ii](#12) Nibley wrote:

> "Salvation for the dead . . . was believed in the early church to have been the main theme of Christ's teaching after the resurrection . . . Both Jews and Christians thought of the world of the dead as a prison . . . in which the dead were detained but not necessarily made to suffer any other discomfort. In the Jewish tradition the righteous dead are described as sitting impatiently in their place of detention awaiting their final release and reunion with their resurrected bodies and asking, 'How much longer must we stay here?' The Christians talked of 'the prison of death' to which baptism held the key of release. Baptism for the dead, then, was the key to the gates of hell [spirit world] (*Matthew 16:18-19*). . . .The 'gates of hell' then, does not refer to the devil at all. The gates of hell are the gates of hell—the 'holding 'back of those who are in the spirit world from attaining the object of their desire . . . Following *1 Peter 4:6*, it was believed in the early church that Christ preached 'to them that are dead' . . . In the first place, the evidence is more than sufficient to establish the presence and prominence in the early church of belief in the salvation of the dead through ministrations that included preaching and baptism. The actual practice of vicarious baptism for the dead in the ancient church is equally certain, even the hostile commentators, with their seventeen different interpretations, agreeing on that one thing alone . . . The earlier the work is, the more it has to say about baptism for the dead. After the third century no one wants to touch the subject . . . Work for the dead is an all-important phase of Mormonism about which the world knows virtually nothing. Not even the most zealous anti-Mormon has even begun to offer an explanation for its discovery, which in its way is quite as remarkable as the Book of Mormon. The critics will have to go far to explain this one" (*CWHN 4:100-149*).

[iii] (#22) For scriptural examples: Enoch speaks of the morning of the first resurrection when "the saints arose, and were crowned at the right hand of the Son of Man, with crowns of glory; and as many of the spirits as were in prison

came forth, and stood on the right hand of God..."(*Moses* 7:56-57) The righteous "dead had looked upon the long absence of their spirits from their bodies as a bondage [prison]" (*D&C 138:50; 45:17*). Peter spoke of Christ's visit to those in spirit prison (*1Peter* 3:18-20); while Joseph F. Smith added more specific knowledge that His visit was only to those in paradise within the spirit prison or spirit world (*D&C 138:20-23*). The righteous who Christ visited were "rejoicing in the hour of their deliverance from the chains of death." (*D&C 138:18*).

[iv] (#28) Millions across the world have strong convictions of life after death. Pim van Lommell, MD in his book, *Consciousness Beyond Life,* wrote:

> "In the United States. between 72 percent and 74 percent of people believe in life after death. (*Introduction, xii*). A representative Gallup poll in 1982 concluded that about 5 percent of the U.S. population may have had a near-death experience (*108*). Those who believed in life after death before their NDE have become absolutely certain after their experience" (*55*).

There are 309 million U.S. residents per the 2010 Census. Using the numbers above, believers in life after death amount to approximately 225 million. If 5 percent of those have had a near-death experience then at least 11 million in the U.S. alone have a strong conviction of life after death by virtue of their near-death experience. Researchers estimate there are at least 50 million Americans that have had a "direct and spontaneous" communication with a "deceased family member or friend" without the use of mediums (*Hello From Heaven! Book Jacket*). Undoubtedly millions of those have a conviction of life after death. There are millions of others (such as Latter-day Saints) who have a conviction or testimony through the Spirit or light of Christ.

[v] (#35) "The most striking test of the reality of out of body reports has been Michael Sabom's research. He asked thirty-two patients who claimed to have watched their resuscitation to describe the medical procedure involved. None made mistakes. Then he asked a control group of twenty-five 'medically savvy' patients to describe the procedure. Twenty-three of the twenty-five made major mistakes." (Kevin Christensen, *Journal of Book of Mormon Studies, FARMS 2:1, 1993*)

[vi] (#59) Orson Pratt elaborated:

> "The dealing of God towards his children from the time they are first born in Heaven, through all their successive stages of existence, until they are redeemed, perfected, and made Gods, is a pattern after which all other worlds are dealt with . . . The creation, fall, and redemption of all future worlds with their inhabitants will be conducted upon the same general plan; . . . The Father of our spirits has only been doing that which His Progenitors did before Him. Each succeeding generation of Gods follow the

example of the preceding ones: . . . by which more ancient worlds have been redeemed . . . Thus will worlds and systems of worlds . . . be multiplied in endless succession through the infinite depths of boundless space; some telestial, some terrestrial, and some Celestial, differing in their glory . . ." ("The Pre-existence of Man," *The Seer, 1853, 134-35*).

vii (#82) Brigham Young taught: "[T]he veil begins to be thinner, and will be withdrawn for us, if we are faithful. The work that God has commenced in this our day is calculated to remove the veil of the covering from all the face of the earth, that all flesh may see His glory together" (*JD 8:114*). John Taylor observed: "We can have a portion of that Spirit by which we can draw back the veil of eternity and comprehend the designs of god that have been hidden up for generations past and gone. We can go back to our former existence and contemplate the designs of God in the formation of this earth and all things that pertain to it; unravel its destiny and the designs of god in relation to our past, present, and future existence" (*Gospel Kingdom, 111*).

viii (#130) Joseph Smith taught: "God set the sun, the moon, and the stars in the heavens, and gave them their laws, conditions and bounds, which they cannot pass, except by His commandments; they all move in perfect harmony in their sphere and order, and are as lights, wonders and signs unto us. The sea also has its bounds which it cannot pass . . . Upon the same principle do I contend that baptism is a sign ordained of God, for the believer in Christ to take upon himself in order to enter into the kingdom of God . . . It is a sign and a commandment which God has set for man to enter into His kingdom. Those who seek to enter in any other way will seek in vain; for God will not receive them, *neither will the angels acknowledge their works as accepted,* for they have not obeyed the ordinances, nor attended to the signs which God ordained for the salvation of man (*TPJS, 197-198; italics* added) Monte Nyman opines: "Therefore, it seems that a requirement for entrance to what Alma calls the spirit world paradise is the ordinance of baptism." (*The Book of Mormon: ALMA, The Testimony of the Word, 180*).

ix (#131) Joseph Smith indicated: "There is nothing in the original word in Greek from which this was taken that signifies paradise; but it was – This day thou shalt be with me in the world of spirits."(*HC 5:424-25*).

x (#142) Joseph Smith saw in vision: "I also beheld that all children who die before they arrive at the years of accountability are saved in the celestial kingdom of heaven," (*D & C 137:10*) and "little children are redeemed from the foundation of the world through mine Only Begotten" (*D & C 29:46*; *JST Matthew 19:13-15*). "Children will be enthroned in the presence of God and the Lamb; ... they will there enjoy the fulness of that light, glory, and intelligence, which is prepared in the celestial kingdom" (*TPJS, 200*).

[xi] (#156) Harold B. Lee warned that we should not judge and draw conclusions on any individual's chance to inherit the celestial glory:

> "Who will say what kind of teacher that person had? Maybe it was a very poor missionary, inadequately prepared, who taught him. Or suppose the individual didn't have the mentality to grasp the gospel; or suppose something else behind the scenes that we are unaware of has to be considered in order for a righteous judgment to be rendered. Who will say which degree of glory he shall merit because of his life here? The only judge who can render a righteous judgment will be the Infinite Judge who knows all things from the beginning of man upon the earth, even to the end of man. He will take all things into His view, and the judgment that will be rendered, you may be sure, will be a righteous judgment where mercy tempers justice, and yet justice has its part." (*The Teachings of Harold B. Lee,* 66)

[xii] (#156) Neal A. Maxwell said: "One dimension of not being 'valiant' is a lack of a real, personal effort to emulate Jesus (*see 3 Nephi 27:27*). It is one thing to acknowledge Jesus as Lord and Savior, but another to worship Him to the point of striving to become more like Him. Only the valiant really do the latter." (*That Ye May Believe, 93*).

[xiii] (#227) The scriptures talk of certain angels who will not be exalted because they didn't fully obey the gospel. They will be "angels of God forever" and not gods (*D&C 132:16*). Perhaps the apostolic fathers and Hugh Nibley are referring to these angels who envy us for our ability to forgive and repent.

SOURCES

Latter-day Saint Scriptures

The Book of Mormon – Another Testament of Jesus Christ, Salt Lake City: The Church of Jesus Christ of Latter-day Saints, 1981

The Doctrine and Covenants, Salt Lake City: The Church of Jesus Christ of Latter-day Saints, 1981

The Holy Bible (Authorized King James Version), Salt Lake City: The Church of Jesus Christ of Latter-day Saints, 1979

The Pearl of Great Price, Salt Lake City: The Church of Jesus Christ of Latter-day Saints, 1981

Other Sources

Aaronic Priesthood Manual, 3 Vols., Salt Lake City: The Church of Jesus Christ of Latter-day Saints, 1993-1995

American Dictionary of the English Language-Noah Webster 1828 Facsimile Edition, San Francisco: Foundation for American Christian Education, 2002

American Heritage Dictionary of The English Language, 4th Ed., Boston: Houghton Mifflin, 2006

American Heritage Medical Dictionary, Boston: Houghton Mifflin Harcourt Publishing Co., 2010

Andrus, Hyrum L. and Helen Mae Andrus, *They Knew the Prophet, Personal Accounts from over 100 People who knew Joseph Smith*, American Fork, Utah: Covenant Communications, 2004

Ballard, Melvin J., *Crusader for Righeousness*, Salt Lake City: Bookcraft, 271.

SOURCES

Barclay, William, *The Apostles' Creed*, Louisville: Westminster John Knox Press, 2001

Benson, Ezra Taft, *The Teachings of Ezra Taft Benson,* Salt Lake City: Bookcraft, 1992

Bible Dictionary, bound with *The Holy Bible, Authorized King James Version*, Salt Lake City: The Church of Jesus Christ of Latter-day Saints, 1979

Book of Mormon Student Manual, Religion 121-122, CES 2nd Edition, Salt Lake City: The Church of Jesus Christ of Latter-day Saints, 1981

Brigham Young University (BYU) Speeches, Provo, Utah: BYU, 1949-2010

Brinley, Douglas E., *Heavens are Open, Sperry Symposium*, Provo, Utah: BYU, 1992

Busche, F. Enzio, *Yearning for the Living God*, Salt Lake City: Deseret Book, 2004

Calvin, John, *Institutes of the Christian Religion*, trans. H. Beveridge, Grand Rapids, Michigan: Eerdmans, 1953

Cannon, George Q., *Gospel Truth*, 2 Vols., comp Jerreld L. Newquist, Salt Lake City: Deseret Book, 1987

Church Section, Church News, and Deseret Weekly of Deseret News, Salt Lake City: 1850-2011

Conference Reports, Salt Lake City: The Church of Jesus Christ of Latter-day Saints, 1899-2010

Crowther, Duane S., *Life Everlasting-A Definitive Study of Life after Death*, Springville, Utah: Horizon Publishers, 2007

Church Almanac, The Church of Jesus Christ of Latter-day Saints, Salt Lake City: Deseret News 2011

Davidson, Karen Lynn, *Our Latter-day Hymns-The Stories and Messages*, Salt Lake City: Deseret Book, 1988

SOURCES

Deseret News, Utah's oldest newspaper, includes *Church News, Church Section, and Deseret Weekly*, Salt Lake City: 1850-2011

Diary of Charles Lowell Walker, 2 vols., ed. A. Karl and Katherine Miles Larsen, Logan, Utah: Utah State University Press, 1980

Dunn, David, *Try Giving Yourself Away*, Englewood Cliffs, New Jersey: Prentice-Hall, 1956

Dyer, Alvin R., *Who Am I?*, Salt Lake City: Deseret Book, 1976

Encyclopaedia Britannica Online, www. Britannica.com,. April 17, 2011

Encyclopedia of Mormonism, ed. by Daniel H. Ludlow, 4 vols., Macmillan Publishing Co. 1992

Ensign of The Church of Jesus Christ of Latter-day Saints, Salt Lake City: 1971-2011

Faith-Promoting Series, 17 Vols., George Q. Cannon and other authors, Salt Lake City: Juvenile Instructor Office of The Church of Jesus Christ of Latter-day Saints, 1879-1915

Flake, Lawrence R., *Three Degrees of Glory*, American Fork, Utah: Covenant Communications, 2000

Gaskill, Alonzo L., *Odds Are, You're Going to be Exalted*, Salt Lake City: Deseret Book, 2008

Gibson, Arvin S., *Glimpses of Eternity: New Near-death Experiences Examined*, Bountiful, Utah: Horizon Publishers, 1992

Gibson, Arvin S., *They Saw Beyond Death*, Springville, Utah: Horizon Publishers, 2006

Goates, L. Brent, *Harold B. Lee: Prophet and Seer*, Salt Lake City: Bookcraft, 1985

Gospel Fundamentals, Salt Lake City: The Church of Jesus Christ of Latter-day Saints, 2002

Gospel Principles, Salt Lake City: The Church of Jesus Christ of Latter-day Saints, 2009

SOURCES

Gospel Topics, Salt Lake City: The Church of Jesus Christ of Latter-day Saints, 2011 online at: www.lds.org

Guggenheim, Bill, and Judy Guggenheim, *Hello From Heaven! A new field of research – After-Death Communication-confirms that life and love are eternal,* New York: Bantam Books, 1996

Hafen, Bruce C., *The Believing Heart,* Salt Lake City: Bookcraft, 1986

Hale, Heber Q., *Vision Given to Heber Q. Hale*, Boise, Idaho: Manuscript 1920, available on-line at: www.byui.edu/onlinelearning , June 2011

Hales, Robert. *Return: Four Phases of Our Mortal Journey Home*, Salt Lake City: Deseret Book, 2010

Harper, Steven C., *Making Sense of the Doctrine & Covenants*, Salt Lake City: Deseret Book, 2008

Heinerman, Joseph, *Spirit World Manifestations*, Salt Lake City: Magazine Printing and Publishing, 1986

Hinckley, Bryant S., *The Faith of Our Pioneer Fathers*, Salt Lake City: Deseret Book, 1956

Hinckley, Bryant S., *Sermons and Missionary Services of Melvin Joseph Ballard,* Salt Lake City: Deseret Book, 1949

Hinckley, Gordon B., *Standing for Something*, New York: Times Books, 2000

Horne, Dennis, *Faith to Heal and to be Healed*, Springville, Utah: CFI, 2009

Hunter, Howard W., *The Teachings of Howard W. Hunter*, ed. by Clyde J. Williams, Salt Lake City: Deseret Book, 2002

Hymns of The Church of Jesus Christ of Latter-day Saints. Salt Lake City: 1985

Improvement Era, The Church of Jesus Christ of Latter-day Saints, Salt Lake City: 1897-1970

SOURCES

Instructor, The Church of Jesus Christ of Latter-day Saints, Salt Lake City: 1929-1970

Jensen, Margie Calhoun, *When Faith Writes the Story*, Salt Lake City: Bookcraft, 1973

Jenson, Andrew, *Latter-day Saint Biographical Encyclopedia*, 4 Vols , Salt Lake City: Deseret News Press, 1936

Journal of Book of Mormon Studies, Provo, Utah: FARMS, Brigham Young University.

Journal of Discourses, 26 Vols. London: Latter-day Saints Book Depot, 1854-1886

Journal of Near-Death Studies, International Association for Near-Death Studies, 1982-2011

Juvenile Instructor, The Church of Jesus Christ of Latter-day Saints. 1886-1929

Kimball, Spencer W., *Miracle of Forgiveness*, Salt Lake City: Bookcraft, 1977

Kimball, Spencer W., *Tragedy or Destiny*, Salt Lake City: Deseret Book, 1977

Latter-day Saint Biographical Encyclopedia, 4 Vols. comp. Andrew Jenson, Salt Lake City: Andrew Jenson Memorial Association, 1936

Lee, Harold B., *The Teachings of Harold B. Lee*, ed. by Clyde J. Williams, Salt Lake City: Bookcraft, 1996

LeBaron, E. Dale, *Benjamin Franklin Johnson: Colonizer, Public Servant, and Church Leader*, Thesis: Dept. of Graduate Studies in Religious Instruction, Provo, Utah: BYU, 1966

Lewis, C.S., *Mere Christianity*, New York: Macmillan, 1960

Lewis, C.S., *The Quotable Lewis*, comp. Wayne Martindale and Jerry Root, Wheaton, Illinois: Tyndale House, 1989

Lewis, C.S., *The Problem of Pain*, New York: HarperCollins, 2001

Lommel, Pim van, MD, *Consciousness Beyond Life: The Science of the Near-Death Experience*, New York: Harper Collins, 2010

Long, Jeffrey, MD, *Evidence of the Afterlife: The Science of Near-Death Experiences*, New York: Harper Collins, 2010

Ludlow, Daniel H., *Latter-day Prophets Speak*, Salt Lake City: Bookcraft, 1978

Ludlow, Daniel H., *Selected Writings of Daniel H. Ludlow*. Salt Lake City: Deseret Book, 2000

Ludlow, Victor L., *Principles and Practices of the Restored Gospel*, Salt Lake City: Deseret Book, 1992.

Lundwall, N.B., *The Vision*, 4th ed., Independence, Missouri: Zion's Printing and Publishing, 1944

Lundwall, N.B., *Temples of the Most High*, 7th ed., Salt Lake City: Bookcraft; 1949

Luther, Martin, *Luther's Works II*, St. Louis: Concordia, 1976

Madsen, Truman G., *The Radiant Life*, Salt Lake City: Bookcraft, 1994

Matthews, Robert J., *A Bible! A Bible! How Latter-day Revelation Helps Understand the Scriptures and the Savior*, Salt Lake City: Bookcraft, 1990

Matthews, Robert J, *Selected Writings of Robert Matthews*, Salt Lake City: Deseret Book, 1999

Maxwell, Neal A., *A Wonderful Flood of Light*, Salt Lake City: Bookcraft, 1990

Maxwell, Neal A., *Men and Women of Christ*, Salt Lake City: Bookcraft, 1997

Maxwell, Neal A., *Moving in His Majesty and Power*, Salt Lake City: Deseret Book, 2004

Maxwell, Neal A., *That Ye May Believe*, Salt Lake City: Bookcraft, 1992

SOURCES

Maxwell, Neal A., *The Promise of Discipleship*, Salt Lake City: Deseret Book, 2001

Maxwell, Neal A., *Whom the Lord Loveth*, Salt Lake City: Deseret Book, 2003

McConkie, Bruce R., *A New Witness for the Articles of Faith*, Salt Lake City: Deseret Book, 1985

McConkie, Bruce R., *Doctrinal New Testament Commentary*, 3 vols., Salt Lake City: Bookcraft, 1970

McConkie, Bruce R., *Millennial Messiah: The Second Coming of the Son of Man*, Salt Lake City: Deseret Book, 1982

McConkie, Bruce R., *Mormon Doctrine*, 2nd ed. Salt Lake City: Bookcraft, 1977

McConkie, Joseph Fielding, *Answers: Straightforward Answers to Tough Gospel Questions*. Salt Lake City: Deseret Book, 1998

McConkie, Joseph Fielding, *The Bruce R. McConkie Story*, Salt Lake City: Deseret Book, 2003

McConkie, Joseph Fielding, and Robert L. Millet, *Doctrinal Commentary on the Book of Mormon*, 4 vols., Salt Lake City: Bookcraft, 2007

McConkie, Joseph Fielding and Robert L. Millet, *The Man Adam*, Salt Lake City: Bookcraft, 1990

McConkie, Joseph Fielding, and Craig J. Ostler, *Revelations of the Restoration, A Commentary on the Doctrine and Covenants and Other Modern Revelations*, Salt Lake City: Deseret Book, 2000

McConkie, Oscar W., *Aaronic Priesthood*, Salt Lake City: Deseret Book, 1977

McKinlay, Lynn A., *Life Eternal*, Salt Lake City: Deseret Book, 1959

Messages of the First Presidency of The Church of Jesus Christ of Latter-day Saints, Ed. By James R. Clark, Vols. 1-5, Salt Lake City: Bookcraft 1976

Migliore, Vince, *A Measure of Heaven: Near Death Experience Data Analysis*, Folsom, California: Blossom Hill Books, 2009

Millet, Robert L., *Life After Death*, Salt Lake City, Deseret Book, 1999

Millet, Robert L. and Joseph Fielding McConkie, *The Life Beyond*, Salt Lake City: Bookcraft, 1998

Moody, Raymond, MD, PhD, *Glimpses of Eternity*, New York: Guideposts, 2010

Moody, Raymond, MD, PhD, *Life After Life*, New York: HarperCollins, 2001

Moody, Raymond, MD, PhD, *Reflections on Life After Life,* New York: Bantam Press, 1977

Moody, Raymond MD, PhD, *The Light Beyond,* New York: Bantam Books, 1989

Morse, Melvin, MD, *Closer to the Light-Learning from the Near-death Experiences of Children*, New York: Random House, 1990

Nelson, Russell M., *The Gateway We Call Death*, Salt Lake City: Deseret Book, 1995

Nibley, Hugh, *The Collected Works of Hugh Nibley*, 19 Vols. Salt Lake City: Deseret Book, and Provo, Utah: Foundation for Ancient Research and Mormon Studies, The Neal A. Maxwell Institute for Religious Scholarship, Brigham Young University, 1986-2010

Nyman, Monte S., *Book of Mormon Commentary*, 6 vols. Orem, Utah: Granite Publishing, 2004

Nyman, Monte S., *Book of Mormon: ALMA, The Testimony of the Word*, Sixth Annual Book of Mormon Symposium, 1991, ed. Monte S. Nyman and Charles D. Tate, Jr., Provo, Utah: Brigham Young University, 1992

Packer, Boyd K., *That All May be Edified*, Salt Lake City: Bookcraft, 1982

Parry, Jay A., and Donald W. Parry, *Understanding the Book of Revelation*, Salt Lake City: Deseret Book, 2003

Parry, Jay A., and Donald W. Parry, *Understanding Death and the Resurrection*, Salt Lake City: Deseret Book, 2003

Peek, Fran, *The Life and Message of The Real Rain Man*, Port Chester, New York: Dude Publishing, 2008

Petersen, Boyd Jay, Hugh Nibley*: A Consecrated Lif*e, Salt Lake City: Greg Kofford Books, 2002

Pratt, Parley P., *Autobiography of Parley P. Pratt*, Salt Lake City: Deseret Book, 1975

Pratt, Parley P., *Key to the Science of Theology*, Salt Lake City: Deseret News Steam Printing Establishment, 1874

Relief Society Magazine, The Church of Jesus Christ of Latter-day Saints, Salt Lake City: 1914-1970

Relief Society Personal Study Guide 3, Come Unto Me, Salt Lake City: The Church of Jesus Christ of Latter-day Saints, 1991

Richardson, Lance, *The Message, Idaho Falls, Idaho: American Family Publications,* 2009

Ring, Kenneth, PhD, *Lessons from the Light—What we can Learn from the Near-death Experience,* Needham, Massachusetts: Moment Point Press, 2006

Ritchie, George G., MD, *Return from Tomorrow*, Carmel, New York: Guideposts, 2007

Scrapbook of Mormon Literature, 2 Vols, Religious tracts by various authors, Chicago: Ben R. Rich, 1855-1913

Sabom, Michael, MD, *Light & Death*, Grand Rapids, Michigan: Zondervan, 1998

Skinner, Andrew, *The Garden Tomb*, Salt Lake City: Deseret Book, 2005

Smith, Joseph,. *Encyclopedia of Joseph Smith's Teachings*, ed. by Larry E. Dahl and Donald Q. Cannon, Salt Lake City: Deseret Book, 2000

Smith, Joseph,. *History of The Church of Jesus Christ of Latter-day Saints.* Edited by B.H. Roberts. 2d. rev. 7 vols. Salt Lake City: The Church of Jesus Christ of Latter-day Saints, 1932-1951

Smith, Joseph, *Teachings of the Prophet Joseph Smith*, comp. Joseph Fielding Smith, Salt Lake City: Deseret Book, 1974

Smith, Joseph, *Teachings of the Presidents of the Church-Joseph Smith*, Salt Lake City: The Church of Jesus Christ of Latter-day Saints. 2005

Smith, Joseph, *The Words of Joseph Smith*, comp. Ehat, Andrew, and Lyndon Cook, Provo, Utah: Grandin, 1991

Smith, Joseph F, *Gospel Doctrine*, Salt Lake City: The Deseret News, 1919

Smith, Joseph Fielding, *Answers to Gospel Questions*, 5 vols., Salt Lake City: Deseret Book, 1975

Smith, Joseph Fielding, *Determining Doctrine*, BYU Discourse, 105

Smith, Joseph Fielding, *Doctrines of Salvation*, 3 vols. 2d edition, Salt Lake City: Bookcraft, 1954-1956

Smith, Joseph Fielding, *Man: His Origin and Destiny*, Salt Lake City, Deseret Book, 1954

Smith, Joseph Fielding, *The Way to Perfection*, Independence, Missouri: Press of Zion's Printing and Publishing Co., 1943

Stuy, Brian H., comp. *Collected Discourses Delivered by President Wilford Woodruff, His Two counselors, the Twelve Apostles, and Others.* 5 Vols. Burbank, Calif.: B.H.S. Publishing, 1987-92

Talmage, James E., *Articles of Faith*, Salt Lake City: The Church of Jesus Christ of Latter-day Saints, 1969

Taylor, John, *Gospel Kingdom: Selections from the Writings and Discourse of John Taylor*, Salt Lake City: Deseret Book, 1943

Taylor, John., *The Mormon*, New York City weekly newspaper founded and edited by John Taylor, 1855 to 1857 1857

SOURCES

The Family A Proclamation to the World, The Church of Jesus Christ of Latter-day Saints, Salt Lake City: Intellectual Reserve, Inc., 1997

Times and Seasons, The Church of Jesus Christ of Latter-day Saints, Nauvoo, Illinois: 1839-1846

Top, Brent L. and Wendy C., *Glimpses of The Life Beyond*, Orem, Utah: Granite Publishing, 2009

Top, Brent L., *The Life Before*, Salt Lake City: Bookcraft, 1989

Topical Guide with Selected Concordance and Index, bound with *The Holy Bible, Authorized King James Version*, Salt Lake City: The Church of Jesus Christ of Latter-day Saints, 1979

Turnbow, Samuel, *Genealogical and Blessing Book of Samuel Turnbow with a Brief Sketch of his Life, 1804-1876*, Provo, Utah: Brigham Young University, 1940

Whitney, Orson R., *The Life of Heber C. Kimball*, Salt Lake City: Deseret Book, 1888

Whitney, Orson F., *Saturday Night Thoughts*, Salt Lake City: Deseret News, 1921

Widtsoe, John A., *Program of the Church of Jesus Christ of Latter-day Saints, Manual for the Senior Department of the M.I.A.*, Salt Lake City: Mutual Improvement Associations, 1938

Woman's Exponent, Salt City Utah: The Church of Jesus Christ of Latter-day Saints, 1872-1914

Woodruff, Wilford, *The Discourses of Wilford Woodruff*, comp.G. Homer Durham, Salt Lake City: Bookcraft, 1946

Woodruff, Wilford, Wilford *Woodruff, History of His Life and Labors, as Recorded in His Daily Journals*, comp. Matthias F. Cowley, Salt Lake City: Bookcraft, 1975

Worldwide Leadership Training, Salt Lake City: The Church of Jesus Christ of Latter-day Saints, 2003-2011

SOURCES

Young, Brigham, *Discourses of Brigham Young*, comp. John A. Widstoe, Salt Lake City: Deseret Book, 1983

Young, Brigham, *Manuscript History of Brigham Young*, journal comp. Elden J. Watson, Salt Lake City: Self-published, 1971

Young, Susa Gates, *History of the Young Ladies Mutual Improvement Association of The Church of Jesus Christ of Latter-day Saints from November 1869 to June 1910*, Salt Lake City: Deseret News, 1911, 25-26)

Young Women's Journal, The Church of Jesus Christ of Latter-day Saints, Salt Lake City, 1889-1929

INDEX

(SEE APPENDIX D FOR LIST OF QUOTED PERSONS)

INDEX

INDEX